Koreans in the Persian Gulf

Analyzing the Korean Peninsula's contemporary engagement with the Persian Gulf region from the 1950s to the present day, the book begins by asking the following question: What drew Koreans to the region in the first place and under what circumstances were they drawn there?

While taking into account a combination of both external and internal factors shaping the dynamics of the Korean Peninsula's interactions with the Persian Gulf region, this book largely concentrates on the agency factor to analyze the nature and scope of a rather multifaceted relationship between the two areas. The Republic of Korea has, in fact, maintained diverse connections to every single country in the Persian Gulf over the past several decades, and its rather considerable activities and accomplishments in the region all justify such an overwhelming focus. The Democratic People's Republic of Korea's record in the Persian Gulf, however, is mostly limited to its relationship with Iran, though Pyongyang has pursued relationships with some other states in the region. This book studies the elements of Pyongyang's actions in the region as an appendage to South Korea's various political and economic achievements.

Employing a process-tracing approach, this book will be of interest to policymakers, as well as to students and scholars of International Relations, Middle East Studies and Asian Studies.

Shirzad Azad is a visiting scholar at Seoul National University's Department of Political Science and International Relations.

T0347338

Routledge Studies in Middle Eastern Politics

Koreans in the Persian Gulf

Policies and International Relations

Shirzad Azad

LONDON AND NEW YORK

First published 2015
by Routledge

2 Park Square, Milton Park, Abingdon, Oxfordshire OX14 4RN
52 Vanderbilt Avenue, New York, NY 10017

Routledge is an imprint of the Taylor & Francis Group, an informa business

First issued in paperback 2019

British Library Cataloguing in Publication Data
A catalogue record for this book is available from the British Library

Library of Congress Cataloging in Publication Data
Azad, Shirzad.
Koreans in the Persian Gulf : policies and international relations / Shirzad Azad.
pages cm. -- (Routledge studies in Middle Eastern politics ; 74)
Includes bibliographical references and index.
1. Persian Gulf Region--Foreign relations--Korea (South) 2. Korea (South)--
Foreign relations--Persian Gulf Region. 3. Persian Gulf Region--Foreign
relations--Korea (North) 4. Korea (North)--Foreign relations--Persian
Gulf Region. I. Title.
DS326.A93 2015
327.5190536--dc23
2014029732

ISBN: 978-1-138-84247-2 (hbk)
ISBN: 978-0-367-87146-8 (pbk)

Typeset in Times New Roman
by Taylor & Francis Books

Contents

Preface

The present book probes the Korean Peninsula's contemporary engagement with the Persian Gulf region from the 1950s until the present day. The bulk of the work concentrates on South Korea's policies and achievements as if the whole project had been initiated for just such a purpose. The Republic of Korea (ROK) has, in fact, maintained diverse relations and multifaceted connections to every single country in the Persian Gulf over the past several decades, and its rather considerable activities and accomplishments in the region all justify such an overwhelming focus. On the other hand, North Korea's record in the Persian Gulf is mostly limited to its relationship with Iran, though Pyongyang has of course periodocially attempted to engage some other countries in the region. The paucity of reliable sources on the Democratic People's Republic of Korea's (DPRK) activities and its virtually identical goals in the Persian Gulf provide the rationale for sketching Pyongyang's actions in the region as an appendage to South Korea's various political and economic achievements.

The Persian Gulf has been virtually the only part of the greater Middle East region to receive Koreans from both sides of the 38th Parallel, comingling the tumults of global politics with the torments of economic transformations pushed back and forth between the two turbulent yet thoroughly contrasting worlds. This incredibly significant region has indeed become a regular rendez-vous of sorts in modern times for South Koreans, who have achieved many milestones in the Persian Gulf at a staggeringly low cost and who have experienced many "firsts" in the area: from signing their largest ever construction contract abroad to obtaining a buyer for the most expensive defense export in their country's history.

The time span that will be covered and the issues that will be discussed in this book are both somewhat considerable, but such a scope is somehow inevitable for an academic project about an astonishingly understudied subject. As an Iranian with firsthand experience of the Korean Peninsula, I have made an endeavor to inquire into this largely untold story as far as possible. And it goes without saying that any errors or omissions in the book are mine alone.

Shirzad Azad
December 26, 2013

Introduction

Research idea

South Korea had very few, if any, formal contacts with Middle Eastern[1] countries until about the mid-1950s. By the end of that decade, Koreans could establish diplomatic relations only with Turkey, turning Ankara into a beach-head from which to initiate early official communications with a number of other major states in the wider Middle East region. In the midst of these initial attempts, which were undertaken mainly through diplomatic channels, Seoul also dispatched, for the first time, a goodwill, or more accurately, a fact-finding mission to a dozen influential Middle Eastern countries, large and small, in order to curry favor and set up some sort of official connection with their governments. Despite the fact that these initial efforts did yield some positive results, both in the short term and the long term, the fact remains that South Korea's early official undertakings toward the Middle East region were not diligent, well-coordinated, or carried out according to proper diplomatic procedures. These initial political strides, moreover, were basically stymied by a lack of long-term goals and an absence of a broader diplomatic vision, two things that are essential when trying to establish official ties with foreign nations.

In the early 1960s, South Korea took steps once again to establish ties with Middle Eastern countries – steps that were in line with its previous policy toward the region. This time, however, they capitalized on the use of much better contemplated moves pursued simultaneously through standard diplomatic means as well as through the deployment of special envoys. A clear corollary of this fresh approach was the establishment of official diplomatic relationships with a number of key countries in the region, particularly Iran and Saudi Arabia. For a period of about a decade, the South Korean government followed a similar pattern, seeking to make formal connections with as many Middle Eastern nations it wished to approach. Seoul also stationed its earliest plenipotentiary ambassadors in the region during this period. However, this latter move was not subsequently reciprocated by those Mideastern nations which Korean envoys had already counted as a springboard for broader bilateral political and economic ties; more importantly, in spite of the fact that they had performed better in the region than they had in the 1950s, the Koreans still lacked a degree of tenacity and persuasiveness in their missions to the Mideast.

South Korea, however, pushed at the highest level of its political establishment for greater engagement with the Middle East sometime in 1974, a policy that differed markedly from the rather mundane and lackadaisical approach to the region that it took during the late 1950s to the early 1970s. The new move focused particularly on the Persian Gulf area,[2] which Koreans had already recognized as the most crucial part of a broader Middle East region, even though their level of attachment to the area was yet to be commensurate with their expanding interests there sometime later. The Persian Gulf (encompassing Iran, Iraq and the six members of the Gulf Cooperation Council (GCC), i.e. Saudi Arabia, Oman, the United Arab Emirates (UAE), Qatar, Kuwait and Bahrain), subsequently dominated South Korea's Mideast foreign policy. Over time, the region became a crucial element in the East Asian nation's overall national security and economic growth strategies. One other striking development in this period was an unprecedented flow of South Korean citizens and corporations to the Persian Gulf, a phenomenon which required the Korean government to come up with more sophisticated policies toward and broader perspectives on the region.

After nearly a decade of robust political and business activity in the Persian Gulf, South Korea's interactions with the region started to slow down as its diplomatic moves returned once again to a nebulous, unbalanced, and less productive state. South Korean citizens also began leaving the Gulf in large numbers along with many Korean companies, the only elements of the private sector to remain being several big businesses, which could still find a feasible way to base their economic activities there. In addition, some of the ROK's diplomatic connections to the region, developed gradually over previous decades, were inevitably downgraded both in scope and extent, while there were even fewer official initiatives to make up for the ensuing economic damage. This was a time when two of the region's major powers, namely Iran and Iraq, were busy fighting a protracted war with negative implications for political stability and business activity in the Persian Gulf, endangering in particular the vested interests of various foreign stakeholders in the region, be they large countries like the United States or small-sized beneficiaries like the ROK.

In the beginning of the 1990s, however, South Korea found itself wanting to re-energize its relatively lukewarm policy toward the Persian Gulf region. Since economic and business matters were no longer occupying its entire agenda, politics – and the nature of international relations in the Persian Gulf more generally – turned out to be the key drivers of diplomatic engagement. However, this new political outlook on the region did not lead to proper policy behaviors in due course, since the follow-up measures undertaken by the South Koreans were still widely discursive in nature and their depth and duration often waxed and waned according to different economic and political circumstances. As far as purely economic and business-related issues were concerned, interactions with the region in the long run were to gradually get

re-energized. This trend (towards increasing economic interactions) was particularly relevant to South Korea's exports to the region rather than to its
conventional imports from the region. Noteworthy in this trend was a change
in finance and banking regulations, since the East Asian nation was required to
meet some of the essential prerequisites demanded by members of the GCC.

In addition to all the starts and stops in South Korea's economic and political
relations with the Persian Gulf during the 1990s, the 2000s ushered in still more
distinctive developments in political, security, economic and even cultural interactions between the ROK and its counterparts in the region. Among these was
the follow-up presence of Korean military forces in the region after the outbreak
of the Iraq War (2003), frequent visits to the region by Korean political leaders,
and an accentuated emphasis on the Persian Gulf as the focal point of a new
approach to the greater Middle East region that was referred to by Min-soon
Song, minister of foreign affairs and trade from 2006 to 2008, as a "spreading
road of the future" (*"apeuro ppeodeo nagal gil"*). All these events coupled with
the many achievements of South Korean businesses in the Persian Gulf made
the region one of Seoul's major economic partners in the world. Noteworthy
during this period of increased activity is the recognition on the part of the ROK
of the importance of investing in various non-economic aspects of its Persian
Gulf policy, including, but not limited to, the promotion of cultural programs,
various kinds of touristic activities, and educational programs. This decision
by South Korea came as a result of its desire to better cultivate its position in
the Persian Gulf, which was expanding and yet vulnerable at the same time to
the emerging presence of some of its Asian rivals in the region.

The foregoing sketch highlights the inconsistency and variegated nature of
South Korea's policy and behavior toward the Persian Gulf region since the late
1950s. During this long period of over five decades, the ROK's approach to the
Persian Gulf has not rested on intelligible policy guidelines, and the level and
scope of its engagement with the region has quite often waxed and waned (as
mentioned above) under different economic and political circumstances. Such a
palpable disparity in South Korea's policy goals and in the means in which it has
tried to achieve them has almost become a major characteristic of the country's
overall approach to Persian Gulf nations during this period. One therefore has to
ask: What does this policy variation really indicate? How do its key components
differ from one period to the next? Is there any defining mechanism behind
such a peculiarity that can help us better grasp the dynamics of South Korea's
Persian Gulf strategy? To come up with a concrete answer to these questions,
the present study seeks to explain in some depth the contours of Korean Persian
Gulf policy from the 1950s until the present time; it will begin with a brief look
at the theoretical approach on which the present book's research relies.

Framework of analysis

South Korea's Persian Gulf policy has been molded, to a large extent, by
an external and an internal element. The external element underscores the

structure of the international system and all the constraints and incentives which are either intrinsic or extrinsic to it. Since the nature of the international system is anarchic or devoid of any supreme authority, states are all subject to its impediments in one way or another. In such a competitive environment, perpetually pushed and pulled by an exogenous yet determining factor, the survival and success of states greatly depend on their overall capabilities or the relative power and position they enjoy within the international pecking order. The external milieu is even more crucial in the case of small states such as South Korea because such vulnerable players are more susceptible to the diktats of the international system and might not be a prime or proper candidate for the potential benefits and inducements that it offers to its members.[3]

Meanwhile, the internal element highlights the role of foreign policymakers in deciphering the external milieu and working accordingly. Their understanding (or misunderstanding) of the structure of the international system provides them with a crucial part of the data which they use to craft relevant foreign policy initiatives. Their apprehension is also a major force behind the implementation of a state's foreign policy agenda. It is plausible to assert that the political equilibrium of a certain state and various social and economic forces within it all may play a part in foreign policy formulations as well as their follow-up application. Moreover, the understanding of these players about the international system and the way they subsequently fashion their countries' foreign policies are already subject to different material and non-material influences.[4] South Korea's foreign policy with respect to the Persian Gulf region, therefore, has been palpably affected by both an external and an internal element. But the question one must ask is: How?

The impact of the external element is essentially embodied by the so-called "US–ROK security alliance" that has functioned for many decades as a master framework of sorts, prescribing and proscribing major directions and crucial issues in South Korea's foreign policy toward the Persian Gulf region as well as other parts of the world. For the ROK, the benefits stemming from its relationship with the United States include a virtual promise from the Americans to provide it with a stable and safe, though not necessarily cheap, supply of energy resources from Gulf countries. The benefit of stable energy supply has turned out to be of paramount importance for Korea over time because the flow of petroleum does not always follow the same rules and procedures that many other commodities in international markets must follow. This has afforded the ROK the opportunity to occasionally give political and non-economic matters a more important role to play over economic and financial matters *vis-à-vis* the oil trade. On top of that, it must be noted that it would never have been possible for non-regional stakeholders such as South Korea to have convenient and nonstop access to Gulf oil and fossil fuels – in addition to other commercial benefits – there without the firm support and cooperation of a powerful patron that itself had an enormous vested interest in the region.

As far as Seoul's Persian Gulf policy is concerned, the internal element is closely associated with the story of South Korea's industrialization and economic development. Whether South Korea was under bona fide authoritarian or post-authoritarian political systems, the state generally functioned as an intervening variable between the international system and the requirements of the country's development program to initiate and implement relevant policies toward the Persian Gulf region. While political leaders such as Park Chung-hee[5] and later Lee Myung-bak played a more direct role in Seoul's Persian Gulf policies, any South Korean approach to the region was to first and foremost serve the interests of the country's political economy. If fact, there has been little, if any, serious disagreement among successive South Korean governments of different political backgrounds regarding the East Asian nation's main attitudes toward and key interests in the Persian Gulf – in spite of their differing political backgrounds and ideologies. However, their strategies and the level of their interest in the region have often contrasted from time to time based on changing circumstances both at home and abroad.

Throughout the past several decades, therefore, the process of industrialization and economic development has been the main driving force behind various Persian Gulf-related policies designed and enacted by the entire political establishment in the ROK from presidency to the parliament to the bureaucracy. As a matter of fact, even the early attempts of the South Koreans to approach the major states of the Persian Gulf in the late 1950s were partially affected by searing economic conditions at home. It is worth noting that the East Asian nation's economy was in such a poor state during this period that it would not have greatly improved from a robust commercial trade with the region. Indeed, it was a time when the sinews of the South Korean economy were so feeble that the South Korean government had a hard time trying to convince Persian Gulf nations to initiate diplomatic ties. As time went by and the South Korean economy underwent crucial developments and significant growth, Seoul's Persian Gulf policy needed, inevitably, to adjust to those changes over time in order to meet the demands of the nation's political economy. A stronger economy both at home and abroad later significantly bolstered the ROK's status among Persian Gulf countries, paving the way for multifaceted relations between both sides in many political, economic and even military and cultural areas.

Besides those systemic and domestic developments, South Korea was often subject to abrupt yet seismic developments in the Persian Gulf which occasionally forced Seoul to take another course of action that was not quite germane to the conventional policy it used (or craved) to cleave to. The first oil shock of 1973–1974 was, for instance, one such development, and in order to adjust to its ramifications, South Korea declared an ostensibly pro-Arab foreign policy, hoping to assure itself a supply of oil from the region. The epoch-making political earthquake that shook Iran in 1979 and North Korea's close ties with Baghdad and Tehran before and after 1980, respectively, were two other crucial developments; they required more pragmatic approaches to be taken by Seoul in order to achieve its coveted policy goals and partially counterbalance Pyongyang's growing clout in the Persian Gulf. Such precipitous developments as these, however, only affected specific issues and did not have long-lasting impacts: They brought about a change in tactics rather than a fundamental change in South Korea's overall foreign policy toward the Persian Gulf region, an overall policy that it had pursued intently over the course of more than five decades.

Significance of the study

The Persian Gulf has for some time now been the focal point of the Middle East and has played a pivotal role in world politics and the global economy. The region has equally been the center of attention of both regional and non-regional players for quite a long period of time. Some of the region's importance can be attributed to the fact that a bulk of the Middle East's natural, human, financial and military resources are to be found there. The region also lies at the juncture of three continents, straddling Asia, Africa and Europe, and its overall impact on world politics has been truly indispensable, both in ancient times as well as in more recent history. More specifically, when the global economy in the post–World War II era had to increasingly rely on the region for basic energy resources, the impact of the region on global politics – and the impact of global politics on the region – became a stark reality. For these fundamental reasons, newcomers to the Middle East in the postwar period have preferred the Persian Gulf region as a launching pad for their regional activities and as the main focus of their foreign policies toward the broader Middle East.

The approach of the Koreans to the Middle East region in the late 1950s and the ensuing decades was no exception to the foregoing pattern. South Korea strove to establish closer diplomatic ties with countries in the Persian Gulf rather than with states in other parts of the Middle East. Such a subtle move became of particular importance in the period following the first oil shock of 1973–1974. The Persian Gulf also became the hub of South Korean construction businesses, the major destination for its migrant workers, and the main market for the manufactured products that Seoul exported to the region. In comparison to the rest of the Middle East, therefore, the ROK's connections to the Persian Gulf became evidently multifaceted over the years, covering a wide range of political, economic, financial, technical, military and even cultural exchanges with the region. Such white-hot interest in and developing connections to the Persian Gulf inevitably demanded an equivalent obsession and an equivalent effort on the part of South Korean policymakers and diplomatic representatives. Only a glimpse at relevant official documents published by the South Korean government about the Middle East attests to the fact that the Persian Gulf has indeed been the cornerstone of the ROK's foreign policy toward a vast swath of the Mideast region from the late 1950s until the present day.

Koreans were, after all, newcomers who safely arrived in the uncharted waters of the Persian Gulf and who at times realized significant achievements, arousing a sense of surprise and jealousy among many of their foreign counterparts in the region. They succeeded in engaging Gulf nations on a long-term basis and laid down the foundations of numerous diplomatic connections to the region throughout the course of nearly six decades. And yet, their story there has largely gone unreported. Over the course of South Korea's encounter with the Persian Gulf, moreover, many significant and unpredictable events occurred in the region, many of which had far-reaching consequences and many of which involved the Koreans themselves in one way or another. The wide-ranging social and economic implications of such occurrences were not restricted to certain aspects of the ROK's bilateral relationship with Persian Gulf countries: They had significant ramifications for the country's domestic affairs as well. And this study, for its part, will shed some light on them.

Despite the importance South Korea has attached to the Persian Gulf, the region has not yet received a proportionate amount of academic attention among Korean scholars, particularly those active in the field of political science and international relations (IR). An unbalanced academic approach has often led some subjects to be heavily studied, if not overstudied, by IR specialists in South Korea at the expense of other subjects, including Middle East studies. As a case in point, South Korea's much vaunted elite institution of higher learning, Seoul National University (SNU), does not offer any Mideast-related courses at the undergraduate or graduate levels across a rather large number of its academic departments and research centres, and it suffers from being almost bereft of relevant specialists. The whole business has been largely assigned to a number of third-tier universities, and the subject has hardly ever received any significant consideration from major scholarly works produced in various areas of the IR discipline. Although the Middle East is not the only region to receive such poor treatment from Korean academics, the centrality of the Persian Gulf region in world politics and the global economy certainly warrants its being given a lot more attention that it has received thus far.

As far as the literature is concerned, a bulk of the existing treatments, particularly those in the Korean language, focus for the most part on economic, cultural and historical issues in Korea's relationship with the broader Middle East, rather than with the Persian Gulf itself. Such works have been produced largely by people whose bailiwick is in the fields of economics, history and literature. The problem with much of their work is that it lacks methodological sophistication as well as systematic sketches of relevant topics that follow an acceptable social-scientific analytical framework. Moreover, many of these scholars were somewhat disinclined to being impartial in their research, an approach which is very much favored by many academics engaged in various social science disciplines. What's worse is that a dozen of their works do not even pose a research question, opening them up to being considered pieces of long-form journalism – even in spite of the fact that they were published as academic works or policy papers. There is also a slew of books and articles on the subject which have been mainly produced by governmental institutions or private-sector stakeholders in order to educate Koreans and get them excited about investment and business opportunities in the Middle East region.

By the same token, academic studies about relations between the Persian Gulf and the Korean Peninsula undertaken in various Middle Eastern countries do not fare any better. The available literature about the subject in both Arabic and Persian shows that academics in Gulf countries have been more much negligent regarding this topic than their Korean counterparts, who had at least produced some work on the economy, society and culture of the Middle East. As a matter of fact, a relative lack of area specialists in various Persian Gulf countries choosing Korean foreign policy as their primary or even secondary area of academic interest has been a major reason why this topic has received such limited attention. For many plausible reasons such as language barriers, scholars who are not affiliated with any of these two regions, especially those active at various academic institutions and research centers in the West, have been even less willing to undertake a major research project about the dynamism of Korea's relationship with the Persian Gulf or the broader Middle East region. All in all, the present study aims to humbly contribute to the existing literature on this topic and fill out a tiny fraction of the lacuna partially discussed here.

Methodological approach

The present study's analysis and interpretation of available materials largely concentrates on three types of sources. First, it will look at official documents accessible from the archives of the South Korean foreign ministry which cover the ROK's diverse interactions with the broader Middle East region from the late 1950s to the early 1980s. Such declassified records, partly dealing with the Persian Gulf region, neither cover the entire time span of this study nor provide enough substance about many issues related to the period they deal with. Second, it will be using academic books and research papers available in English, Korean, and a number of other languages in addition to research reports, yearbooks, bulletins, investigative treatises, memoirs, and other data published by governmental agencies and private-sector entities. Third, but not last, this study will use a set of materials that include a pool of relevant newspaper articles and commentaries which are available either online or in hard copy at various libraries. While this study does make use of pertinent information as yet unobtainable from conventional sources, these three categories of material supply the bulk of the raw data on which this study's research relies.

With regard to the method of analyzing these relevant sources, this study applies a process-tracing approach in order to examine, in a more organized pattern, the distinctive evidence accumulated in line with the study's research question and its core hypothesis. The main purpose is to reify, in a subtle way, the causal relationship between the variables of the study (or research variables) through an extended application of process-tracing, which is, as we will see, a rather appropriate analytical tool for this study. Process-tracing analysis here describes a sequence of major developments and events closely related to the research variables; such a process will in this case be tinged, however, with additional related inputs which may appear to be unconnected to a particular occurrence. Of course, such descriptive inference heavily relies on a constant process of analysis and interpretation, and on the selection of a wide range of indicative and appropriate data from both primary and secondary sources which this study has collected during a relatively long period of time.

The relevancy and aptness of process-tracing analysis for this study has much to do with three important issues. First, process-tracing analysis is actually a scientific research method because it primarily depends on a key hypothesis to proceed. A particular focus on establishing a causal mechanism between potential variables both boosts its scientific claim and curtails some of the problems associated with non-scientific methods. Second, process-tracing analysis is based on the chronology of key events, which plays a major role, in this case, in substantiating the relationship between the research variables in an attempt to sketch the process of industrialization and economic development in South Korea and its ramifications for the dynamics of the ROK's foreign policy toward the Persian Gulf region throughout the past six decades. Third, the specific data extracted from a sequence of major events over a considerable period of time plausibly fits the methodology of this study. A unique pool of data that has necessarily been gathered from numerous sources is very much a requirement for process-tracing analysis as a social-scientific research method.

Book structure

Excluding this introduction and the conclusion, this study comprises six chapters. Chapter 1 focuses primarily on how the initial program of economic development and industrialization in South Korea made it essential for the ROK to set up basic diplomatic connections to the Persian Gulf region; it roughly covers a period of a decade and a half from the late 1950s to the early 1970s. In order to avoid becoming a simple reiteration of the issues that have already been covered by other works, this chapter will include a brief sketch about some crucial non-economic matters ranging from the political upheavals in the Korean Peninsula in the aftermath of the Korean War to the encounter of Koreans with the labyrinthine complexities of Middle Eastern politics and the ROK's development of a rivalry with North Korea in the Mideast region. In Chapter 2, particular attention is paid to both the positive and negative implications of the first oil shock (1973–1974) and the following construction bonanza in the Persian Gulf which involved a swarm of Korean construction firms and workers – in addition to other subsequent repercussions on global trade and international export markets. The chapter later highlights South Korea's relations with Iran and Saudi Arabia in order to better examine the ROK's various steps toward expanding its diplomatic ties with the region during the 1970s.

Chapter 3 assesses another turning point in Korea's relationship with the Persian Gulf, namely, the outbreak of the Iran–Iraq War in 1980, when the regime of the DPRK unexpectedly developed a relationship with Tehran chiefly for military purposes. The whole episode significantly influenced the ROK's interactions with Iran for most of the decade, though the regional strife itself brought about the East Asian country's first arms exports to the region. In spite of the involvement of hard politics, South Korea's commercial ties to the region, such as those with the GCC, remained virtually intact throughout the decade. Seoul was able to rekindle its relations with Tehran soon after the war came to an end, an issue which is covered in Chapter 4. That was a transitional period epitomized by the end of the Cold War, but its early ramifications for the Persian Gulf turned out to be the harbinger of a true catastrophe, i.e. the Iraqi invasion of Kuwait and the ensuing regional conflict (the Gulf War) of 1990–1991. Seoul's policy toward the crisis further increased its political engagement with the region, which was to be soon coupled with an acceleration in the country's economic ties there.

In Chapter 5, the analysis is extended to South Korea's Persian Gulf policy in the wake of the Asian financial crisis of 1997 and focuses particularly on the country's attempt to forge better trade ties and establish new markets for investment and business. Besides the new controversy surrounding of North Korea's trade relations with Iran, a subsequent watershed moment was upheaval caused by the Iraq War in 2003 that paved the way for the presence of Korean military forces – for the first time – in the region following the ROK's policy response to the crisis. South Korea's connections to the Persian Gulf, moreover, experienced a very critical momentum shift in the decade following the war, which is the period when the East Asian country reached the pinnacle of its economic interactions with Iran and its growing ties with the GCC led to serious talks on many new issues, including the idea of concluding a free trade agreement (FTA) and a strategic partnership. Lastly, Chapter 6 is primarily an appraisal of South Korea's diplomatic and economic achievements in the Persian Gulf during the presidency of Lee Myung-bak (2008–2013), including the formation of stronger links to the GCC; a move into Kurdistan; a somewhat quiet triumph over the quandary of sanctions against Iran; and a more serious focus on the daunting issue of energy security.

Notes

1 "Middle East" is a widely disputed term in contemporary history, and a loose definition of this term encompasses all countries located in Western Asia, the Caucasus, and North Africa. The geographic borderlines of this vast swath of territory extend from the Caspian Sea in the north to the Gulf of Aden in the south and from Uyghuristan (Xinjiang) in the east to Morocco in the west. Arabic, Persian and Turkish are the three main languages spoken in this broad region,

while the constitution of its population includes many ethnic groups following various religions – Islam being the most widespread among them. Such striking variation is also reflected in other important aspects of the Middle East including climate, political institutions, and economic and social organization.

2 The Persian Gulf region encompasses Iran, Iraq and the six members of the GCC, namely, Saudi Arabia, Oman, the United Arab Emirates (UAE), Qatar, Kuwait and Bahrain. The Persian Gulf lies at the heart of the Middle East, and its water mass of 251,000 square kilometers is linked to the Gulf of Oman by the Strait of Hormuz. And while there is no single agreed-upon definition of the Middle East, the boundaries of the Persian Gulf are palpably demarcated and recognized around the world. This study is adamant in its use of the term "Persian Gulf" to refer to the waterway and the littoral countries, even though a number of Arab countries have made certain strides in recent decades toward distorting the geographical definition of the term, which had more or less been consistent since 550 BC. Despite such recent controversy, most academics around the world faithfully adhere to the original definition presented here.

3 For an extensive analysis of the dynamics of the relationship between states and the international system, see Kenneth N. Waltz, *Theory of International Politics* (New York: Random House, 1979).

4 In international relations, different schools of thought, from liberal institutionalism to constructivism, sharply differ on which parameters really matter most in shaping the mind-set of foreign policymakers.

5 This book follows the English convention for writing proper names, singling out only a number of widely known political figures such as Park Chung-hee and Kim Il-sung, whose names are spelled using the Korean (East Asian) convention of putting the family name before the given name.

1 Early encounters and rivalries: Reaching out to the Persian Gulf

Post–Korean War politics and economy: A securitized peninsula

When the 37-month Korean War (June 1950–July 1953) came to a conclusion, the internecine conflict had already done extensive damage to both warring parties: to their militaries, to their economies, and to their citizens. The bloody war between the two Koreas further fractured the long-established ethical mores and ethnic bonds of a people highly renowned for its homogeneity, marking the bloody confrontation as the most devastating conflict in Korean history. A small, but significant indicator of the nature of this tragic event was the audacious and injudicious boast of Syngman Rhee, then South Korean president, that he could reduce the population of North Korea from 12 million to 3 million by the time the war was over.[1] Despite being constrained to the Peninsula itself, the human cost of the three-year war was particularly heavy, leaving 4 million, roughly 10 percent of the population, dead or maimed, and about 5 million as refugees. Moreover, as much as one half of Koreans on both sides of the 38th Parallel had to see a family member or close relative become separated from them permanently.[2]

Although the war had temporarily marginalized Japan from South Korean affairs both politically and militarily – but not necessarily economically – the conflict managed to substantially increase the role of other stakeholders in the Peninsula, including the United States, China (Communist China) and the Soviet Union. Moreover, the Korean War had far-reaching significance not only for Koreans, but for the entire world: the Peninsula was to later be known for many decades as the last remaining relic of the Cold War after having been looked upon as a launching pad for its first major conflict. In fact, the line that divides the Peninsula into "North" and "South," often referred to as the Demilitarized Zone (DMZ), was a crucial symbol of the ideological division between the two major blocs in the Cold War, the United States and the Soviet Union: It represented the opposition between capitalism and communism. The Korean conflict saw a war of nerves turn into an actual war between two antagonistic blocs (i.e. the capitalist and the communist), setting the stage for a number of similar tragedies to take place outside the Peninsula, most notably the Vietnam War.

As much as the two Koreas were enmeshed in the Cold War, the signing of a ceasefire agreement in 1953 turned what had been a brutal war back into what was to become a war of words, and the Peninsula was to remain a militarized zone – and remains so until the present day. An important factor behind such protracted animosity and such an invidious situation was the fact that the ideological divide between the two Koreas had been principally coupled with sovereignty claims that were buttressed by a high degree of material and moral support from the larger coalitions or blocs with which each party was associated. The core political establishment in both Seoul and Pyongyang asserted that it was the legitimate sovereign power of the entire Korean Peninsula and that the other side needed to surrender once and for all and forfeit its claim to sovereignty without any preconditions. Such a sense of entitlement to legitimacy had ripple effects for the securitization of society throughout the entire Peninsula because each party had its own plans for unification, couched in numerous caveats, and left the entire population of its own constituency with no option but to think and behave, *pari passu*, in accordance with its vision of a united Korea.

In the southern part of the Peninsula, there was another reason why political and security issues were given priority by the ruling regime in Seoul. Simply put, South Korea was economically insignificant to the Western bloc in comparison to the rising importance of Japan within the anti-communist camp's postwar program for Asia as a whole. This view of the ROK during the 1950s was closely related to its small size as well as its domestic politics: There were various leftist organizations that were sympathetic to the North. This meant that for the West, Seoul was more of a security concern than an economic prize. And while the northern part of the Peninsula managed to launch its economic plan under a strong security umbrella, the south only securitized; it paid scant attention, if any, to economic matters. This situation was bearable for the Western bloc in the short run, but in the long run the political elites in Seoul often found themselves having to make penance because the West was no longer willing to defend and coddle a political regime which was failing to put its basic domestic affairs in order.[3]

Postwar politics

Basically, the South Korean president Syngman Rhee epitomizes much of the country's politics from the late 1940s until 1960, when his regime was toppled by a student uprising that began as a protest against his policies. During this period, South Korean politics was all about Rhee's ambitions, his style of leadership, and his enemies inside and outside the country. Despite Rhee's paramount impact on South Korean politics from 1948 to 1960 and his influential role in anti-Japanese liberation activities prior to 1945, many people have viewed (and continue to view) him as a man shrouded in mystery.[4] The enigma of Syngman Rhee has a lot to do with the many contradictions that can be found in his personal and political lives, and in the various policies he had put into place during his time in office. More importantly, Rhee's image became even more mysterious because so little has been credited to his legacy by succeeding South Korean elites of every bent, from proponents of development and economic growth to pro-democracy policy wonks to progressive pro-unification pundits.

For instance, developmentalists and pro-growth proponents largely ignore the impact of his government in the early rise of South Korean conglomerates, which first came into existence through benefiting from special economic circumstances during the Korean War. Instead, they widely criticize Rhee for his authoritarian political leadership style which paved the way for rampant corruption amongst – and rent-seeking relationships between – business interests and government officials. They also very much tend to highlight Rhee's autocratic approach to power which saw him marginalize the independent role of technocrats within the state bureaucracy and fail to pay enough attention to forming a sophisticated long-term economic plan for the country.[5] For obvious reasons, leaders of pro-democracy movements and some other leftist thinkers – many of whom were later to place themselves under the progressive banner – had even far less sympathy for Syngman Rhee and were therefore even less eager to credit any of their subsequent achievements to policies implemented under his leadership.

All in all, Syngman Rhee was most renowned for his fierce anti-communism and his lack of tolerance for leftists and North Korea supporters in South Korean society throughout his presidency from 1948 to 1960. This ferocious anti-communism on the part of the president was combined with his ardent nationalism: He longed for "one nation, one country." Rhee was competing with his counterpart in the North, Kim Il-sung, for a united Korea – that would be run from Seoul – to such an extent that he was even willing to personally appeal for the application of the nuclear weapons in order to achieve a Cadmean victory over Pyongyang.[6] The Korean War had simply strengthened his anti-North rhetoric *vis-à-vis* his enemies at home and abroad, and consolidated the political power of the establishment he was leading. Coupled with crippling economic conditions and burdened by ineffective bureaucratic management, such an accentuated advocacy of security issues only made matters worse and dragged the country into a chaotic sea of vexing domestic and foreign policy dilemmas – in spite of Rhee's ignominious exit from South Korean politics and from South Korea proper in the early 1960s.

A dire economic situation

From the end of the Korean War until the early 1960s, when the economy was in the doldrums, daily life for ordinary citizens became quite difficult, as most South Koreans were living in hunger in a country where "people were literally eating the bark off trees" to survive.[7] Since the political system was substantially dysfunctional and mostly obsessed with witch-hunts and branding opponents as "enemies of the state," the economic paralysis exacerbated by rent-seeking practices ensured that South Korea would largely remain a poverty-stricken and cash-strapped state strangulated by widespread social disorder. Such social and economic chaos was only aggravated by the psychological pressure of foreign occupation and constant saber-rattling from the communist North. On the surface, the country still continued to function on a primarily agrarian economy, with agriculture and fishery forming the principal sources of income for most South Koreans just as they had for many centuries. However, the war had taken its toll on this traditional way of living as well, making agriculture and fishery less productive and an insufficient means to meet the needs of a growing population in the postwar period.

This was a time when South Korea was one of the world's most indigent nations; it was even poorer than some of the moribund economies of Africa such as those of Sudan and the Democratic Republic of Congo (formerly Zaire).[8] Because the Korean War had virtually devastated nearly two-thirds of the South's production capacity, the nation's total industrial production at the end of the war had been scaled back to nothing more than one third of what it was in the 1940s.[9] The average per capita income of the East Asian state stayed well below $100, roughly the same as that of India, which had over 430 million inhabitants at the time, and much less than that of Taiwan ($150) and far below that of Japan ($400).[10] Taiwan (the Republic of China, Nationalist China) is perhaps the most similar case to that of South Korea partly because both states had already experienced Japanese colonization and partly because the membership of the two countries in an anti-communist camp had significantly contributed to the securitization of their domestic politics (though both states also shared many other political and economic characteristics, and also had cultural traditions in common).

As its manufacturing capacity was infinitesimal and seriously handicapped by the paucity of relevant natural resources, the ROK had to increasingly rely on massive American aid in order to manage to keep its population alive and get the most rudimentary affairs of state back on track. In fact, from the mid-1940s until the early 1960s the supply of foreign aid was the only viable source of foreign capital, and two-thirds of it was provided by the Americans. Moreover, foreign aid financed more than two-thirds of South Korea's imports, which largely consisted of food and consumer goods. This almost uninterrupted flow of foreign aid was only an ephemeral stimulus, with little long-term benefits, simply because this funding further dragged the country into a vicious circle of abject poverty and dependency, turning it into a "bottomless pit." In addition, the foreign aid did not come unconditionally: Certain strings were attached to it, including the stringent implementation of specific political and economic measures, one of which was a thoroughgoing land reform that was implemented by the government of Syngman Rhee.[11]

The purpose of the preceding sections has been to present an overall picture of the major political and economic circumstances in which Korea found itself just prior to its modern encounter with the Persian Gulf region.

Approaching the Persian Gulf: Goodwill missions

Despite the obsession of Syngman Rhee's government with domestic affairs and with matters affecting the Korean Peninsula more generally, it was still very much attuned to the ROK's international relations and interactions with the nations of the world. The Korean War had not only made the ROK more visible in many parts of the globe, it had also made the quixotic quest for legitimacy and international recognition a major goal for both Koreas in the postwar period. This was a time when both Seoul and Pyongyang needed to fiercely, and often frantically, jostle with each other to court the sympathy of as many nations as they could and disaffect the rest from rallying behind the other party. As an important player in the politics of the Cold War and a key voting bloc at major international meetings, the broader Middle East, including the Persian Gulf region, captured the attention of Rhee's government in a big way in the second half of the 1950s. It is therefore safe to say that the ROK's overture to the region at that particular period in time was driven predominantly by political, as opposed to economic, considerations – even though economic matters were not completely off the diplomatic agenda.

After a string of contacts made by South Korean delegations in a third country, President Syngman Rhee sent a goodwill mission to ten countries in the Middle East and North Africa from April 15 to June 24, 1957. Dispatched with the aim of "cultivating and promoting the friendship and the spirit of mutual cooperation" with the receiving nations, the more than two-month mission led by General Chung-yul Kim, qua special representative of the ROK's president, visited Morocco, Tunisia, Libya, Lebanon, Saudi Arabia, Sudan, Ethiopia, Iraq, Iran and Afghanistan.[12] This diplomatic step was a breakthrough for three compelling reasons. First, it provided the mission with an opportunity to experience the region firsthand and observe its vastly different set of political and economic circumstances – thus enabling it to compare them to those of the Korean Peninsula. Second, the Korean delegation had a unique opportunity to introduce its country to many high-level political officials in the Middle East region and seek their sympathy and support for the ROK. Finally, a rather long report, containing a whole host of observations, remarks and recommendations made by the mission, was submitted to the president and more or less came to serve, in subsequent years, as a guide to be consulted by the South Korean government when it sought to make significant decisions regarding its Mideast policy.

In the Persian Gulf region, Kim's goodwill mission visited Iran, Saudi Arabia and Iraq. From among the ten countries visited by the mission, Iran was surprisingly the only state which had already recognized the ROK. The mission's confidential report for the president also reveals that following the outbreak of the Korean War, in addition to denouncing both Pyongyang and Beijing, the Iranian government had at one point even seriously considered the idea of sending its military forces to participate in the fight against the communists, but the Persian Gulf country's long border with the Soviet Union had dissuaded its government from taking the idea any further.[13] Saudi Arabia, for its part, exerted a great deal of influence on many Arab nations in the region, and its top leader, King Saud, was known to be a heavyweight in the anti-communist camp. Iraq was yet to play any crucial role beyond its frontiers partially because the country's young and inexperienced leader, twenty-two-year-old King Feisal II, could hardly rival King Saud's position and power among the anti-communist Arabs in the region.

Throughout the mission's time abroad, the South Korean delegation was also particularly concerned with the status and activities of both the Chinese and Japanese in the region. The people of the mission surprisingly found out that the Chinese were as active as the Soviets and that their trade halls and cultural exhibitions, buttressed by well-staffed embassies, were astonishingly well represented in nearly every country they visited. The mission was especially envious of Japanese activity in the region. For instance, Japan had already exchanged diplomatic envoys with almost every nation that the South Korean mission was visiting, and dozens of Japanese technical experts were working as part of various development programs in the region. Furthermore, the Japanese had not ignored some of the most remote and landlocked countries in the region (e.g. Afghanistan). Their activities were mainly concentrated on the promotion of foreign trade, which differed somewhat from China's "politics-first" approach, which was contextualized by its serious rivalry with the Soviet Union in the Mideast.[14]

Taking the diplomatic activity of its Asian neighbors into account, the mission recommended to the South Korean government that it try to get recognized by as many non-communist countries in the greater Middle East region as it possibly could. The government also needed to try to establish diplomatic missions in several Mideast countries so that the South Koreans could jostle with the fledgling and poorly fortified positions of the Chinese and Japanese in the region. The mission particularly highlighted the increasing activity of Chinese missions in the Middle East and warned the government that once Beijing nurtures its nascent presence in the region through establishing more diplomatic relationships, it would make it harder for the South Koreans to gain recognition and push forward their potential political and economic interests there. In order to achieve such important objectives, the ROK could somehow capitalize on the rising anti-colonial sentiments in the region, particularly among many former colonies which might come to a better understanding of Seoul's fragile status (at least partially) because of their own previous experiences of colonial subjugation.[15]

When the South Koreans approached the Persian Gulf region in 1957, therefore, they were in a very vulnerable position – sitting ducks as it were – and had to start almost everything from scratch. Britain, and not the United States, was still ruling the roost as the dominant foreign power in the region, and the Americans themselves were relative newcomers who had just realized the region's potential; their primary interest at that time was oil, and they were focused on their relationship with Saudi Arabia. With a smattering of the region's religious and politico-economic affairs, moreover, the Koreans lagged far behind their East Asian counterparts, including China and Japan, both regarded as enemies by Seoul at the time, and even Taiwan. For instance, when General Chung-yul Kim's mission arrived in Saudi Arabia, it needed to be kept *au courant* with the nuts and bolts of Middle Eastern politics by Taiwan's consul to Jeddah, Wang Shih Ming, who was a Muslim and a former class-mate of the Saudi Arabian ambassador to the United States and who had decades of experience in the region, including an education at Egypt's Cairo University. It was again a Taiwanese counselor to Baghdad who saw off Kim's goodwill mission when his Korean delegation left Baghdad on June 5, 1957.[16]

Contacts from Turkey

From the time Seoul established its diplomatic relationship with Ankara in March 1957, Turkey virtually became South Korea's bridgehead for direct contacts with and convenient connections to the Persian Gulf region for a period of about ten years. There was a range of motivations behind the South Korean government's decision to earmark Turkey for such important busi-ness. Ankara had voted in Seoul's favor with respect to its membership in the UN in the 1948 General Assembly and extended its recognition to the coun-try in the following year. Turkey also decided to establish diplomatic relations with the ROK much earlier than many of its fellow Mideast nations and received a resident Korean ambassador soon after. Moreover, a Turkish bri-gade of 4,500 men was among the first foreign military units to arrive in South Korea after the start of the Korean War in 1950. Later, during the brigade's twenty-one-year mission, from 1950 to 1970, 60,000 Turkish soldiers were stationed in the ROK, 878 of whom, according to one Turkish source, lost their lives and 2,246 of whom sustained injuries.[17]

Despite its decision to develop relations with Turkey as a convenient way in which to keep in direct contact with Gulf countries and a number of other nations in the Middle East during the second half of the 1950s, the ROK (i.e. the Ministry of Foreign Affairs) considered it, albeit dubiously, to be a European country. This approach to Turkey has always been in sharp contrast to that of South Korea's East Asian neighbors. For instance, the Ministry of Foreign Affairs of Japan considers Turkey to be a Middle Eastern country, while the Ministry of Foreign Affairs of China considers Turkey to be a country in West Asia,[18] as does the Ministry of Foreign Affairs of Taiwan. Of course, taxonomy of this type can, over time, have significant implications for a veritable smorgasbord of different things, from developing educational curricula to orga-nizing cultural exchanges, and from keeping historical archives to booking airline tickets.

Some historically significant, and surprisingly rarely discussed, racial and linguistic connections have indubitably influenced the attitudes and behaviors of Koreans, as well as Japanese, toward their Turkish "brothers" for quite a long time; however, such issues are beyond the scope of the present study.

Even if the legacy of the Korean War played a role in South Korea's dubious classification of Turkey, the latter's policy of dispatching troops to the Peninsula has since been a contentious one – even amongst the Turks themselves. Opponents of the policy contend that the measure was a violation of Turkey's constitution and that it disregarded the will of the Turkish National Assembly, whose approval the government needed in order to deploy military forces to a war zone. Others attribute the move to Turkey's self-interested calculations *vis-à-vis* their standing with the West rather than to any genuine infatuation with the East. In their view, Turkey's Korean War policy had a lot to do with Ankara's desire to join the alliance system which had been carved out by the West in the post–World War II era. They substantiate such a claim by pointing to the rewards given to Turkey by the Western powers for its Korean War policy, which include their meaningful support for Ankara's inclusion as a non-permanent member in the UN Security Council for the first time in 1951; the acceptance of the country into the North Atlantic Treaty Organization (NATO) in 1952; and its membership in other international bodies established by the West during the 1950s and 1960s.[19]

Following the establishment of diplomatic ties with Turkey in 1957, the South Korean plenipotentiary ambassador to Ankara was assigned the task of approaching the countries of the region in an effort to establish diplomatic relations. A couple of months after the return of the goodwill mission to Seoul, South Korea's then ambassador to Turkey, Il-kwon Chung, engaged in a string of correspondences with Syngman Rhee through a channel facilitated by the foreign ministry. The ambassador's study and close observations of the region highlighted four major issues. First, the Korean government was urged to establish diplomatic relations with Iran, Iraq, Saudi Arabia and Ethiopia as early as possible in order to maintain its interests in a vast swath of the Middle East region, including North Africa. The choice of Ethiopia among North African nations, *de novo*, was probably due to Addis Ababa's dispatch of the Kagnew Battalions to South Korea during the Korean War: the only African nation that sent more than 3,000 soldiers there – soldiers that remained in the ROK until 1965.[20]

Second, a permanent embassy in any of these countries[21] could cost approximately $1,000 per month, whereas a goodwill mission – like the one dispatched in 1957 for a temporary visit to the Middle East – could cost approximately $15,000. Therefore, the overall cost of two goodwill missions could be sufficient to run three permanent embassies in the region for a year. Third, South Korea's permanent embassies in the Middle East could help states in the anti-communist bloc counteract the influence of communist states in the region, particularly China and its ally, the DPRK. Finally, the South Korean government inevitably had to do something in order to scale back the effectiveness of Japanese economic development in order to prevent the recurrence of Japanese militarism. This was a delicate issue because the Japanese, in Ambassador Chung's view, enjoyed popularity in the region and many people there still had "wrong impressions" of Japan. Short of setting up permanent missions, therefore, the Koreans could hardly counterbalance Japan's growing role and expanding economic interest in the region.[22]

Such hostile sentiments toward Japan created quite a few obstacles for Seoul's foreign policy in the Middle East. For example, Chung recommended that the Korean government swiftly establish diplomatic relations with Iran, which he considered to be the most desired country in the region with which to develop ties: It was one of the most pro-Japan countries in that part of the world; a key member of the Baghdad Pact; and the gate to the Middle East region, with powerful ties all over Asia. But the problem was, somewhat ironically, that Iran had proposed to have its ambassador to Tokyo be accredited to Seoul for the time being to be its representative to the ROK. The South Korean government was completely against the idea, and so it asked Tehran to instead accredit its Taiwan ambassador to the ROK. A similar problem arose when the Scandinavian countries requested – through Seoul's diplomatic mission in Washington, D.C. in 1958 – that the Korean government accept their ambassadors to Japan as their diplomatic representatives to the ROK, which was an idea, as we have just seen, that Seoul had already rejected.[23]

As Iran did not have a dedicated ambassador to Taiwan, instead accrediting its Tokyo ambassador to Taipei simultaneously,[24] and as the Korean government was adamant about establishing diplomatic ties with Tehran, the issue became the subject of heated discussions that took place during several cabinet meetings in November 1958. The general view of the Korean cabinet was that the ROK needed to stick to its conventional policy and not acquiesce to the idea of accepting a Tokyo-stationed foreign diplomat being accredited to Seoul. However, taking various matters into account, including the insistence of both President Syngman Rhee and Foreign Minister Chung-whan Cho that the need for a policy shift trumped their general dislike of the newfangled arrangement, the cabinet eventually agreed to take an unprecedented decision in early December 1958, according to which the South Korean government would agree to let Iran have its plenipotentiary ambassador to Tokyo be accredited to Seoul as the Persian Gulf nation's top official representative to the ROK. Soon after this diplomatic aberration, the foreign ministry asked South Korea's ambassador to the United States, You-chan Yang, to inform the Scandinavian diplomats about the possibility of arranging similar diplomatic exchanges with their governments.[25]

Establishing diplomatic relations

While South Korea was keen on establishing diplomatic relations with Iran and to exchange ambassadors with Tehran as early as 1958, some confusion in the later stages of the negotiation process and the replacement of Seoul's Ankara envoy, Ambassador Il-kwon Chung – who had personally taken part in the initial stages of the negotiations through Tehran's embassy in Turkey – impeded the process. In early 1959, Seoul's new ambassador to Ankara, Eung-kyun Shin, was instructed to take care of the issue and continue negotiating with both Iran and Saudi Arabia simultaneously. Once Iran's plenipotentiary ambassador to Japan, Abbas Aram, returned to Tehran to become foreign minister in 1960, the Korean government was even more eager to finish the negotiation process, which finally ended in the establishment of diplomatic relations between the ROK and Iran in October 1962. Seoul appointed its Ankara envoy as an accredited ambassador to Iran before dispatching a resident ambassador and opening its embassy in Tehran in April 1967. Unlike South Korea, Iran's limited interests in Seoul allowed Tehran to take a more lackadaisical approach to dispatching their envoy, appointing its Tokyo ambassador, Nouredin Kia, as an accredited ambassador to Seoul only in 1968 and setting up its embassy in the South Korean capital in 1975.[26]

In addition to Iran, South Korea had plans to establish political ties with Iraq, but its efforts were thwarted by a *coup d'état* in 1958 and by the rise of the socialist Ba'ath Party in 1963: Seoul was left with no choice but to shelve its plans for more than three decades. Although the ROK still communicated with the new political system that had surfaced in Baghdad – as is evidenced by a congratulatory message sent by the Korean foreign minister, Chung Huh, to his Iraqi counterpart, Hashim Javad, on the occasion of the second anniversary of the new republican regime in July 1960[27] – the Ba'ath Party's significant tilt toward North Korea made it quite difficult, to say the least, for Seoul to further engage in serious discussions with the Iraqi government with respect to establishing diplomatic ties between the two countries. It was only the end of the Iran–Iraq War in the late 1980s that would pave the way for bilateral negotiations; they were started in earnest and culminated in July 1989 with the setting up of formal diplomatic relations between Seoul and Baghdad.

As for Saudi Arabia, South Korea established diplomatic ties with the Arab country in October 1962 and appointed its Ankara ambassador to be an accredited envoy there. Seoul later opened an embassy in Jeddah in 1973 which later moved to Riyadh in 1982. In 1967, Saudi Arabia accredited, for the first time, its Tokyo ambassador, Nasser al-Mankour, to Seoul; al-Mankour was also holding a concurrent post in Taipei at the time. In 1974, Saudi Arabia became the first Arab country to establish an embassy in the ROK. Meanwhile, compared to its ties with Saudi Arabia, South Korea's official relations with Oman, the UAE, Qatar, Kuwait and Bahrain did not start so quickly. With the exception of Oman, these small Gulf states only gained independence during the decade between 1961 and 1971. Later, a relatively long process of bilateral negotiations with these states led to the signing of a joint *communiqué* on the conclusion of a diplomatic relationship between the ROK and Oman in March 1974, Qatar in April 1974, Bahrain in April 1976, Kuwait in June 1979 and the UAE in June 1980.[28]

A new national agenda: Industrialization and economic development

In the early 1960s, when South Korea's economy was in the doldrums due to a combination of internal and external causes (as discussed above), and when a panoply of political and economic predicaments had engrossed South Korea internally and externally – to the extent that poverty-stricken Koreans were dreaming of the Philippines as their cloud-cuckoo-land – an abrupt military *coup d'état* led by General Park Chung-hee ushered in a new era which the country had never thought possible before. The army-executed political putsch of May 16, 1961, which toppled the short-lived government of Dr. John Chang (Myon Chang), was dubbed a "military revolution to reconstruct the nation"[29] in a book that was ostensibly penned by Park Chung-hee himself.[30] A political manifesto and an economic prospectus significantly drawn from the German experience of the post–World War II era,[31] the book particularly illustrates Park's[32] displeasure with the situation, compelling him to denounce, with a melancholic sentiment, whatever previous generations of Koreans had carried out, good or bad, and remind his fellow citizens that "sorrow is the only reward we can get from surveying our past history ... on the whole, our history is just a long process of desolation and despair ... our history, which is just a Pandora's box of evils, had better be burnt. We must not boast about our history."[33]

To overcome a wide range of economic and social ills delineated in some detail throughout Park's book, the junta soon embarked on a national agenda of economic development and industrialization in earnest. Going even further, the new regime designated the elimination of poverty as a "national goal," promising to turn a predominantly agricultural society into a modern industrialized society that would enable ordinary Koreans to escape poverty and enjoy a higher standard of living.[34] The junta, consisting of a group of military men dressed in civilian clothing, declared that it was incumbent on each individual to disengage from worthless political disputes and instead invest their energy on productive economic activities: This was the *sine qua non* of getting the ROK out of an economic slumber. This "economy-first" and "nationalism-first" approach declared by Park and his fellow officers assured a better future for South Koreans in exchange for an *ad interim* halt on the many political demands they had long quarreled over with previous governments. In fact, such a concentration of political will and compatible social support was simply a precondition for a successful implementation of the ambitious policies pursued by the new government so that, in Park's own words, "as the Aswan Dam stands for Nasser's revolution, so must the Ulsan Industrial Complex and the first Five-Year Plan for Economic Development stand for our May Revolution."[35]

The first five-year plan (1962–1966) subsequently encapsulated the essence of policies which the junta had pledged for a prosperous South Korea under its leadership. Crafted largely by a group of economists and development-oriented bureaucrats mandated by the military government, the first economic plan particularly underscored the important contribution that exports would make to national success – a stark contrast with the futile strategy of import-substitution that had been carried out by previous governments. The policy plan also highlighted the necessity of building up domestic savings, from

2 percent of Gross National Product (GNP) in 1962 to more than 8 percent of GNP in 1966 – or roughly 5 percent on average during the entire plan period – so that the flow of both foreign and domestic revenues could partially be used to finance the implementation of a dozen new industrial projects.[36] Moreover, the policy document specifically underscored the unassailable yet facilitating role that the state had to play in the process of industrialization and economic development: Without the state, there would be no hope of achieving the plan's basic objectives.

A strong state in charge

From the time of Park Chung-hee's military coup in 1961 until early 1988, the army in civilian clothing uninterruptedly took the helm of both political and economic affairs in South Korea. It created a Byzantine security system known as the Korean Central Intelligence Agency (KCIA) to watch the citizenry intently and suppress dissent at all levels.[37] Moreover, Park assigned many of his officers to top-level positions at various state-sponsored institutions so that they could effectively manage and control state economic policy.[38] These moves were justified by the military's role as the righteous defender, the Praetorian Guard as it were, of South Korea's "guided capitalism" and its determination to enact the reforms that were desperately needed for the new national agenda. The state's policy of intervening in economic development and its close cooperation with the business sector – known as "*chungkyung yuchak*" (the tight coalition of government and conglomerates) – became a crucial element of South Korea's economic success in the ensuing decades.[39]

The military's direct and indirect involvement in the stringent implementation of industrialization and economic development programs assisted South Korean businesses in different ways over the years. At the highest level, whether through the president and prime minister or through a relevant planning bureaucracy, the government developed guidelines for the state's industries and trade sectors. The government then provided businesses with the certification and funding they required through its tight control over the banking system and through the use of a highly efficient credit allocation system – it wanted to ensure their success. In addition to removing the various financial and technical obstacles that had impeded the progress of Korean companies, the state still had to work hard to promote Korean products around the world. Such an undertaking turned out to be an immense challenge, to say the least. It is no wonder that the East Asian country's top diplomatic bureaucracy was later renamed as the Ministry of Foreign Affairs and Trade for many years, clearly indicating how commercial interests dominated South Korea's export-oriented economic policy – not to mention its foreign policy.

Foreign trade was of paramount importance to the export-based approaches taken by the government. On the one hand, the state used all its diplomatic and other international connections to advance the interests of Korean businesses, promoting their products in different parts of the world and occasionally sorting out their legal and trade disputes. On the other hand, the government closed the domestic market to foreign competition, thus helping domestic producers increase and single-handedly gobble up all the money people were spending. To make this an achievable goal, the national currency was devalued by 50 percent in order to encourage exports at the cost of imports – though decreasing inflation was a motive behind this measure as well. The state, meanwhile, did not treat all businesses with such benevolence, as its strategy of selectiveness largely favored certain enterprises which gradually formed the backbone of South Korea's colossal conglomerates (*chaebol*) and were to be run by the ROK's foremost captains of industry. The government's biased policies favored these companies at the expense of many other small businesses that were incapable of surviving in the domestic market let alone of entering into international competition with their big rivals, which could thrive in both markets thanks to huge advantages given to them by the Blue House.[40]

International components

In spite of the interventionist role played by the state, external factors were equally important, if not far more important, to South Korea's eventual economic success. The ROK commenced its program of industrialization and economic development in the heyday of the ideological confrontation between the capitalist and communist blocs, a time when an overwhelming majority of the world's population was thoroughly obsessed with non-material matters. In the midst of this period of ideologically driven conflicts, which also saw the reorganization of industrial and trade relationships throughout the globe, South Korea, together with a carefully selected handful of countries, was given a special mandate to develop its economy and catch up with the industrialized world.[41] It was this unique opportunity that eventually catapulted the ROK from a starving state to a prosperous state over the course of three decades. The propitious international environment also brought with it some other advantages which the Koreans were blessed enough to take advantage of. The benefits included easy access to the markets of the more affluent nations of the developed world, whose lenient attitudes toward new products imported from a new competitor assured the survival and success of Korean brands – even as their home country still continued to protect its domestic markets from similar treatment in the absence of a *quid pro quo*.

Generous financial assistance and foreign loans of various sorts, moreover, contributed considerably to the early phases of many industrial and commercial projects which South Korea had started but was unable to finish due to a lack of funds. Upon the normalization of bilateral relations with Japan and the signing of the Treaty on Basic Relations in 1965, Tokyo paid a total of 288 billion yen ($800 million)[42] in grants and soft loans as compensation for its colonial past and to stymie any further claims related to the issue. The monetary value of Japan's compensatory payment was roughly equivalent to four times South Korea's total exports in 1964 and around one-and-a-half times larger than its national budget at the time.[43] Another crucial development was the benefits given to the ROK for its active participation in the Vietnam War,[44] timely assistance which reached more than $1 billion in economic and non-economic aid soon after the war. For instance, South Korea's foreign exchange earnings from the Vietnam War amounted to approximately $546 million between 1965 and 1969, though it was possibly less than Japan's and only a little more than what Taiwan received – and these countries had not even partaken in the conflict.[45]

One other factor that played into South Korea's economic growth was the availability (or lack) of various raw materials, particularly energy and fossil fuels. By and large, the Korean Peninsula is bereft of sufficient natural resources, and the northern part of the Peninsula has been ironically endowed with a far better share of such resources than the southern part. An example of this asymmetrical distribution of natural resources is the fact that during Japanese colonial rule (1910 to 1945), the North was turned into a hub for mining and industrial activities and the South, because of its warmer and wetter climate, had to serve as an agricultural center dominated by the production of rice. Contrary to this odd background, when the East Asian state embarked on an ambitious program of turning an agrarian economy into an industrialized economy in the early 1960s, it was the unavoidable and unenviable task of the Korean government to look somewhere else for the raw materials it required. At that time, the only natural assets at its disposal domestically were deposits of tungsten, sea ports, fishing grounds, some raw materials for cement production, and a small percentage of arable lands that were fortunate enough to receive a high level of annual rainfall.[46] Fossil energy, chiefly crude oil, was the most crucial resource that the government needed to purchase from other parts of the world, and it was to obtain a great deal of it from the Persian Gulf region.

An increase in economic and political interaction: The energy factor

As an agricultural nation, South Korea had long been inured to the use of wood as the chief source of its domestic energy, and it was only after the end of the Korean War that the government started to encourage the production of coal as a complementary source of energy. In 1960, both wood and charcoal accounted for no less than 60 percent of domestic energy consumption in South Korea, while the production of coal still increased rapidly in the early 1960s only to become stagnant sometime later.[47] When the national industrialization and economic development program began to take shape in 1962, labor seemed to be the only resource available in a large quantity that could be readily exploited. However, the Korean experience of Japanese colonialism – and its emphasis on labor and economic productivity – had already convinced the new regime that its new economic policies could succeed in spite of the lack of indigenous sources of fossil fuels and other natural resources vital to industrial production. This was also the case in the late 1960s: The absence of a sufficient amount of iron ore in local mines did not cause the ROK to give up on its efforts to become a self-sufficient steel producer.[48]

It therefore comes as no surprise that as the South Korean economy started to become industrialized, the pattern of energy consumption had to change accordingly. The government now gave priority to the importation of raw materials, petroleum in particular, at the cost of consumer goods while simultaneously asking the citizenry to save more and consume less. Once South Korea's economic growth started to gain traction, its consumption of energy began to grow by leaps and bounds. The soaring pattern of oil consumption inescapably came at the cost of traditional energy sources, so that the share of wood and charcoal in domestic energy utilization shrank to just 16 percent by 1973. In 1964, South Korea imported 5,835,000 barrels of crude oil, and by 1968 petroleum gradually became the country's chief source of energy. In addition, the ROK completed its first major oil refinery in 1964, which could process as much as 35,000 barrels of crude oil per day.[49] But two key questions remain. First, where did this vital oil supply come from? And second, which countries were its prime purveyors?

The very first supply of oil was imported by South Korea from the Persian Gulf state of Kuwait in 1962.[50] In 1964, Kuwait still provided 100 percent of the ROK's oil, but Seoul soon started to buy petroleum from Iran. Iran and Kuwait, then, became the major suppliers of the East Asian nation's oil throughout the 1960s. In 1968, Iran and Kuwait along with Saudi Arabia were the Persian Gulf region's top petroleum producers, and while oil had become the mainstay of Kuwaiti and Saudi Arabian export revenues, its role in the Iranian economy was yet to achieve a dominant role. The more the Korean economy came to depend on oil, the more it had to depend on the Persian Gulf for the requisite petroleum. Such strong concentration and one-way dependency on a single region for the importing of energy was neither logical geostrategically nor beneficial economically, putting pressure on South Korea to later make new plans to considerably transform its unvaried and almost routine relationship with Persian Gulf nations: It needed to be about more than just oil.[51]

Economic exchanges

South Korea's export-oriented industrialization and economic growth policies required having access to a myriad of porous international markets. In order to introduce Korean products to foreign markets, Seoul established the Korea Trade Promotion Corporation (KOTRA) in 1962, which came to be renamed the Korea Trade-Investment Promotion Agency in 1995. The East Asian country's comparative advantage of having a large pool of cheap labor played a crucial role in the promotion of export products that mostly comprised labor-intensive manufactured goods. This achievement made it possible for the Koreans to gradually shift the country's principal exports from primary goods and labor-intensive commodities to light-industrial items throughout the 1960s and the early 1970s.[52] During this early period, when Korean brands were both unknown and devoid of internationally competitive quality standards, South Korea could still ship its primary export items to Middle Eastern markets, particularly to the bazaars of the Persian Gulf, thus partially counterbalancing its swelling trade deficit with the region.

KOTRA launched its first Middle East branch in Tehran in August 1964, the same year it opened an office in Tokyo, where the lion's share of Korean exports had currently been heading. KOTRA's second branch in the Persian Gulf region was opened in Kuwait in 1969, the year that the Korean agency also established its third Mideast branch in Tunisia.[53] By 1967, South Korea's exports to the Persian Gulf amounted to $911,000 with Saudi Arabia ($607,000) and Kuwait ($304,000) being the largest markets in the region. In 1973, on the eve of the first oil shock, Seoul's commodity shipments to Persian Gulf countries had shot up to a total of $38 million with Iran ($16 million), Saudi Arabia ($13 million) and Kuwait ($7.5 million) as its top export markets. More interestingly, these three countries were the ROK's top export destinations in the entire Middle East at the time, receiving a huge chunk of its manufactured products that were sent to the region. South Korea did not export much to Qatar at that time, and its next smallest market in the Persian Gulf was the UAE, which received annual South Korean exports valued at just $71,000.[54]

In spite of South Korea's growing commercial exchanges with the Persian Gulf, as its largest export market throughout the Middle East, Seoul was nevertheless rather despondent about its stupendous trade deficit with the region. In 1967, it imported $19.4 million (Kuwait $19 million and Saudi Arabia $418,000) worth of petroleum from the Persian Gulf, which significantly increased to $250 million in 1973, when its three import partners in the region consisted of Saudi Arabia ($154 million), Kuwait ($82.5 million) and Iran ($13.5 million).[55] In fact, South Korea imported more than twenty times the total value of its exports to the Persian Gulf in 1967. By 1973, Seoul still imported seven times more than what it could ship to its trading partners in the Gulf. In both years, therefore, the expanding importance of petroleum as the single most valuable raw material Seoul had to import enabled the Persian Gulf to reify its hegemonic position *vis-à-vis* South Korea's overall two-way trade connections to vast swathes of the Middle East region. The weight of this peculiarity, which never faded away in terms of quantity or quality, compelled the East Asian state to constantly adjust its political and economic policies toward other parts of the Middle East in order to bring them into line with its vested interests in the Persian Gulf – and not *vice versa*. Such delicacy entailed a cautious yet prudent approach to some contentious issues, foremost among which was Pyongyang's increasing diplomatic maneuvers in the Middle East – a threat that could potentially endanger the ROK's growing interests in the Persian Gulf.

Rivalry with North Korea

Although the growing economic clout of the Persian Gulf compelled Seoul to map out necessary political strategies *pari passu* with its Gulf interests, the North Korean issue had always been an important element of the ROK's policy considerations toward the region and toward the Middle East in general. Even when the first South Korean ambassador to Turkey, Il-kwon Chung, warned his government, in one of many letters he sent to Seoul in January 1959, about the urgency of establishing diplomatic relationship with Iran, Chung ascribed part of the latter's dominant position in the Middle East to Tehran's indisputable posture "as a bulwark against communist infiltration."[56] In the southern part of the Persian Gulf, South Korea's first goodwill mission to Saudi Arabia in 1957 had already acknowledged King Saud's steadfast approach to safeguarding his country and maintaining what he referred to as an impenetrable barricade to counter the spread of communism and the infiltration of communist agents. His political power and anti-leftist leanings were therefore sought to contain, as far as possible, the dissemination of communist ideology among Arabs over which the king had influence.[57]

Over time, the anti-communist stance of these two key states, one on the northern and one on the southern shore of the Persian Gulf turned out to be of great use to South Korea. Still, this advantage could secure neither sure-fire support for Seoul in all North Korean-related matters nor the occurrence of occasional blunders in the region involving Pyongyang. For instance, during the visit of a goodwill mission from South Korea to Iran in August 1968, the South Korean ambassador to Tehran objected to his host country's frequent application of the words "North" and "South" to the two Koreas, claiming – quite out of the blue – that "if some people thought that North Korea is a country, they would better pick up another name for it."[58] Another problem, which occurred to a certain extent in the smaller Gulf countries, and more often in other parts of the Middle East, was the simultaneous visits by both South and North Korean delegates and their respective quests for recognition and political support at meetings of the United Nations (UN), which would lead to diplomatic complications for their host nations – as epitomized by two separate cases[59] in Kuwait and Lebanon in 1968.[60]

The rivalry between South and North Korea, in principle, dated back to the immediate post–World War II period, when the arbitrary division of the Korean Peninsula generated the "Korean Cause" or "Korean Question." Each party feigned ostentatiously an exclusive legitimacy over the entire Peninsula, striving to gain as much international support as it could in its favor. To further gain the sympathy of other nations by presenting their own sovereign territory as eminently successful and a far better model to be embraced by the other side, the two Koreas also attempted to refashion their political and economic situation: The North began this process no later than the end of the Korean War, and the South started, as we have seen, in the early 1960s. North Korea was able to accomplish unexpected economic achievements and stay well ahead of South Korea during the 1950s and 1960s because of a combination of factors, including its colonial legacy, a staggeringly unified political system, and the *Juche* (often translated as "self-reliance") political ideology.[61] Pyongyang got a great deal of international support throughout the 1970s, while Seoul benefited from the earlier support it gained during the 1950s.[62]

In that period, South Korea's international standing was partially hampered by its strong attachment to the so-called "Hallstein Doctrine,"[63] according to which Seoul could not establish diplomatic relations with any nation that maintained diplomatic ties with Pyongyang. However, coupled with the necessity of achieving economic objectives through developing bilateral relations with a greater number of countries, South Korea eventually had to discard this policy in the early 1970s. The South Korean government had already announced its desire to expand diplomatic ties with member nations of the Non-Aligned Movement (NAM), a rising international bloc of political power that rose in popularity in the 1970s.[64] For its part, North Korea had made relentless efforts to drum up the support and sympathy of the movement, and these efforts culminated in Pyongyang's official membership in the NAM in 1975. On the contrary, South Korea's less appealing image within the NAM, worsened further by Seoul's dedicated participation in the Vietnam War, made its subsequent attempts to join the movement far less successful (for instance, its bid to join the organization in 1975 was rejected).[65]

While the movement was officially established at a summit in Belgrade in September 1961, it was the outbreak of the Korean War in the early 1950s that had propelled many members of the NAM onto the international scene. The movement's championing of the Korean Cause led to member states later meeting at the UN and urging the two Koreas to abide by the 38th Parallel, which had already bifurcated the Peninsula. Egypt and India in particular mediated on behalf of the NAM in order to iron out the problem.[66] Despite the fact, mentioned above, that South Korea suffered a setback in its overall approach to the movement compared to that of North Korea, Seoul's foreign policy did not encounter any serious objections among the NAM member states of the Persian Gulf, with the exception of Iraq. A case in point is Iran, which was an active member of the movement right from the beginning, having even attended its Bandung conference in April 1955. Seoul was able to develop significant political and economic relations with Tehran during the 1960s and especially during the 1970s.

In a nutshell, the rivalry between the two Koreas in the Persian Gulf was very distinctive because of the contrasting objectives they were trying to achieve in the region throughout the 1960s and 1970s. North Korea was mainly after political recognition, though it occasionally adopted economic measures in order to secure it. With South Korea, it was the reverse: Seoul was committed to achieving economic relations with the countries of the Persian Gulf, using political means to ensure a steady supply of energy and better access to the region's markets. Alliance politics particularly allowed the ROK to cultivate closer connections to Iran and Saudi Arabia, while North Korea could benefit only from mutual ties with Iraq – even though Pyongyang's relationship with Baghdad was almost devoid of the camaraderie it enjoyed from bilateral interactions with some other Middle Eastern countries including Egypt and Libya. South Korea's accomplishments therefore remained stable and incremental, while North Korea's accomplishments were provisional in nature and were often inconsistent.

Notes

1 Wilfred G. Burchett, *Again Korea* (New York: International Publishers, 1968), p. 66.
2 Carter Malkasian, *The Korean War* (Oxford: Osprey Publishing, 2001), p. 88.
3 Edwin O. Reischauer, *Beyond Vietnam: The United States and Asia* (New York: Vintage Books, 1967), p. 188.
4 See Robert T. Oliver, *Syngman Rhee: The Man behind the Myth* (New York: Dodd, Mead and Company, 1954).
5 Stephan Haggard and Chung-in Moon, "The State, Politics, and Economic Development in Postwar South Korea," in H. Koo (ed.), *State and Society in Contemporary Korea* (Ithaca: Cornell University Press, 1993), pp. 51–93.
6 Barry Gills, *Korea versus Korea: A Case of Contested Legitimacy* (New York: Routledge, 1996), p. 78.
7 Hakan Hedberg, "International Government Financing Survey: Special Report on South Korea," *The Institutional Investor*, Vol. 12, No. 4 (1978), pp. 113–121, 140.
8 Robert Wade, *Governing the Market: Economic Theory and the Role of Government in East Asian Industrialization* (Princeton: Princeton University Press, 1990), p. 35.
9 Charles R. Frank, K. Kim and Larry E. Westphal, *Foreign Trade Regimes and Economic Development: South Korea*, Vol. 7, National Bureau of Economic Research (New York: Columbia University Press, 1975), p. 9.
10 W.D. Reeve, *The Republic of Korea: A Political and Economic Study* (London: Oxford University Press, 1963), p. 125.
11 Haggard and Moon.
12 Republic of Korea, Ministry of Foreign Affairs, *Wegyo Munseo* [Diplomatic Archives] (Seoul: Ministry of Foreign Affairs, 1996).
13 *Wegyo Munseo* [Diplomatic Archives], 1996.
14 *Wegyo Munseo* [Diplomatic Archives], 1996.
15 *Wegyo Munseo* [Diplomatic Archives], 1996.
16 *Wegyo Munseo* [Diplomatic Archives], 1996.
17 Ismail Soysal, *Soguk Savas Donemi ve Turkiye: Olaylar Kronolojisi (1945–1975)* [*The Cold War Period and Turkey: Chronology of Events (1945–1975)*] (Istanbul: ISIS Yayincilik, 1997), p. 179.
18 Apart from a number of such major official bodies, however, this taxonomy has been gradually treated as antediluvian in recent years, as more and more Chinese institutions and media outlets are no longer hesitant to use the term *zhōngdōng* (the Middle East) to refer to any sort of development relating to West Asia.
19 Yucel Bozdaglioglu, *Turkish Foreign Policy and Turkish Identity: A Constructivist Approach* (London: Routledge, 2003), pp. 57–59.
20 Michael J. Varhola, *Fire and Ice: The Korean War, 1950–1953* (El Dorado Hills, CA: Savas Publishing Company, 2000), p. 134.
21 Seoul established its diplomatic relationship with Addis Ababa in December 1963.
22 Ambassador Il-kwon Chung's Correspondence with President Syngman Rhee, in Republic of Korea, Ministry of Foreign Affairs, *Wegyo Munseo* [Diplomatic Archives] (Seoul: Ministry of Foreign Affairs, 1994).
23 *Wegyo Munseo* [Diplomatic Archives], 1994.

24 Additionally, Iran's envoy to Turkey, who had been concurrently accredited to Greece, had already encountered some troubles because of a tense situation between Ankara and Athens, and the Iranian government did not want its Tokyo ambassador to have a similar unpleasant experience.
25 *Wegyo Munseo* [Diplomatic Archives], 1994.
26 After serving in the post for four years, Ambassador Kia was awarded the Order of Diplomatic Service Merit, Kwanghwa, by South Korea's Prime Minister Jong-pil Kim in April 1972 for his "constant efforts to promote mutual cooperation between Korea and Iran" since the time he had been assigned the accredited position in 1968. See "Iranian Envoy Cited," *Korea Times*, April 26, 1972, p. 1.
27 "Message to Iraq," *Korean Republic*, July 15, 1960, p. 1
28 Dates are according to the information released by the Ministry of Foreign Affairs' website, which is available at http://www.mofa.go.kr.
29 Chung-hee Park, *Kunggawa hydngmydngiwa na* [*The Country, the Revolution, and I*] (Seoul: Hyangmunsa, 1963).
30 A number of other books were subsequently published under his name during the 1960s and 1970s, but it seems unlikely that Park himself penned a single page of those works.
31 The book sings the praises of Germany's "Miracle on the Rhine River" and explores some of the key characteristics of the German people that led to the project's success; he then uses the example of Germany to lay the groundwork for the national task of achieving South Korea's "Miracle on the Han River" over the years to come.
32 Park, "the granite-faced general who turned nation-builder," does in no way gloss over Japan's development story throughout the book. Serving Japan as Masao Takagi in the colonial period, Park Chung-hee's attachment to the Japanese was in fact far stronger, so that upon his assassination on October 26, 1979, Tokyo's ambassador to Seoul, Hisahiko Okazaki, mourned Park's death as the demise of "the last soldier of Imperial Japan."
33 Park, pp. 249–250.
34 A famous motto ascribed to Park Chung-hee is "urido hanbon chal sara bose" ["Let's live well at least once"].
35 Park, p. 266.
36 Gilbert T. Brown, *Korean Pricing Policies and Economic Development in the 1960s* (Baltimore: Johns Hopkins University Press, 1973), p. 46.
37 In a letter to President Syngman Rhee on November 11, 1958, South Korea's ambassador to Ankara, Il-kwon Chung, had already proposed that Rhee emulate the Turkish security system and establish a central intelligence unit to monitor everything, including all South Korean armed forces. It is not clear to what extent such an idea subsequently influenced Park's security apparatus. See *Wegyo Munseo* [Diplomatic Archives], 1994.
38 Graham Field, *Economic Growth and Political Change in Asia* (London: Macmillan Press, 1995), p. 156.
39 Based on one observation, South Korea's relentless yet rather ruthless policies of industrialization and economic development "produced a 58-hour work week, the longest of any country surveyed by the International Labor Organization; the world's highest industrial accident rate; and a working class that remains relatively impoverished. In 1985, 60% of South Korean workers earned less than $110 per month, far below the government's estimated minimum monthly income of $335 needed to support a family of five." See Walden Bello, "Asia's Miracle Economies: The First and Last of a Dying Breed," *Dollars & Sense*, Vol. 143 (1989), pp. 12–15.
40 The World Bank, *The East Asian Miracle: Economic Growth and Public Policy – A World Bank Policy Research Report* (New York: Oxford University Press, 1993), p. 127.

41   Barry Gills, "The Political Economy of Diplomacy: North and South Korea and Competition for International Support," in D. Kim and T. Kong (eds.), *The Korean Peninsula in Transition* (London: Macmillan Press, 1997), pp. 199–223.
42   In 1965, $1 bought 360 Japanese yen.
43   Hideo Suzuki and Yoshii Satoshi, *Rekishi ni miru nihon to kankoku & kitachousen* [*Japan's Relations with South and North Korea from a Historical Perspective*] (Tokyo: Akashi Shoten, 1999), p. 138.
44   South Korea dispatched roughly 320,000 soldiers to Vietnam throughout the course of the war, and its maximum troop participation peaked at 50,000 in 1968. During a period of eight years and six months of involvement in the war from September 1964 to March 1973, approximately 4,407 soldiers were killed and 17,060 were injured. South Koreans also claimed that they killed 41,000 Vietcong fighters ("1965 nyeon jeontubyeong beteunam pabyeong uigyeol" ["Decision on Combat-Troop Dispatch to the Vietnam War in 1965"], *Dong-A Ilbo*, July 2, 2008).
45   Claude A. Buss, *The United States and the Republic of Korea: Background for Policy* (Stanford: Hoover Institution Press, 1982), p. 82.
46   Michael E. Porter, *The Competitive Advantage of Nations* (New York: Free Press, 1990), p. 464.
47   Haider A. Khan, *Technology, Energy and Development: The South Korean Transition* (Cheltenham, UK: Edward Elgar, 1997), pp. 80–81.
48   Garth L. Mangum, S. Kim and Stephen B. Tallman, *Transnational Marriages in the Steel Industry: Experience and Lessons for Global Business* (Westport, CT: Quorum Books, 1996), p. 123.
49   Khan, pp. 79–81.
50   "Kuwait, Korea Mark 20 Years of Growing Partnership," *Business Korea,* Vol. 16, No. 2, (1999), pp. 68–69.
51   Christopher M. Dent, *The Foreign Economic Policies of Singapore, South Korea and Taiwan* (Cheltenham, UK: Edward Elgar, 2002), p. 148.
52   Daniel Metraux, "The Economy," in Andrea Matles Savada and William Shaw (eds.), *South Korea: A Country Study*, 4th edition. (Washington, D.C.: Library of Congress, Federal Research Division, 1992), pp. 135–196.
53   Cited from KOTRA's website: http://kotra.or.kr.
54   Data is taken from the website of the Korean Statistical Information Service: http://kosis.kr.
55   Korean Statistical Information Service.
56   *Wegyo Munseo* [Diplomatic Archives], 1994.
57   *Wegyo Munseo* [Diplomatic Archives], 1996.
58   "Hazf shomali va jenubi az donbal nam kore!" ["Leaving Out North and South after Korea"], *Kayhan*, August 4, 1968.
59   Lebanon was particularly sensitive about the issue, as its foreign ministry sources later revealed that the country had become embarrassed by the pressure exerted upon it to favor one Korea over the other, though the Middle Eastern nation had already announced that Beirut was neither willing to receive a political delegation from Pyongyang nor wanting to develop political ties with Seoul. Despite the trouble, Lebanon still evinced its diplomatic grace and treated both visiting North and South Korean delegates equally.
60   "N., S. Korea Delegations Pose Problem," *The Daily Star*, July 23, 1968.
61   *Juche* was basically promoted to function as the fundamental principle behind every North Korean domestic and foreign policy initiative.
62   Gills, *Korea versus Korea*, p. 19.
63   Named after Walter Hallstein, the doctrine worked as West Germany's basic foreign policy guideline from 1955 to 1969 when Willy Brandt became German chancellor and later abandoned some of the main elements of its core principles.

64 *Daehan minguk wegyo yeonpyo* [*Republic of Korea, Annual Report on Foreign Policy*] (Seoul: Ministry of Foreign Affairs, 1970), p. 280.
65 Deon Geldenhuys, *Isolated States: A Comparative Analysis* (Cambridge: Cambridge University Press, 1990), p. 73.
66 Peter Willetts, *The Non-Aligned Movement: The Origins of a Third World Alliance* (London: Frances Pinter, 1978), p. 8.

2   The oil boom and the ensuing construction bonanza

The Korean Cause meets the Arab Cause: The first oil shock

After more than a decade of relative political stability and continuous economic growth at home, South Korea suddenly experienced a new upheaval that was to significantly affect its economy as well as its Persian Gulf policy. For the first time since the beginning of the ROK's industrialization and economic development program, events in the Middle East seriously tested the power and flexibility of the South Korean economy and posed a formidable challenge to the nation's foreign policy toward the region – and especially toward the Persian Gulf. The Arab-Israeli war of 1973 and the ensuing oil shock would propel South Korea through a very crucial period in its history, a period that would start and end poorly, but that would otherwise bring about a great deal of prosperity. The crisis, which soon turned out to be a blessing in disguise, led to highly important developments – political, economic and even cultural – in South Korea's relations with various Gulf countries. The South Koreans strove to make the most of this milestone in their ties with the Persian Gulf region, feeling very proud of their newfound commercial achievements, which were far greater than any that had come before.

In the wake of the Yom Kippur War in October 1973, Arab members of the Organization of the Petroleum Exporting Countries (OPEC) pushed for an oil embargo against Western countries unless they stopped arming Israel and pushed Tel Aviv to withdraw from the territories it had occupied during the Six-Day War in 1967.[1] At the same time, non-Arab members of OPEC, especially Iran, were discontented with low oil prices and took the opportunity to demand better prices at the organization's Tehran meeting in January 1974.[2] Iran, for instance, argued that Western nations had already increased the price of their exported wheat and cement by 300 percent and that it was only logical for stalwart importers of oil to be prepared to pay a higher rate for OPEC's petroleum.[3] A combination of these two matters along with the subsequent oil shortage in world markets brought about the so-called "first oil shock." The Arab states that triggered the problem in the first place, however, did not fully cooperate with the measure taken by OPEC. A case in point is Saudi Arabia, the presumptive leader of the Arab countries of OPEC, which not only opposed unflinchingly Iran's call for a price hike, thereby causing further disunity within the cartel, it also made sure that quantities of its petroleum poured into American markets during the height of the oil embargo.[4]

The oil crisis of 1973–1974, which came from out of the blue and which had no precedent, sent a sudden electric shock through the South Korean economy, causing significant instability and uncertainty. Besides a disruption in the daily life of Korean citizens, the earliest reverberations of the first oil shock that were felt by the ROK's nascent economy included an inflation rate of just over 20 percent, an exorbitant bill for energy imports, and, consequently, a significant trade deficit. All at once, South Korea's oil bill shot up from less than $300 million in 1972 to over $1 billion in 1974, roughly 15 percent of the total value of its imports. Moreover, the fledgling East Asian nation's existing trade deficit of about $1 billion in 1973 ratcheted up to approximately $2.4 billion in 1974, adding yet another blow to the country's economic prospects.[5] Such an abrupt payment imbalance, largely caused by the importing of oil at higher rates, was particularly harmful to many Koreans; the quickest – and practically the best – remedy was to be unexpectedly found in the Persian Gulf region itself, where a sizeable chunk of Korea's oil payments were headed.

While the painful ramifications of the first oil shock were much more severe for some other energy-importing nations such as South Korea's East Asian neighbors Japan and Taiwan, the South Korean government soon managed to successfully pull the country from the brink of economic disaster. An early sign of its success was exemplified by the ROK's maintaining a 30 percent average export growth rate in 1974–1975, when the volume of world trade had substantially decreased.[6] In the midst of this global oil calamity, more importantly, the South Korean government maintained its policy of making large investments in energy-consuming heavy industries *pari passu* with Park Chung-hee's statement, made in 1972, that "steel equals national power."[7] Additionally, the improvement of a poor economic situation coupled with sanguine forecasts about its swift return to previous growth rates coincided with the end of diplomatic squabbles that had been going on in the Arab world, paving the way for a stable oil supply and the inordinate penetration of South Korea's contractors and its manufactured products into Gulf markets. It did not take long for the energy nightmare of the early 1970s to end.

The Israeli factor in Korean–Arab relations

The ROK and Israel established diplomatic relations in April 1962, and Tel Aviv set up its embassy in Seoul the following year before it appointed a resident ambassador two years later. Contrary to Israel, South Korea did not open an embassy or consulate in Israel, and the South Korean ambassador to Italy with non-resident status in Greece and Israel, Duk-choo Moon, never presented his credentials to Tel Aviv. The main stumbling block was that such a move could simply incur the wrath of many Arab countries – including

Saudi Arabia – which were already unhappy with Seoul's diplomatic ties with Israel.[8] Such a diplomatic game of running with the hare and hunting with the hounds continued even after the Yom Kippur War of 1973 and the ensuing oil shock; as far as the public eyes of the Arab world were concerned, the South Korean government did its utmost not to appear to be on good terms with Israel. The Israelis objected on several occasions to South Korea's failure to reciprocate their diplomatic gestures toward Seoul; eventually, they became so disgruntled that they decided to shut their embassy down in 1978, announcing that budgetary reasons were behind the move to end the Jewish state's diplomatic presence in the ROK. It took Israel another decade and a half to overturn this policy and reopen its embassy in Seoul in 1992.

Until just prior to the first oil shock, South Korea had tried to stick more or less to a "dual" diplomacy by trying to balance its ties with Israel and the Arabs. In principle, South Korea's sympathy for Israel was strong prior to the Six-Day War of 1967; however, after the war, Seoul gradually started to have some sympathy for the Palestinians as a sign of apparent solidarity with the Arab Cause. In the aftermath of the war and the following oil shock, Seoul became even more obsessed with finding harmless ways to evince its understanding of and support for the Arab Cause. The crux of the dilemma, stemming largely from an attachment to the double-track policy, was how to get the name of South Korea listed as a friendly nation to the Arabs – the *sine qua non* of securing a safe supply of oil – while simultaneously not appearing to be an anti-Israel country in the Western media and policy circles. The very fact that the South Korean government was highly obsessed with finding out how its neighbor Japan and the Association of Southeast Asian Nations (ASEAN) reacted to the crisis in order to figure out its own course of action indicates that the problem was actually quite delicate and that it required a very calculated policy response.[9]

After dragging its feet for some time, the South Korean government finally declared its official position regarding the Arab–Israeli conflict, the root cause of the oil embargo. The four-article statement, announced by the South Korean foreign ministry on October 23, 1973, contained a view quite similar to those announced by Japan and Indonesia, the ASEAN representative, as if all of them had been paraphrased from a single text. In a nutshell, the political statement accentuated four points, including a refrain from using force to acquire territory or adjudicate an international dispute; the withdrawal of Israeli forces from the territories that Tel Aviv occupied during the conflicts of 1967 and 1973; recognition and respect for the legitimate claims of the Palestinians; and respect for the integrity and independence of every sovereign state.[10] In addition to a series of visits to some influential Arab countries that were conducted subsequently by its cabinet ministers and parliamentarians in order to further consolidate Seoul's approach to the region, South Korea also prohibited all government officials from visiting Israel and even barred any ROK representatives from attending "Book Trade-Faro," which was scheduled to be held in Jerusalem in April 1975.[11]

It comes as no surprise, then, that in the aftermath of the 1967 Arab–Israeli war, the South Korean government needed to equipoise contrasting attitudes affiliated with both conflicting camps in order to safely secure Seoul's national interests in the Middle East. On one side, some Korean media outlets and businesses were calling on the government to openly support the Arab Cause following the 1967 war and even more so after the 1973 war and subsequent embargo. The other side included many pro-Israeli elements within the American media and American policy circles that often used to remind South Korea about "tremendous sacrifices" they made for the Koreans, obliging them not to favor the Arabs at Israel's expense. A case in point is the fact that two American senators, Edmund Muskie and Hush Scott, contacted the South Korean ambassador to the United States, Dong-jo Kim, in January 1973 in order to caution his country about rumors related to an imminent pro-Arab shift among South Korean media organizations and politicians. Enclosed in their letters to Kim was a copy of a forthcoming editorial that was to be published by the *Near East Report* highlighting critical assessments of some putatively pro-Arab attitudes expressed by South Korean newspapers and politicians.[12]

South Korea's relationship with Israel was actually such a sensitive issue that even a private and non-governmental entity run by Korean citizens could potentially jeopardize the ROK's Arab policy: A paid advertisement by the Unification Church and its leader, Reverend Sun-myung Moon, appeared in the *New York Times* on December 19, 1976, insisting that Israel, the United States and South Korea, "the nations where Judaism, Christianity and the Unification Movement are based, must also be brothers." The advertisement, which raised eyebrows among many Arabs, forced the South Korean government to nix any affiliation with the Church and the message it had aired. The South Korean foreign minister, Tong-jin Park, made it clear both quickly and publicly that the Unification Church did not have anything to do with the South Korean government and that Church's leader did not represent the government's position. Moreover, the South Korean embassy in Jeddah sent a letter to Saudi Arabia's foreign ministry to let the relevant Saudi officials know that the ROK could not be held responsible for the Unification Church's activities and that Seoul would unswervingly observe its (rather flimsy) commitment to support the Arab Cause as specified previously through its policy statement delivered on December 15, 1973.[13]

North Korea seizes the occasion

The ROK's reactions to developments in the Arab world were not determined solely by local media interests, the views of its politicians or the expectations of its foreign partners. South Korea's rivalry with North Korea with regard to the Arab states of the Middle East was also an influential consideration, particularly throughout the 1970s, when Seoul capitalized rather significantly on building better relationships with a large number of countries in the region. This approach was crucial to South Korea's interests and achievements in the Persian Gulf, where the Arab Cause could at last compel Arab leaders in the region to push for an oil embargo, which would in turn endanger the life-blood of the fledgling South Korean economy. Moreover, the rivalry to capture the heart of Arab leaders was not confined to Seoul and Pyongyang, as India and Pakistan had already set a precedent throughout the Middle East, each country campaigning fiercely in order to drum up the support and recognition of as many Arab countries as it could – even to the detriment of its neighbor and archrival.

The fact that the Arab nations of the Middle East initially perceived South Korea and North Korea in much the same way significantly advanced the latter's profile throughout the 1950s, 1960s and 1970s. North Korea built close relationships with both Egypt and Syria, as Pyongyang wasted no time in recognizing their political alliance when the two countries merged to become the United Arab Republic (UAR) in February 1958 – though they were later to split up in 1961 when Syria withdrew from the union. The ruler of the DPRK regime, Kim Il-sung, became the first Korean leader to have a summit with an Arab head of state, meeting Egypt's Gamal Abdel Nasser in Cairo in 1964. At that time, Nasserism was at its zenith and Egypt was thereby able to wield a significant amount of influence as the *de facto* leader of the Arab world. Later, Kim Il-sung attended another summit, this time with the Syrian president, Hafiz al-Asad, in Pyongyang in 1974, only a few years after a state visit to the DPRK by al-Asad's predecessor, Nureddin al-Atassi.[14] Unlike North Korea, South Korea was only able to establish a relationship with Egypt at the consular level and it was not able to establish any sort of relationship with Syria because of Damascus's serious reservations about Seoul's political ties with Israel.[15]

The Arab–Israeli conflicts of the late 1960s and the early 1970s provided North Korea with yet another opportunity to move closer to its Arab allies. When the 1967 war broke out, the DPRK threw its unwavering support behind the Arabs,[16] while in 1973 Pyongyang went one step further and provided military support as well. Once the Yom Kippur War of 1973 broke out, Kim Il-sung personally received both the Egyptian and Syrian envoys to Pyongyang, offering them moral and material support: North Korea dispatched more than 300 military technicians and pilots to both Egypt and Syria. It did the same for Libya in 1979, when it sent 280 air force personnel to the regime of Colonel Muammar Gaddafi in order to assist the government in quelling a local rebellion.[17] Despite North Korea's passionate support of the Arabs in the 1973 war, the ensuing oil shock did not work in Pyongyang's favor at all. This was a time when the North Korean economy first embraced some commercial exchanges with a number of European (and other) capitalist nations. The dramatic spike in petroleum prices following the first oil shock coupled with the fall of prices for Pyongyang's nonferrous mineral exports caused the North Korean economy to default.[18]

North Korea's public flirtation with the Arabs was not enough to tarnish South Korea's image, as Pyongyang's occasional damaging claims often threatened to endanger Seoul's interests in the region.[19] As revealed during an interview with the *Korea Herald* in June 1972, the leader of a South Korean trade mission to Beirut, Mogan Yun, had already complained that North Korea's propaganda about South Korea was really damaging Seoul's image and interests in the region.[20] One such case occurred on January 25, 1975, when the North Korean News Agency (KCNA) reported that the ROK had offered military assistance to Israel following the Yom Kippur War in October 1973. The news made the South Korean foreign ministry vehemently deny the claim as a "groundless allegation," emphasizing Seoul's apathy toward the idea of giving Israel any kind of assistance.[21] Such ruinous accusations, which led to bitter feuds between Pyongyang and Seoul over their respective policies toward the Arab world, were not without precedence; they go back at least as far as 1956, when North Korea claimed that the then South Korean president, Syngman Rhee, had offered to dispatch troops to assist Britain and France in their fight against Egypt during the Suez Crisis.[22]

Petrodollars and a new desire for foreign goods

One immediate result of the first oil shock in 1973–1974 was a sudden inflow of cash into the coffers of OPEC member states – especially those of the Persian Gulf member states. When oil prices started to creep up from $1.50 per barrel in 1972 to approximately $9 per barrel in 1974, oil incomes of OPEC countries likewise shot up from $13.7 billion in 1972 to $87.2 billion in 1974.[23] In one sense, the fluctuation in oil prices was not something new and could be traced back to the discovery of oil in 1859. For example, one year after the initial discovery of oil in Pennsylvania, the price of the commodity was a staggering $20 per barrel, but at the end of that year it was a only $0.10 per barrel – occasionally, the price would drop to such an extent that a barrel of oil became cheaper than a barrel of water.[24] Despite historical variations in petroleum prices since then, the price hike following the first oil shock was unprecedented, and it had tremendous implications for petroleum producers in the Persian Gulf region.

In the aftermath of the oil price explosion, Iran reached its highest ever output, producing 6 million barrels per day (bpd) in 1974. Encouraged by the rise of oil prices, such a level of production brought in so much revenue, that per capita income increased from about $180 before the oil shock to approximately $810 in 1973–1974 and probably more than $1,500 a year later.[25] This phenomenon transformed, abruptly, almost everything from the pattern of imports to the standard of living among ordinary citizens for the better part of the 1970s. In Saudi Arabia, the first oil boom helped the country's national incomes grow stupendously from less than $6 billion in 1972 to more than $25 billion by 1974. Such a sudden surge in the Arab state's mainstay put the very stability of the Saudi establishment at stake, spawning a famous remark by King Faisal: "Revolution can come from thrones as well as from con-spirators' cellars. We need everything in this country, but stability is the first priority."[26]

Faisal's concern with instability was particularly relevant to Iran, as the flow of petrodollars virtually turned the country's economy into an oil-based economy and derailed its development programs and economic plans, which had previously experienced significant progress. While income from petroleum exports comprised less than 50 percent of Iran's foreign exchange revenues in 1971–1972, its share increased to a whopping 70 percent by 1975–1976, when the country's oil revenues reached about \$23 billion.[27] Not only did the flow of oil dollars fail to help Iran in the form of a panacea to its fundamental economic ills, it also exacerbated those ills in the long run once the govern-ment and the general public got badly addicted to foreign imports at the cost of national production. What's worse was that the flood of petrodollars instantly enhanced the people's expectations for better wages and a higher standard of living, killing off the country's early prospects for a cheap labor force with which to shoulder the financial burden of industrial programs and domestic production.

The ardor with which the citizens of the Gulf states now sought foreign-made consumer goods was, therefore, one phenomenon that now characterized the region in the wake of the first oil boom. During this period, the nations of the Persian Gulf started allocating huge sums of money to their militaries – with Iran at top of the list; the latter increased its defense expenditures from \$1.93 billion in 1973–1974 to a mind-blowing \$10.41 billion in 1975–1976, when the country's food imports were then estimated to be \$1.6 billion or roughly 13 percent of total imports.[28] Moreover, the oil producers channeled some of their surplus income into foreign banks, mostly in the West, and to other developing countries – the funds serving as loans designed to stimulate economic growth. Another, more important, destination of petrodollars was the state bureaucracy and, consequently, the many new government-initiated development plans and infrastructure projects that it underwrote, many of which came into existence after the first oil shock. It was the implementation of these infrastructure projects that made the Persian Gulf region the desti-nation of choice of various international construction companies, including many from South Korea.

Hitting the jackpot: The construction bonanza

In the wake of the first oil shock, virtually all OPEC member countries embarked on large-scale infrastructure and development plans at a rate that was unprecedented in their respective histories. In the Persian Gulf region, Iran, and to some extent Iraq, went on to achieve full-fledged industrialization within a generation or so due to the success of many ongoing development programs that had been launched long before the oil price hike. Saudi Arabia and the five other smaller states in the region still initiated their own development projects, but the lack of a large domestic workforce with the requisite knowledge and experience made these nations much more dependent on the whims of international contractors and foreign workers who were all too eager to carry out those projects.[29] It was therefore the implementation of extensive infrastructure projects and the suitability of international bidding to these projects that turned the Persian Gulf into a hive of construction and a magnet for foreign contractors, many of whom came from South Korea, from about 1974 onward. While the flow of foreign contractors into the region was subject to its own vicissitudes and uncertainties over the years, it never dwindled.

And while the South Koreans were new to the construction industry of the Persian Gulf, they possessed significant construction and building experience. In addition to completing many domestic reconstruction projects after the Korean War and building military bases and other facilities for the American forces stationed in South Korea, many Korean subcontractors were engaged in dozens of construction projects during the Vietnam War, which served as their first exposure to international work. In December 1973, the Samwhan Construction Company became the first South Korean firm to be awarded a contract in the Gulf. Having been granted a contract valued at approximately $25 million, its objective was to construct a 164 km highway in Saudi Arabia between Khayba and Alula.[30] This development opened the region up to a whole host of Korean companies throughout the 1970s and beyond, shaping a new, yet much-vaunted, chapter in South Korea's engagement with the Persian Gulf. By the late 1970s and early 1980s, Korean companies could extend their construction businesses to other parts of the Middle East, including Libya and Egypt, even though their country had no formal diplomatic relations with those nations.

In the Persian Gulf region, Saudi Arabia was the largest construction market and the *ne plus ultra* of overseas building for South Korean companies as well as for other foreign firms from the West and the East heading to the Arab country. For instance, there were more than 260 international contractors in Riyadh by the late 1970s, 50 of which belonged to South Korea alone, with possibly the same number in Jeddah. This phenomenon had much to do with Saudi Arabia's lavish spending on building projects, which grew seventeen-fold from 1973 until the end of 1979.[31] The Saudi market was indeed very crucial to South Korean companies in terms of lucrative construction contracts that they could sign anywhere in the world at that time. For example, they signed about $2.6 billion in overseas contracts in 1976, the lion's share of which came from Saudi Arabia – the equivalent of $2.1 billion.[32] And while the earnings of Korean contractors from the region's construction business was nil prior to 1973, one lucrative contract signed by Hyundai to build an industrial port in Jubail (Saudi Arabia) was worth nearly 25 percent of South Korea's national budget in 1976.[33]

This provides a glimpse into the impact of the construction boom on the South Korean economy as well as the country's commercial interactions with the Persian Gulf during that period. In a broad sense, the presence of Korean construction businesses in the Persian Gulf region had significant internal and external implications for South Korea. On the domestic side, large incomes obtained through the work of construction companies helped South Korea easily chip away at the debt it had incurred in the wake of the first oil shock and then contribute to the growth and success of its economy for many years to come. Construction revenues were large enough to assist South Korea with its balance of payments, with the reimbursement of its foreign debts, and with the employment of its workforce. As a part of their contribution, South Korean companies took home more than $45 billion from Saudi Arabia alone over the decade between 1973 and 1984, accounting for about 61 percent of South Korea's overseas construction contracts during that period.[34] In addition, the construction industry helped South Korean companies eventually become the cornerstone of the ROK's economy; Hyundai, for example, was to become the largest *chaebol* in South Korea by 1978.

On the international side, the oil boom helped solidify the presence of South Korean companies in the Gulf. They entered the Persian Gulf as newcomers in 1973–1974, and by the end of the decade they came to be seen by their East Asian rivals as well as by established Western contractors as serious competitors. And while many Korean firms started their businesses as subcontractors for Japanese or other more experienced companies, they swiftly managed to outstrip their competitors in the international construction industry; in some cases, they even managed to overtake firms for whom they had initially been subcontractors. Once they had firmly established their position in the Gulf, they were no longer willing to aggressively engage in one-upmanship with rival companies in order to land a small or medium-sized contract they had previously been more than happy to take on as subcontractors.[35]

Korean workers in the Persian Gulf

Construction companies took hundreds of thousands of Koreans over the course of a decade to Persian Gulf countries to work intently on various projects that they had contracted for. An overwhelming majority of these workers were manual laborers, but a fraction of this enormous group consisted of skilled laborers and professionals – the latter including nurses, doctors, engineers and technicians. Though most Korean workers were hired – as one might expect – by South Korean companies, a tiny minority of them were recruited by Japanese and Western contractors (even if they had been initially brought to the Gulf by Korean agents). Korean laborers made it into nearly all Persian Gulf countries, but Saudi Arabia received the greatest number of workers throughout the entirety of the construction boom: A combined total of 720,000 Korean laborers were hired for construction projects across Saudi Arabia from 1973 until 1984. The largest number of them arrived in 1982, when more than 110,000 Koreans formed the third largest group of foreign workers stationed in Saudi Arabia.[36]

South Korean contractors enjoyed certain advantages when they hired their fellow citizens to carry out construction projects throughout the Persian Gulf region and (on occasion) the broader Middle East. Although the imported workforce was not the only factor that contributed to the overall success enjoyed by Korean companies in the region – companies that became veritable stars of the international construction industry by the early 1980s – it was nevertheless an extremely important one: Korean laborers were, for the most part, hard-working, disciplined and obedient, and their physical energy played a con-structive role in the completion of contracted projects, many of which were finished ahead of schedule. Not only were they a selling point for Korean companies to be used over and against their rivals, they also had very little in common, culturally or politically, with the local population and so were therefore less likely to socialize with the Saudis and become a source of concern for the government. Another great advantage of employing fellow Korean laborers flown in from thousands of miles away was that they received, on average, 20 percent of their wages in local currency and the bulk of the outstanding 80 percent in Korean won. This afforded the contractors a unique opportunity to ship home a hefty tranche of their desperately needed foreign exchange earnings.[37]

While Korean companies were often envied by their international competitors as well as policy analysts, they were simultaneously blamed for the exploitation and poor treatment of their workforce. They were particularly blamed for paying much lower salaries in comparison to their Western and Japanese competitors and for forcing their laborers to work longer hours under (what were often) extreme hot weather conditions. Such accusations turned out to be credible when 3,000 Korean workers rioted against their employer, Hyundai, at Saudi Arabia's Jubail Industrial Harbor Project in March 1977, killing two managers and wrecking property and equipment estimated to be worth $48 million.[38] The incident was so sensitive and disastrous that it forced the South Korean gov-ernment to immediately form a task force to resolve the labor disruption in less than ten days. This effort to resolve the situation included an early appearance by Kyu-ha Choi, then South Korean prime minister, at the scene of the strike to make a formal apology to both the government of Saudi Arabia and the workers themselves.[39] While it is true that there were conscripts among the Korean workforce whose terms of service in the Persian Gulf had let them discharge from military service early with some money in their pockets as a further incentive to do so, the rest of it comprised people who were neither accustomed to complaining nor taught to object to unfair and inappropriate working conditions. They were eager laborers who had to toil away for 14 to 16 hours a day in the scorching heat on a construction site which some observers have described as having been "nothing more than a military barracks."[40]

The government assumes the mantle

From the beginning to the end, the South Korean government played an indispensable role in the arrival, performance and accomplishments of Korean construction companies in the Persian Gulf region. It was Park Chung-hee who personally pushed Hyundai and other contractors to sail far out into the uncharted waters of the Persian Gulf soon after the first oil shock disturbed the Korean economy. At that time, South Korea was particularly desperate to ramp up its foreign exchange earnings and – in order to do so – to dispatch its surplus labor somewhere abroad; the majority of these workers were unskilled laborers and were not a productive element in the domestic economy. The government, therefore, established extensive programs that were designed to help send Korean construction companies and Korea's surplus workforce to Persian Gulf countries throughout the 1970s and the early 1980s. Not only did the government turn its embassies into a rendezvous for contractors – a construction *attaché* at the embassy was always the first point of contact in case of an emergency – at the national level, the construction ministry and the construction industry were virtually interchangeable because they had become one single entity with one single function.[41]

The government also established various agencies, research institutions and training facilities to supervise the activities of the construction companies and promote their interests in the Persian Gulf. Various laws and regulations were also passed in many instances to accelerate the inroads of South Korean contractors into the region. For example, one law enacted in 1979 aimed to assist the contractors with the export of plant and equipment, especially through tax incentives. The main provision of the law allowed for a 50 percent tax reduction on revenues earned through exported plant.[42] On top of the government's supportive measures came its efforts, at the outset, to provide construction enterprises with financial aid as well as supplementary services both inside and outside South Korea. An example of the latter was the establishment of the government-controlled Korean Exchange Bank in Bahrain, as South Korea's first offshore banking facility, to meet the pecuniary and commercial requirements of the many Korean companies throughout the Persian Gulf region.[43]

Occasional recommendations by the government, even when they were not put into writing or afforded any official status, could also play a role in the enhancement of the *esprit de corps* and camaraderie among Korean construction companies working in unfamiliar surroundings far away from home. One such recommendation included advice to Korean companies to refrain from "excessive competition" between them. The government did not pass on "tips" of this type only to Korean companies, as it had already suggested that skilled workers not work for international companies to the disadvantage of their fellow Korean contractors in the Persian Gulf region. The government was partially entitled to such guidance because it was spending, in some cases, millions of dollars to train specialists and skilled workers in order to help provide its construction companies with the human capital they required. With the exception of those soldiers-turned-workers who had been trained at military camps, the government needed to write a check for approximately $3 million to educate 5,000 skilled laborers in professions such as carpentry, plumbing and welding.[44]

Once South Korean construction companies became more experienced and moved from labor-intensive to technology-intensive projects, their ever-increasing dependency on the government for technological assistance became a stark reality. The early projects won by Korean firms in the Persian Gulf were largely constrained to channeling water supply and sewerage lines or setting up housing estates and ordinary low-rise buildings. In order to walk away with larger, more technologically sophisticated contracts for the construction of power supply systems or oil industry installations, Korean contractors had to equip themselves with knowledge of more advanced engineering techniques so that they could compete with well-to-do rivals from Japan or the West that had already possessed an advanced level of technological know-how.[45] To overcome such an obstacle, the South Korean government tried to incentivize foreign construction firms in the region to enter into joint ventures with the Korean firms in the area. Such an initiative paid off over time, and construction-related foreign investments in South Korea amounted to more than 4 percent of all foreign investment plans approved by the mid-1980s, of which more than 80 percent were only to materialize after 1977.[46]

Less visible factors

South Korea's construction companies were widely accused of offering their services at cutthroat prices and significantly underbidding the competition. While many agreed that Korean companies did underbid for their contracts, there was no agreement as to what extent their bids differed from those of their rivals; estimates put the discounted bids at anywhere from 15 to 50 percent. Other observers with a keen interest in the actions of Korean entities believed that "often South Korean bids are 30–40 percent below Western bids."[47] Western companies in particular cried foul over this Korean practice, condemning it as a means of unjustly cornering the market; it ate into their profit margins to such an extent as to make the cost of doing business in the Gulf way too high. The crux of the problem was that sometimes the total value of a contract offered by a Korean firm did not exceed what a Western contractor had estimated would be the cost of its building materials.[48] After all, Korean construction companies were importing raw materials from their home country, and, on top of that, they were further privileged with a cheaper workforce as well as with access to a whole host of subsidies provided by their government in Seoul.

Another less debated and even far less investigated issue is the extent to which companies paid additional agent fees and made illicit offers to the authorities in order to win construction contracts. The dearth of investigative reports, the absence of public inquiries, and self-censorship have made it nearly impossible to determine with any certainty just how many Korean contractors made such payments and to what extent they actually used bribes and slush funds for the purpose of gaining influence and winning lucrative (or even modest) contracts. However, in spite of this difficulty, two well-known bribery scandals involving Hyundai were exposed in Saudi Arabia, leading to the arrest of the company's managers, who apparently had the audacity to take millions of dollars to a Saudi military complex in order to bribe government officials. Not only did the scandals result in Saudi Arabia immediately black-balling Hyundai from its market for about two years (1980–1981), they also tarnished the image of Korean contractors in the Persian Gulf region and gave some less fortunate firms a chance to fare better, even if only for a while.[49] In the words of Chung-in Moon, who studied the history of Korean construction companies in Saudi Arabia in more detail, "most Korean firms have reportedly engaged in such practices. The utilization of 'non-conventional' business practices was thought to be quite common among Korean firms."[50]

Finally, ideological and cultural factors may have played a significant role in the success of Korean firms in the Arabic-speaking nations of the Persian Gulf region. After all, the political chaos in the Middle East in 1973 and the ensuing oil shock had been triggered by the West's support for Israel. Those in charge of construction projects, if they were biased, could potentially associate Western contractors with Israel, whereas the same could not be said of contractors from the East, including those from South Korea, Japan and Taiwan. At the same time, Western firms were well aware of the impacts that such a prejudice might have on their chances of winning contracts and had found a way to overcome this problem. In one case, Bechtel, one of the largest American contractors in the Persian Gulf, went out of its way to disregard its own country's Sherman Antitrust Act by refusing to deal with those American subcontractors and suppliers which had been blackballed through the Arab League's boycott of Israel.[51] However, it remains hard to determine whether or not ideological and cultural proclivities as well as a desire for diversification among the pertinent politicians in the region substantially worked to the advantage of Korean contractors.

The promotion of exports

Besides the advent of the construction bonanza, as it were, the steep rise in imports and spending seen in Persian Gulf countries in the aftermath of the oil shock dovetailed neatly with South Korea's policy of promoting its exports overseas, a policy which had long been heavily reliant on the American and Japanese markets. The South Korean government from the top down intended not only to diversify the country's export destinations, but, more importantly, to also increase the volume of manufactured goods it was shipping abroad. At a ceremony marking the 9th Export Day on November 30, 1972, Park Chung-hee vowed that his government "will provide every possible support and cooperation to help industries attain the annual export target of $10 billion by the early 1980s."[52] Construction and trade with the Persian Gulf region in the aftermath of the first oil boom, then, emerged as the *deus ex machina* that helped such an expectation come to fruition much earlier than Park had envisioned. Over a relatively short time span of seven years (1970–1977),

South Korea increased its merchandise exports from $1 billion to $10 billion, achieving a major breakthrough *pari passu* with that long-cherished national goal uttered so succinctly by the South Korean president.[53]

While South Korea's exports to world markets, therefore, increased by only 21.7 percent in 1975 as compared to a year earlier, its exports to the Persian Gulf region during that same year skyrocketed, increasing by more than 220 percent to approximately $290 million from $108 million in 1974.[54] Iran remained far and away the biggest market for Korean exports, receiving $42 million in 1974 and $126 million in 1975, indicating a surprising jump of roughly 300 percent in one year alone. By 1979, Saudi Arabia, Kuwait and Iran were the ROK's top three export markets in the Persian Gulf, importing $704 million, $228 million and $186 million worth of Korean products, respectively. In 1974, South Korea's exports to these three countries accounted for $101 million of the $108 million the country shipped to the entire Persian Gulf region. By 1979, South Korea's combined exports to the Gulf reached about $1.3 billion, the lion's share of which consisted of commodities shipped to the aforementioned three nations (about $1.1 billion). When South Korea's combined global exports had shot up to $10.5 billion in 1977, the share headed to the Persian Gulf region was, astonishingly, about $1.2 billion or more than 10 percent of the total.[55]

After all, South Korea's export penetration into the Persian Gulf was part of the East Asian country's overall policy of promoting its exports around the world. Exports, according to this policy, were considered the primary engine of growth in Korea's economy, the yardstick of success, and the touchstone of all microeconomic and macroeconomic policies. Soon after the beginning of state-instituted economic development plans in 1962, achieving significant export growth was explicitly regarded a highly crucial national priority and, in fact, a patriotic obligation for anyone who was in a position to play a role in one way or another. For his part, the South Korean president personally engaged in this priority from crafting relevant policies to observing the stringent implementation of those policies through frequent visits to corporate head offices, during which he would attend export meetings and take part in award ceremonies and other such events.[56] By virtue of the fact that the value of South Korea's manufactured exports reached $14.7 billion by 1979 (from less than $100 million in 1963 and $1 billion in 1970), one can say not only that the country had produced a lot since 1960, but that it had learned a lot since then as well. In 1960, the ROK's total exports accounted for only 3 percent of the GNP, almost all of which was due to commodities such as seaweed, ginseng and minerals.[57]

Among the lessons learned was the need to pay attention to the role of foreign firms in the development of an export-based economy. In order to ramp up exports, South Korea developed what came to be known as Export Processing Zones (EPZs). Korean companies were responsible for a large chunk of the East Asian country's manufactured products throughout the 1960s and the early 1970s. With the aim of attracting foreign investment for export purposes,

South Korea set up two EPZs, Masan in 1970 and Iri (now Iksan) in 1974. The two export zones could absorb, in less than three years, one hundred foreign and joint ventures (many of them from Japan), producing exports worth $175 million. By the mid-1980s, the total value of Korean exports shipped from EPZs reached $890 million, accounting for roughly 3 percent of the ROK's overall global exports. This level of growth for EPZ exports was comparable to that for all products made in South Korea: For a period of one decade from 1975 to the mid-1980s, South Korean exports from the EPZs had grown at an average rate of 41 percent annually, which was close to the national rate of 46 percent per year for the same period.[58]

Working on long-term foundations: Tracing historical roots

As South Korea's political and economic relations with the Persian Gulf region further evolved, attempts were made to track down previous connections in the dim and distant past, aiming to both foster new cultural interactions and promote the ongoing bilateral relationship in other economic and political areas. Academic archives and archeological findings in particular were consulted, even if through Chinese sources, to back up the relevant literature about contact in the ancient past. What was unearthed indicated that Koreans did in fact come into contact with people from Iran in antiquity and that such fortuitous encounters had taken place much earlier than those between Koreans and Arabs. Their initial contacts with Iranians had much to do with official trade and private business activities along the Silk Road, with China serving as a bridge of sorts between the two peoples – especially at a time when the Iranian state extended well into the western provinces of present-day China.

The existence of a unique literature in Iran was also a very valuable instrument to some interested Koreans who were striving to discover additional sources to those that existed in China and Korea. Since dozens of classic works produced by Iranians provide various descriptions of Koreans and remark on the peculiar circumstances of the Korean Peninsula in ancient times, quests of this type turned out to be quite promising and eye-catching. One prominent and widely cited work of the Iranians written around the middle of the ninth century is a book penned by the renowned historian and geographer Abulqasim Ibn Khordadbeh, whose masterpiece, *Kitab al-Masalik va al-Mamalik* (*The Book of Roads and Kingdoms*), gives a fair explanation of the location of the (then) unified Silla Kingdom. What particularly makes Ibn Khordadbeh's work so well-known is that it has since remained the first non-Asian reference to Korea in recorded history[59] (some have deviously dubbed the book "the first Western reference to Korea").[60] And whether his indispensable contribution needs to be regarded only as part of the Iranian historical experience or as a mere quirk of fate, its author Ibn Khordadbeh turned out to be the first scholar to introduce the Korean Peninsula to the world (c. 846).

Contrary to Korea's older connections to Iran, meanwhile, its relations with the Arabs are believed to go back to sometime around the eleventh century. Among the historical investigations that have been launched into the history of Korean–Arab relations, one work has even asserted the existence of blood ties between the two peoples, a claim backed up by the existing sources, especially the Chinese sources, and family genealogies. The work in question is the 90-page piece written by Sang-su Choe, who was the founder and vice-president of the Korea–Saudi Arabia Association based in Seoul at the time when the work was released in both Korean and English versions in 1971.[61] According to Choe's assertion, the genesis of blood relations began to form in the second half of the thirteenth century, when an Arab, Samga (Sanko in Chinese), who had been brought to Korea by the ruling Mongol elite, married a Korean woman and subsequently became a naturalized citizen. Samga was soon given the Korean name of Sun-yong Chang by King Chungyol, and through his three sons he became the progenitor of the Toksu Chang family in Korea.[62] Whether or not Samga, even supposing that both his name and the foregoing story about him were actually genuine, was an Arab by origin and to what extent the historical records kept by his ancestors and the Chinese archives can be considered authentic and accurate will likely remain one of history's unsolved mysteries.

Religious and academic bodies

Infrequent contacts and a few settlements in the distant past could hardly suffice as the basis for the promotion of Iranian traditions or the Islamic culture of the Arabs in the Korean Peninsula on a large scale. Contrary to that anomalous background, however, contemporary connections turned out to be quite regular and highly influential, especially in fostering Islamic symbols and values among Koreans. The Turkish army brigade which entered South Korea following the outbreak of the Korean War played a crucial role in introducing Islam to its host nation, teaching Islamic principles to dozens of Koreans and setting up early Islamic communities such as the Korea Islamic Society in 1955.[63] Following the expansion of bilateral relations between South Korea and the Arab countries of the Middle East from the 1960s onward, the mantle of Islamic stewardship was gradually transferred to Arab-dominated Islamic societies and Arab nationals, a majority of whom often congregated in various parts of Seoul. In 1966, the Korean Muslim Federation was created, and it later became registered as a "juridical person" through the government's Ministry of Culture and Information in 1967.[64]

In 1970, the South Korean government agreed to donate a 5,000 square-meter site in Seoul for the establishment of a central mosque and an Islamic center, a project which was to be fully financed by an Islamic foundation supported by the Arab countries of Saudi Arabia, Kuwait, Libya and Morocco: the World Muslim League. Based in Mecca, it underwrote a $245,398 contract with South Korea's You Won Construction Company in September 1974, covering the total cost of carrying out the project.[65] Once the building was completed and inaugurated in October 1975, the Islamic entity undertook a leading role in the local Muslim community: It served as a proper place of assemblage and an agent of pilgrimage; it hosted religious festivals; and it managed the translation of Arabic texts – the latter being not only for the Muslim community, but for the state as well. Coupled with similar organizations such as the Korea–Arab Friendship Society (formed in 1971), such Islamic societies also became instrumental in South Korea's public diplomacy with and informal (yet influential) connections to many Islamic nations, including the Arab countries of the Persian Gulf region.[66]

As the South Korean government's interactions with the Persian Gulf – and the greater Middle East – developed, its academic institutions began to turn their attention toward the region as well. In 1965, the Department of Arabic Studies was created at Hankuk University of Foreign Studies (HUFS), where the Department of Middle East Studies was established as part of a graduate program one year later. In addition to the dozens of private institutions – many of which were in Seoul – that started to provide language lessons, the Arabic program was subsequently extended to other academic institutions, including Myongji University, Busan University of Foreign Studies and Chosun University. Another sign of the emerging academic focus on the Middle East was the establishment of the Korea Foundation for Middle East Studies (KFMES) by Park Chung-hee in 1975, hosting about 15 trained staff and the same number of economics specialists.[67] Coinciding with the aftermath of the oil shock and the subsequent construction boom in the Persian Gulf, the KFMES was primarily assigned three key tasks: to conduct research on development plans in the oil-exporting nations of the Middle East; to provide Korean enterprises with consultations about business opportunities in the region; and to manage orientation seminars and tutorials for those Korean nationals who were going to take on a typical job as a laborer, or even a plum job, somewhere in the Mideast.[68]

VIP visits

Given the ROK's geographical distance from the Persian Gulf and the fact that its bilateral relations with the countries of the region were limited to formal commercial and diplomatic connections, South Korea desperately needed to capitalize on high-profile meetings in order to secure its growing interests there. Tong-won Lee was the first South Korean foreign minister to visit the Persian Gulf nations of Iran and Saudi Arabia (November 1966) – although he also stopped over in Turkey, Lebanon and Jordan during his trip to the Middle East. His "ice-breaking" visit was rather important because the greater Middle East region was considered at the time to be the "dark corner" of the ROK's foreign policy.[69] The 1973 Middle East crisis and the following oil shock further necessitated official visits to the region and compelled dozens of Korean cabinet ministers and many other high-ranking politicians to fly to

Persian Gulf countries throughout the 1970s and thereafter. Despite many earlier visits conducted by officials of lower rank, President Kyu-hah Choi was the first ever South Korean president to go to Saudi Arabia and Kuwait, traveling to these nations in May 1980. Of course, it should be noted that he had already visited Iran and Saudi Arabia as prime minister in 1977 and as foreign minister in 1971.

Prior to Choi, the only time a South Korean president had a bona fide opportunity to go to the Persian Gulf was in the early 1970s, when the king of Iran extended an invitation to Park Chung-hee to attend "the 25th Centennial Anniversary of the Founding of the Iranian Monarchy" to be held in October 1971. Citing a pending inauguration ceremony and an overwhelming amount of official duties, Park declined the invitation and instead dispatched his relatively large delegation to the region; the group included Prime Minister Too-chin Paik, five cabinet ministers including Foreign Minister Choi, the mayor of Seoul, dozens of business executives, and several academics.[70] One reason why visits of top Korean officials to the Persian Gulf were so rare was a lack of reciprocity, that is, the visits were not responded to in kind. Limited political and cultural interests in and a rather lackluster economic relationship with South Korea did not motivate the leaders and high-ranking officials of Persian Gulf nations to regularly head toward the Korean Peninsula.

To partially overcome this obstacle, the ROK started to invite Persian Gulf officials – from heads of state to members of parliament – to come visit Seoul while they were in the Far East on official visits to Japan. For instance, Park Chung-hee invited the Saudi Arabian king, Faisal Ibn Abdul Aziz Al-Saudi, who was going to visit Japan in May 1967, to have a sojourn in Seoul for a meeting with Korean officials. Unfortunately, the invitation was subsequently declined.[71] The lack of diplomatic ties had previously encumbered South Korea when it wanted to extend an official invitation to the visiting Iranian King, who was on a Far Eastern tour to Japan and Taiwan in June 1958.[72] The Shah of Iran never visited South Korea, but his foreign minister, Ardeshir Zahedi, became the first high-ranking Iranian official to visit the East Asian nation in May 1969, when he also received an honorary doctorate in law from Chung-Ang University in Seoul.[73] Moreover, Zahedi became the first foreign minister from a Middle Eastern country to have ever visited the ROK up until that time.[74] The first official visit to South Korea by a top Saudi official[75] was carried out by Sayed Omar Al-Sakkaf, the minister of state for foreign affairs, in July 1974.[76] The South Korean president at the time, Park Chung-hee, conferred on both Zahedi and Al-Sakkaf the "Order of Diplomatic Service Merit, Kwanghwa" during their official visits to Seoul in 1969 and 1974, respectively.

Developing better ties with the Persian Gulf: Major bilateral relations

South Korea's expanding trade with and bilateral connections to the Persian Gulf gradually turned the region into one of its major commercial partners by the end of the 1970s. As the region alone had already accounted for 80% of South Korea's exports to the entire Middle East by the mid-1970s,[77] the importance of Persian Gulf countries to its Mideast trade was already crystal clear. In 1980, South Korea's total imports were valued at about $22 billion, one fourth of which, $5.5 billion, was from the Persian Gulf region alone, putting Saudi Arabia and Kuwait as its third and fourth largest import partners in the world, respectively. At the same time, the region still accounted for approximately one-ninth ($2 billion) of its total exports ($17.5 billion), making Saudi Arabia and Iran its third and sixth largest export destinations in the world, respectively. This was a significant increase compared to the previous levels of bilateral trade between the two sides in 1970, when trade with the Persian Gulf accounted for around $69 million of the East Asian country's $2 billion in total imports and about $1.7 million of its roughly $800 million in total exports.[78]

In the Persian Gulf, the ROK's general pattern of commercial activity underwent tremendous developments as well. In 1971, the East Asian country had only three import partners in the region, namely, Iran, Kuwait and Saudi Arabia. By 1980, however, South Korea's commercial links to the Persian Gulf had broadened, enabling Seoul to import goods from all eight countries in the region. And while the UAE had no share of South Korean exports until 1972, the tiny Arab nation became one of Seoul's top 20 export destinations in 1980, receiving approximately $190 million worth of Korean products. South Korea's exports to Iraq increased from nil in 1970 to about $35 million in 1980, while its exports to Kuwait soared from about $1.5 million in 1970 to around $250 million in 1980, making Kuwait the East Asian nation's thirteenth largest export market in the world.[79] However, during the decade from 1971 to 1980, South Korea's most beneficial trade relationship in the Gulf, if not the entire Middle East, was with Iran, receiving Iranian imports in the amount of $1.6 billion while shipping $1.4 billion in manufactured goods to the Persian Gulf nation. The ROK's balance of trade with Saudi Arabia and Kuwait, however, was not as balanced; its two-way trade with both countries was far from ideal and was highly asymmetrical. During the same period, namely, 1971–1980, Seoul's total exports to Saudi Arabia and Kuwait amounted to $3.5 billion and $1.2 billion, respectively, while its imports from the two Arab countries amounted to approximately $9.6 billion and $6.2 billion, respectively.[80]

Inasmuch as geographical size and political influence mattered, especially during the 1970s, South Korea conducted the majority of its diplomatic and non-economic exchanges in the Persian Gulf with Iran and Saudi Arabia. With the exception of Iraq, Seoul did have political relationships with the smaller, and less powerful, nations in the region – though such relations were dwarfed by the economic ties that the ROK had with these countries. From the very beginning, Seoul courted these tiny states and, on various occasions, was able to make distinctive deals with each of them. For instance, Qatar agreed to import all of its cement from South Korea[81] following a trade protocol with Seoul in 1977.[82] Bahrain permitted Korean Air Lines (KAL) to fly to Manama three times a week in 1977; this allowed thousands of Korean laborers who worked in Saudi Arabia to fly to Bahrain directly and then take short ferry ride to their destination. Moreover, the Kuwaiti government allowed the Korea Development Bank (KDB) to have a chance to raise 7 million Kuwaiti dinars (approximately $24 million) through issuing bonds for purchase in Kuwait in 1976. About a year later, the Korea–Kuwait Banking Corporation became the first joint Arab–Korean bank to set up a branch in Seoul.[83]

South Korea–Iran relations

For a whole host of political, economic and cultural reasons, Iran was the center of the South Koreans' unremitting attention in the Persian Gulf, and the Middle East in general, from the very outset of their (modern-day) arrival in the region during the second half of the 1950s. As much as alliance politics is concerned, South Korea was able to develop stronger political ties and more considerable economic relations with Iran under the Pahlavi monarchy in the 1960s and (especially) in the 1970s. Even when one factors in the alliance politics between South Korea and its other close partners in the region – Saudi Arabia, for example – Iran was still the ROK's first pick of the bunch; its position was as distinctive as "a crane among chickens." Besides serving as one of the main pillars of the security of the Persian Gulf, part of Iran's unique standing in the region had to do with the vexing dilemma of the Israeli issue in the ROK's overall diplomacy toward the Arab countries of the Middle East. For example, the South Korean government had to frequently reassess its rather ambiguous policy toward Israel in order to please its Arab partners, particularly those petroleum suppliers in the Persian Gulf, while such a stumbling block did not bother Seoul's ties to Tehran – not in the 1960s and not in the aftermath of the Yom Kippur War of 1973.

In addition to its early recognition of the ROK and its sympathy toward the people of South Korea upon the outbreak of the Korean War, the Iranian government often threw its unequivocal support behind Seoul in major international debates involving the Korean Cause, especially at UN meetings. Iran was even willing to help South Korea get out of the quagmire that was the Vietnam War, offering to play a mediating role in order to find a political solution to that internecine conflict which involved a significant number of South Korean soldiers.[84] To further nurture this kind of Iranian goodwill towards their country and to solidify bilateral relations with Iran, the South Korean government often resorted to the slew of political, economic and even cultural measures at its disposal until the fall of the monarchy in early 1979.[85] Every South Korean top official, with the exception of the president, visited Iran before 1979; among them were prime ministers, the speaker of the National Assembly, many cabinet ministers (including the head of foreign ministry), and mayors of Korea's largest cities. On one occasion, a special representative of the South Korean president traveled all the way to the Shah's vacation spot in northern Iran to deliver a letter from Park Chung-hee.[86]

On economic grounds, Iran was alluring to South Korea long before the 1973 oil boom that saw the start of an unprecedented spending spree on imports and new construction projects.[87] Before it suffered the adverse effects of petrodollars, Iran's economic plans had progressed rather significantly and earned a great deal of global appreciation. The ROK was no exception. Korean officials used Iran's economic progress and improved standing in the world at this time as reasons why their country should foster stronger ties with the Persian Gulf nation.[88] In the words of Suk-chan Lo, the South Korean ambassador to Tehran in 1968: "Korea is inclined to improve its relations with Iran, the country whose economic development has impressed all the nations in the world."[89] Recognizing Iran as potentially the largest market in the Middle East for its manufactured exports, South Korea strove to sign a series of lucrative economic packages with the Iranian government in the aftermath of the first oil shock, when Saudi Arabia was gradually becoming the largest construction market for the South Koreans.

Following a dozen smaller deals, the two countries signed a major pact at the conclusion of the "Second Session of the Korea–Iran Ministerial Joint Commission for Economic and Technical Cooperation" held in Tehran from October 31 to November 3, 1976, under which they agreed to expand their two-way trade and to try to do $2 billion in trade during a five-year period ending in 1980. The massive agreement also included the promise of delivering 60,000 barrels of crude oil per day to South Korea for a period of 15 years; the construction of 100,000 housing units; a dramatic increase in the number of Korean unskilled and skilled workers admitted to Iran; the exchange of information on economic development; and cooperation between their respective fisheries.[90] Moreover, the two countries embarked on a number of joint economic projects, including a well-known 50–50 joint venture between the Korean Ssangyong Corporation and the National Iranian Oil Corporation (NIOC) signed in January 1976 to build a crude oil refinery in South Korea. Another joint activity was the formation of a company to produce and sell garments, a venture which was to receive 60 percent of its funding from Iran's Saka Manufacturing Corporation and the other 40 percent from South Korea's Boo Hung Sa & Co.[91]

The Korean contractors in the region, meanwhile, turned their businesses to the Iranian market when Hyundai Construction signed a deal with Iran to build a shipyard for the Iranian navy near Bandar Abbas, a southern port city straddling the Persian Gulf. By April 1979, companies from South Korea had established 5 percent of their overseas businesses in Iran,[92] taking thousands of Korean laborers with them to carry out their projects. Other groups from the Korean migrant workforce also ended up working in Iran, including 32 air technicians employed at National Iranian Airways and around 70 nurses employed at Mofid Hospital in Tehran, the latter actually being the largest group dispatched on a single occasion "in the history of [the] overseas employment of Korean nurses."[93] The increasing number of Korean laborers in Iran made South Korea request that the Iranian government exclude the ROK's working nationals from paying social security and medical insurance, both of which combined to account for roughly 34 percent of their wages.[94] The generous agreement was signed during a visit to Iran by South Korean Prime Minister Kyu-hah Choi in May 1977. This deal saw 3,500 workers stash away no less than a total of $5 million a year working in the Persian Gulf country at this time.[95] Needless to say, this benefited South Korea tremendously.

Besides all of its historical achievements and its influences on modern civilization, contemporary Iranian culture – from folklore to higher education and from sports to the culinary arts – was yet another enticing and illuminating sphere to many Koreans, encouraging the government to seriously work on promoting cultural relations between the two countries.[96] The two countries signed a Treaty of Friendship[97] during Foreign Minister Zahedi's visit to South Korea in May 1969, which was actually the first ever treaty penned on paper since the establishment of diplomatic relations seven years earlier;[98] the measure was later buttressed by other agreements on cultural and sport-related exchanges. As part of these accords, a friendly football (soccer) match was held between the national teams of the two countries in September 1971, an event which was accompanied by an interesting development in South Korea's foreign interactions. The coach of the Iranian national soccer team, Netto Igor Aleksandiovich, was a Russian who became the first Soviet citizen to visit the ROK since 1948,[99] riveting a number of Korean media outlets, many of which put a shot of his arrival at Gimpo International Airport on the front page of major newspapers.[100]

Town twinning with Iran, meanwhile, became one more unprecedented development and a new initiative in South Korea's deepening relationship with a Middle Eastern country. In 1976, the Seoul Metropolitan Government raised the idea of making Seoul and Tehran into "sister cities," so that both capitals could exchange names. Once Iran embraced this suggestion, the two mayors paid official visits to each other's city sometime in 1977 in order to unveil the name of a street in Seoul and a street in Tehran, respectively – the name of the street in Seoul would be named "Tehran" and *vice versa*.[101] The mayor of Tehran, Javad Shahrestani, who had just assumed office in August 1977, was previously in charge of the Ministry of Road and Transportation; and it was in this role that he had significantly helped South Korean contractors start their businesses in Iran.[102] "Seoul Street," located in north Tehran, was a one-horse road in the first place and has inescapably remained so ever since, whereas "Teheran-ro" or "Tehran Street," also colloquially known as "Tehran Valley," has grown to become the center of a bustling business district that plays host to many Korean (and international) financial institutions, the East Asian nation's tallest skyscrapers, and more than half the country's IT venture firms.[103]

South Korea–Saudi Arabia relations

As Egypt and Iraq, two of the most populous and influential Arab nations in the Middle East, had been pushed into the socialist camp, Saudi Arabia became the most important Arab partner for South Korea in the Persian Gulf and in the greater Middle East. South Korea actually attached such importance to its relationship with Saudi Arabia even before the latter became one of Seoul's main sources of petroleum and one of the main destinations for its contractors. The Koreans perceived the Saudis to be growing in popularity and influence in the Arab world and the Muslim world more broadly because it served as the custodian of major Islamic shrines. And it was this perception that encouraged the South Korean government to repeatedly ask the Saudi government to help it gain the support of other Arab nations or to help it strengthen its relations with them.[104] South Korea particularly needed Saudi Arabia's backing in order to set up diplomatic ties with a number of Persian Gulf nations – which included Kuwait, the UAE and Bahrain – and a number of other Middle Eastern countries – which included North Yemen and Algeria. The go-between role that the Saudis played was also instrumental on other occasions: they were especially helpful when the South Korean government needed to rally the support of Arab nations with respect to the Korean Cause and to South Korea's membership in the UN.[105]

As the expansion of the Korean economy largely relied on a stable supply of petroleum throughout the 1970s, the ROK had to rely, time and again, on Saudi Arabia for its oil needs – so much so that the Arab nation was responsible for no less than half of South Korea's fossil fuel imports in 1979. Even when the Saudis categorized South Korea as a friendly nation in December 1973, promising a sure-fire supply of petroleum following the first oil shock, the South Korean government was still in search of other economic favors from them. For instance, in 1974 it asked Saudi Arabia to deposit $1 billion on a long-term basis in the Korean Exchange Bank in order to ease the pressure on South Korea's balance of payments and to help satisfy the cash requirements of its many economic projects. The Saudi government was diametrically opposed to the idea of a $1 billion cash loan, and this forced South Korea to reduce the requested amount to $500 million, or half the initial amount, which was still considered to be a large sum of money at the time.[106]

The first major agreement on economic matters between South Korea and Saudi Arabia, a state of religious resonance and energy eminence, was signed during Foreign Minister Al-Sakkaf's visit to Seoul in July 1974. The accord, which promised acceleration in mutual economic and technical cooperation, served as a bridgehead for a number of other agreements between the two nations in various areas, ranging from construction to trade and from investments to joint ventures.[107] The infiltration of a myriad of South Korean contractors into the Saudi construction market from 1974 onward was yet another crucial development which had tremendous implications for both the fledgling Korean economy[108] and the robust bilateral interactions between the two nations – the latter soon cemented by the presence of a great number of South Korean nationals in Saudi Arabia. Aside from the economic benefits that the construction boom would provide for the Korean economy, this development considerably increased the international experience of many ordinary South Korean citizens who had never before left the confines of the Korean Peninsula: Now they found themselves going to work in Saudi Arabia or in other countries of the Persian Gulf region. For example, while there was only one single South Korean in Jeddah in 1973, there were no less than 1,200 South Koreans in that city by 1975. What's more, they had the opportunity to enjoy their own restaurant and to live in a special residential district there.[109]

Notes

1 In 1973, there were various reports and rumors indicating implicitly that the United States government was seriously contemplating a plan to occupy Saudi Arabia's oil fields. The Saudis themselves are still bewildered by these rumors – even if they were merely concocted on a tactical basis in order to intimidate Saudi Arabia and some other Arab countries at the time. See "MEMRI: Former Saudi Ambassador to the US Slams Obama," *Independent Media Review Analysis (IMRA)*, December 7, 2013.

2 Despite the fact that OPEC's policy of bumping up oil prices made most of the non-oil-producing nations quite uneasy and nervous about their economies, many of them were still willing to regard, for the time being, the oil cartel as the vanguard of third-world demands from the industrialized and developed world. For instance, the Jamaican prime minister, Michael Manley, became emboldened, stating: "I suggest that OPEC, along with its younger cousins like the International Bauxite Association, have changed the fundamental equations of economic power as decisively as did the Industrial Revolution." See Thomas A. Johnson, "Third World Believes New Economic Order Is at Hand," *New York Times*, October 13, 1975, p. 14.

3 William D. Smith, "Price Quadruples for Iranian Crude Oil at Auction," *New York Times,* December 12, 1973.

4 "Saudi Arabia Oil Smuggled to U.S. Despite Embargo," *Korea Times*, January 13, 1974, p. 1.

5 Arthur M. Whitehill, *Doing Business in Korea* (Beckenham, UK: Croom Helm Ltd., 1987), p. 85.

6 Chung-hee Park, *Korea Reborn: A Model for Development* (Englewood Cliffs, NJ: Prentice-Hall Inc., 1979), p. 92.

7 Edmund Burke III, *Global Crises and Social Movements: Artisans, Peasants, Populists and the World Economy* (Boulder, CO: Westview Press, 1988), p. 256.

8 "ROK Mideast Diplomacy Faces Touchy Situation," *Korea Times*, November 23, 1966, p. 2.

9 *Wegyo Munseo* [Diplomatic Archives] (Seoul: Ministry of Foreign Affairs, 2006).

10 *Wegyo Munseo* [Diplomatic Archives], 2006.

11 *Wegyo Munseo* [Diplomatic Archives], 2006.

12 *Wegyo Munseo* [Diplomatic Archives] (Seoul: Ministry of Foreign Affairs, 2003).

13 *Wegyo Munseo* [Diplomatic Archives] (Seoul: Ministry of Foreign Affairs, 2009).

14 "His Excellency Nureddin al-Atassi Pays State Visit to the DPRK," *Pyongyang Times*, October 6, 1969, p. 1.

15 Abdul-Monem Al-Mashat, "The Egyptian Perception of Korean Issues," in J. Rew (ed.), *Korea and Egypt: The Change and Continuity in their Policy and Cooperation* (Seoul: Korean Institute of the Middle East & Africa, 1995), pp. 65–80.

16 "Korean People will Stand Firmly by the UAR, Syria and Other Arab Peoples," *Pyongyang Times*, June 8, 1967, p. 8.

17 Robert A. Scalapino and H. Yi, *North Korea in a Regional and Global Context* (Berkeley: University of California, Berkeley, Center for Korean Studies, 1986), p. 338.

18 Gavan McCormack, *Target North Korea: Pushing North Korea to the Brink of Nuclear Catastrophe* (New York: Nation Books, 2004), p. 85.
19 See, for instance, "South Korean Officials' Impressions on Israel," *Pyongyang Times*, November 24, 1966, p. 3; and "S. Korean Puppets Attempt to Worm into Arab Soil," *Pyongyang Times*, October 5, 1967, pp. 6–7.
20 *Wegyo Munseo* [Diplomatic Archives], 2003.
21 *Wegyo Munseo* [Diplomatic Archives] (Seoul: Ministry of Foreign Affairs, 2005).
22 Burchett, p. 165.
23 Abbas Alnasrawi, "Middle East Oil and Economic Development: Regional and Global Implications," *Journal of Asian and African Studies*, Vol. 19, No. 3–4 (1984), pp. 137–149.
24 Anthony Sampson, *The Seven Sisters: The Great Oil Companies and the World They Made* (London: Hodder & Stoughton, 1975), p. 21.
25 Donald N. Wilber, *Iran: Past and Present*, 8th edition. (Princeton: Princeton University Press, 1976), pp. 256–259.
26 Fouad Abdul Salam Al-Farsy, "King Faisal and the First Five-Year Plan," in Willard Beling (ed.), *King Faisal and the Modernization of Saudi Arabia* (London: Croom Helm Ltd., 1980), pp. 58–71.
27 Keith McLachlan, "Iran," in *Middle East Annual Review 1978* (Saffron Walden, UK: Middle East Review Co., 1979), pp. 203–214.
28 McLachlan.
29 John Roberts, *Visions & Mirages: Middle East in a New Era* (Edinburgh and London: Mainstream Publishing, 1995), p. 157.
30 Bernard Reich, *The Powers in the Middle East: The Ultimate Strategic Arena* (New York: Praeger, 1987), p. 315.
31 James Buchan, "The Meaning of Competition," *Saudi Business*, February 1, 1980, pp. 20–24.
32 "The Koreans Are Coming! The Koreans Are Coming!" *Engineering News-Record*, Vol. 198, No. 13 (1977), p. 16.
33 Shahid Yusuf and Kaoru Nabeshima, *Postindustrial East Asian Cities: Innovation for Growth* (Palo Alto, CA: Stanford Economics and Finance, 2006), p. 249.
34 C. Moon, "Korean Contractors in Saudi Arabia: Their Rise and Fall," *Middle East Journal*, Vol. 40, No. 4 (1986), pp. 614–633.
35 Michael Cassell, "The East–West Battle," *Financial Times*, January 22, 1979.
36 Moon.
37 Nigel Disney, "South Korean Workers in the Middle East," *MERIP Reports*, No. 61 (1977), pp. 22–24, 26.
38 Mark L. Clifford, *Troubled Tiger: Businessmen, Bureaucrats, and Generals in South Korea* (Armonk, NY: M.E. Sharpe, 1994), p. 118.
39 For authoritarian behavior and "martinetesque" management, some laborers were thinking of Ju-yung Chung, the head of Hyundai, as the alter ego of Park Chung-hee, the South Korean president at the time. In Donald Kirk's words, "Hyundai managers viewed their workers as shock troops, equipped and trained to perform under the most grueling conditions." See Donald Kirk, *Korean Dynasty: Hyundai and Chung Ju Yung* (Hong Kong: Asia 2000 Ltd., 1994), p. 84.
40 James Buxton, "Competing in a Seller's Market," *Financial Times*, August 30, 1977.
41 "All Eyes on the Generals," *Middle East Economic Digest (MEED)*, April 1983, pp. 43–65.
42 "Competitors Envy the Record," *MEED*, March 1981.
43 "Korea's Crucial Link to the Middle East," *Business Week*, August 1, 1977, p. 41.
44 "The Koreans Are Coming! The Koreans Are Coming!"
45 John Bunton, "Western Contractors Face New Challenges," *MEED*, April 1979, pp. 3–5.

46 Russell Mardon, "The State and the Effective Control of Foreign Capital: The Case of South Korea," *World Politics*, Vol. 43, No. 1 (1990), pp. 111–138.

47 John Bunton, "The Market Continues Expand Modestly," *MEED*, February 1980, pp. 3–5.

48 James Buxton, "A Big But Demanding Market," *Financial Times*, August 30, 1977.

49 John Whelan, "Arab Contractors Win a Bigger Share of the Market," *MEED*, March 1981, p. 2.

50 Moon. The other party might have occasionally had a skeleton in its closet as well and thereby have needed to be equally blamed for asking to receive some filthy lucre in one way or another. A former Hyundai manager had once told Donald Kirk, a South Korea-based American correspondent, that "there are 5,000 people in the royal family in the Saudi government. By means of allotment of bribes, King Fahd can manage the royal family. Hyundai got many requests unofficially for bribes for giving some favor ... bribery is part of the system ... that's the name of the game ... we call it 'internal favors.'" See Kirk, p. 87.

51 Walter McQuade, "The Asian Building Boom is Making Construction History," *Fortune,* September 1978, p. 115.

52 Cited from *Major Speeches by President Park Chung Hee, Republic of Korea* (Seoul: The Samhwa Publishing Co., n.d.), p. 132.

53 Park, p. 90.

54 Atef Sultan, "South Korea's Middle East Penetration Shows Muscle," *MEED*, July 16, 1976, pp. 3–8.

55 Korean Statistical Information Service.

56 Porter, p. 475.

57 Larry E. Westphal, "Industrial Policy in an Export-Propelled Economy: Lessons from South Korea's Experience," *Journal of Economic Perspectives*, Vol. 4, No. 3 (1990), pp. 41–59.

58 The World Bank, *Export Processing Zones* (Washington, D.C.: The World Bank, Industry and Energy Department & Country Economics Department, 1992), p. 27.

59 Frank Gosfield and Bernhardt J. Hurwood, *Korea: Land of the 38th Parallel* (New York: Parents' Magazine Press, 1969), p. 31.

60 Richard Rutt, "Arabia Ties Searched: Book Review," *Korea Times*, April 16, 1972, p. 3.

61 For the English edition, see S. Choe, *Relations between Korea and Arabia* (Seoul: Omungak, 1971).

62 "Korea–Arab Ties Back to 11th Century," *Korea Times*, February 14, 1974, p. 2.

63 "Turks No Strangers since Korean War," *Korea Times*, July 29, 1973, p. 4.

64 James H. Grayson, *Korea: A Religious History* (New York: RoutledgeCurzon, 2002), p. 196.

65 For a copy of the contract, see *Wegyo Munseo* [Diplomatic Archives] (Seoul: Ministry of Foreign Affairs, 2004).

66 "Muslims in Korea Increasing Steadily," *Korea Times*, September 23, 1975, p. S4.

67 Disney.

68 Sultan.

69 *Korea Times*, November 23, 1966, p. 2.

70 "Premier Kim Off for Iran Fete," *Korea Herald*, October 12, 1971, p. 1.

71 *Wegyo Munseo* [Diplomatic Archives] (Seoul: Ministry of Foreign Affairs, 2001).

72 *Wegyo Munseo* [Diplomatic Archives], 1994.

73 "Iran Foreign Chief Receives Doctorate," *Korea Herald*, May 6, 1969, p. 4.

74 "Korea and Iran Sign Amity Pact Vowing Closer Cooperation," *Korea Herald*, May 6, 1969, pp. 1, 4.

75 Prior to Al-Sakkaf, the Saudi Arabian minister of state and president of the central planning organization, Hisham Muhiddin Nazer, was another ranking Saudi

official who had visited South Korea in February 1974; however, Al-Sakkaf appeared to be seen by the Koreans as a big shot in comparison to Nazer.

76 "Korea, S. Arabia Mull Further Cooperation," *Korea Times*, July 2, 1974, p. 1.

77 Sultan.

78 Korean Statistical Information Service.

79 Korean Statistical Information Service.

80 Korean Statistical Information Service.

81 While the country's only cement factory had been razed to the ground during the Korean War, South Korea later significantly capitalized on its cement industry and became one of the world's largest cement exporters.

82 *Business Week*, August 1, 1977.

83 Disney.

84 "Iran Eyes Viet Mediation Role: King Makes Bid to Lee," *Korea Herald*, November 27, 1966, p. 1.

85 As an indication of just how much importance South Korea attached to Iran back then, 141 pages from the archives of the ROK's foreign ministry, dating to the period from 1967 to 1970, were devoted to the Iranian Foreign Minister Zahedi's visit to Seoul in early May 1969; they covered the major events of his trip, including a speech he delivered at Chung-Ang University upon receiving an honorary doctorate. The 1971 archives related to "the 25th Centennial Anniversary of the Founding of the Iranian Monarchy and the Proclamation of the Charter of Human Rights by Cyrus the Great" goes far beyond that, assigning around 677 pages to coverage of the official correspondence between the two nations regarding an invitation sent to South Korea's top leadership to partake in the ceremony and the follow-up developments, which included the attendance of a rather large Korean delegation led by Prime Minister Too-chin Paik.

86 "Korean Special Envoy Flies Noshahr," *Ettelaat*, August 4, 1968.

87 On many occasions, both in written correspondence and in speeches (e.g. a welcoming statement by Foreign Minister Choi addressed to his visiting Iranian counterpart Zahedi in May 1969), South Korean officials referred to the country as "the Empire of Iran," instead of "the Iranian monarchy," "imperial Iran" or "the Kingdom of Iran." It seems, however, that the application of such a term was intentional and not a diplomatic blunder.

88 Iran's first seven-year development plan (1948–1955), the earliest of its type in the entire Middle East region, had been initiated roughly two-and-a-half decades before the country's industrialization was severely hampered by the first oil shock (1973–1974).

89 "Korean Goodwill Mission in Tehran: Korea Wants to Develop Relations with Iran," *Ettelaat*, August 3, 1968.

90 *Wegyo Munseo* [Diplomatic Archives], 2006.

91 "Trade Volume between 2 Nations Expands in Economic Cooperation," *Korea Times*, July 12, 1978, p. S4.

92 "Overseas Contractors Soar – Survey: South Korea," *Financial Times,* April 2, 1979, p. 19.

93 "70 Korean Nurses Will Be Dispatched to Iran," *Korea Times*, February 20, 1977, p. 8.

94 "Korea–Iran Pact Set on Insurance Dues," *Korea Times*, March 6, 1977, p. 1.

95 "Korea, Iran to Sign 2 Economic Accords," *Korea Times*, May 11, 1977, p. 1.

96 For instance, the president of Kyung Hee University, Young-seek Choue, who was also the president of the International Association of University Presidents (IAUP), a world body with members from all continents, typified "Iran as the best example of national zeal for education" and a sterling model of why "Korea should expand advanced education" and abandon "the strictly imposed enrollment quota for higher learning institutions." For more details on Choue's impression of

Iran after visiting dozens of universities and meeting Iranian leaders, see "Investment in Education Spurs Nat'l Development," *Korea Times*, January 30, 1977, p. 5.

97 The Korean–Iranian Friendship Association (KIFA) was inaugurated in July 1978 on the occasion of a visit to South Korea by Jafar Sharif-Emami, president of the Senate of Iran and prime minister of Iran in 1960–1961.

98 Praising the potential impact of the amity treaty and its "vital" role in developing South Korea's relations not only with Iran but with other countries in the Middle East as well, an enthusiastic editorial by the *Korea Herald* very much appreciated the people who had helped make the move possible, noting fervently that "all concerned authorities and diplomats who have made the conclusion of this significant treaty with Iran a reality deserve our hearty commendation and thanks." See "Korea–Iran Amity," *Korea Herald*, May 6, 1969, p. 2.

99 Aleksandiovich was in fact the second Russian citizen to have been issued an entry permit by the ROK. The first permit had already been issued in early 1971 to G.A. Dorefeev, a Soviet scientist and a member of the secretariat of the International Atomic Energy Agency (IAEA), who was going to partake in an international radiation conference in Seoul. Dorefeev, however, did not attend the scheduled event, instead giving a chance to the coach of the Iranian national soccer team to enter South Korea as the first Soviet citizen to do so since 1948.

100 "Russian Arrives here as Iran Soccer Coach," *Korea Herald*, September 9, 1971, p. 1.

101 General Chung-yul Kim, the first South Korean high-ranking official to visit Tehran, and who did so in June 1957 as the head of the first goodwill mission sent there by the ROK, had a very positive view of the Iranian capital and its people, but it is not clear how much his impression actually influenced his brethren to make this move: "I was very much impressed with the city of Tehran ... it was a pleasant blend of old culture and efficient modern. Its streets are wide and clean with tall verdant trees all along the streets and elsewhere ... its air is refreshing and invigorating ... its men and women almost uniformly handsome and well-built. Its street full of modern cars of all makes, and its shops filled with all sorts of commodities" (*Wegyo Munseo* [Diplomatic Archives], 1996).

102 *Wegyo Munseo* [Diplomatic Archives] (Seoul: Ministry of Foreign Affairs, 2007).

103 MobileReference, *Travel Seoul, South Korea: Illustrated Guide, Korean Phrasebook and Maps (Mobi Travel)* [E-book] (Boston: MobileReference, 2010).

104 The earliest such impression of Saudi Arabia was that of General Chung-yul Kim, the head of the first goodwill mission, who met the Saudi king in May 1957, pointing out that he "came to be impressed with the King's keen sense of responsibility for the welfare of not only his own people but also for the Arab peoples as a whole ... even while he was eating, one of his secretaries was briefing him on the latest news of the world ... he had no time to read the papers, he customarily had the news read to him during meal hours ... Egypt and Syria are now being left out in the cold by the influence of King Saud" (*Wegyo Munseo* [Diplomatic Archives], 1996).

105 *Wegyo Munseo* [Diplomatic Archives], 2004.

106 *Wegyo Munseo* [Diplomatic Archives], 2004.

107 "Korea, S. Arabia Sign Agreement on Cooperation," *Korea Times*, July 5, 1974, p. 1.

108 The contribution of the construction jackpot to the South Korean economy was prodigious enough to be considered by many Koreans to be one of the key factors behind their abrupt success, acknowledging that "the Korean miracle was stimulated greatly by Saudi Arabia through vast construction works." See U. Shim, "Korea's Economic Progress Owes Much to Saudi Arabia," *Diplomacy*, Vol. 9, No. 11 (1983), pp. 30–31.

109 "Seoul–Jeddah Economic Ties Grow," *Korea Times*, September 23, 1975, p. S2.

3 Coping with crisis: The South's loss is the North's gain

Changing circumstances at home and in the Persian Gulf

South Korea experienced an expanding yet relatively stable relationship with the Persian Gulf region during the 1960s and 1970s. Even the previously unknown phenomena that were the energy embargo and the ensuing oil shock of 1973–1974 turned out to be a blessing in disguise, at least for the Koreans. As soon as the trepidation caused by energy shortages and increased oil prices tapered off, the region became the center of a booming construction industry as well as a bustling market for all sorts of imported products. This situation saw South Korea obtain a great deal of material wealth from unprecedented levels of interaction with the Persian Gulf countries and strengthen what seemed to now be its perennial engagement in the region. The ROK's continuous and profitable relationship with the nations of the Persian Gulf was only further solidified by the political and economic situation at home, which was highly stable. Meanwhile, in the late 1970s and especially during the early 1980s, this stability was to be significantly affected in spades by turbulent events in the Persian Gulf region – though it is fair to say that this stability would also be affected by domestic political and economic developments as well.

At home, Park Chung-hee, the strongman who governed South Korea with an iron fist and who guided its economic development for 17 years, was assassinated in October 1979. Park was South Korea's longest serving leader in the post-liberation period, and in the decades following his assassination, a new chain of political events was set in motion that would bring instability to the country – instability that it had not experienced for more than a decade and a half. It all started with the military *coup d'état* led by Major General Chun Doo-hwan in December 1979 and the Gwangju Uprising in May 1980 – the latter ending in a brutal massacre. Even when Chun managed to clinch the leadership of South Korea and get elected as a civilian president in September 1980, his image and achievements could never rival those of Park, and he would remain a very controversial ruler – especially because of the massacre perpetrated at Gwangju – until he left office in February 1988.[1] Economically, South Korea started to show so much improvement, that rising wages, healthier domestic markets, and increased expectations of Korean workers left little motivation for the latter to head to the Persian Gulf, where a cheap labor force was once a selling point for Korean companies (for about a decade from the time they had first entered the region in 1974).

In the Persian Gulf, the fall of the Pahlavi monarchy, which had been a good friend to South Korea, and the ensuing political turmoil in Iran, which had deleterious implications for the production and export of its petroleum, instigated the second oil shock – which negatively affected both the Korean economy as well as the global economy. The oil shock, which stemmed from the unpredictable political developments in Iran, was soon exacerbated by the outbreak of the Iran–Iraq War, placing South Korea's now increasing interests in the region in even more jeopardy. In spite of an expanding relationship during the 1970s, bilateral relations between Seoul and Tehran were downgraded in the aftermath of a regime change in Iran: It was the largest diplomatic setback that the East Asian country had ever suffered in the Middle East since its modern encounter with the region in the late 1950s. The Iran–Iraq War further imperiled South Korea's stakes in both countries, particularly in the former, when the new Islamic regime in Tehran approached Pyongyang for support in exchange for oil, a sudden development which took Seoul by surprise. It was a move that would later result in the denigration of Seoul's image among Iranian officials because North Korean diplomats would begin actively working against Seoul's interests in Tehran.

The second oil shock

In late 1978 and early 1979, in the wake of Iran's domestic chaos and political instability, the global energy market experienced the throes of the second oil shock. The crux of the crisis was massive strikes that buffeted the Iranian oil industry, disrupting the country's oil production markedly from 5.8 million barrels per day (bpd) in July 1978 to about 700,000 bpd in January and February 1979. This low level of petroleum production was only able to meet domestic requirements, essentially cutting off the world from the Iranian crude supply. At first, Saudi Arabia stepped up its oil production in order to make up for the lack of petroleum in world markets that came as a result of the circumstances brought about by the revolution in Iran, but Riyadh soon backtracked on its decision partly because of a production quota that had been set by OPEC limiting the production and supply of oil. And while Iran soon managed to raise its oil production to about 2.5 million bpd and more than 4 million bpd in March and April 1979, respectively, oil prices still kept soaring, leaving no doubt in anyone's mind that the second oil shock was indeed an unavoidable reality. The price of Iranian light crude oil increased sequentially to about $16 per barrel in March 1979, $23 per barrel in July 1979, and over $33 per barrel by March 1980 – or more than twice the previous year's price.[2]

Unlike the first oil shock, the second oil shock (1979–1980) was devastating for South Korea: Skyrocketing petroleum prices were especially detrimental to the Korean economy because the ROK had been importing nearly all of its oil from three Persian Gulf countries, namely, Saudi Arabia, Kuwait and Iran, making the East Asian nation even more vulnerable to any unpredictable oil price increases or supply shortages in the region. Moreover, South Korea had virtually ignored the repercussions of the first oil shock; they passed most of the price increases on to consumers, so that they would have to shoulder a big part of the burden. But the country's energy-intensive heavy industries, which used up increasingly large amounts of oil throughout the 1970s, could no longer remain immune from a sudden price hike; they could not remain indifferent to the chaotic energy markets in the wake of the second oil shock. In addition, local retailers were in no position to absorb the same costs as they had done in 1974. The oil shock of the late 1970s and early 1980s, therefore, had severely affected South Korea on a microeconomic and on a macroeconomic level, dragging the country into the most challenging recession it had experienced since the early 1960s, when it had first implemented its plans for economic development and industrialization.[3]

One important consequence of the second oil shock for South Korea was a palpable peak in the country's oil bill, rising by about 42 percent in 1979 and by about 82 percent in 1980 – the latter figure being roughly equivalent to 30 percent of Seoul's foreign exchange earnings for the year (and both figures being relative to the total oil bill from 1978). This, in turn, led to another immediate consequence that would see oil suddenly account for 25 percent of its overall imports from nearly 15 percent. As a result, South Korea's GNP contracted over 5.5 percent and its real Gross Domestic Product (GDP) suffered a more than 6 percent decrease in 1980, leading to 20 percent inflation and an estimated \$5.5 billion deficit in its balance of accounts.[4] In addition to imposing a wide range of *ad interim* measures on its domestic economy such as rationing energy and electricity – and selling them at higher prices – the government also needed to implement a series of rigid monetary and fiscal policies in order to cope with the crisis. Since the petroleum shortage drained so much money from its treasury, South Korea could not afford but to borrow a hefty amount of cash from abroad at significantly higher interest rates in order to grease the wheels of its economic machine lest it grind to a halt.[5]

Toward energy security

Perhaps the only positive consequence of the second oil shock for South Korea, which is resource-poor, was that the crisis turned out to be a milestone in the country's longstanding approach to energy security: It had come to see its overdependency on imported petroleum – a bulk of which had been supplied by Persian Gulf countries for quite a long time – in a brand new light. Energy insecurity was to be suddenly recognized as an overriding concern and as a matter of national security, obliging a now resolute government to handle the issue much better than it had before: It had to be vigilant and remain on the lookout for anything that could potentially disrupt its energy supply, which was critical to the well-being of the Korean economy and, hence, of

Koreans in general. And while the East Asian country had already established the Ministry of Energy and Resources in January 1978, roughly one year before the outbreak of the second oil shock, the energy issue had long been under the purview of the Ministry of Commerce and Industry, which had typically seen bureaucratic deliberation and concurrent policy consideration as a matter of secondary importance.[6]

Prior to setting up a separate ministry to be responsible for energy, South Korea had also taken two other concrete steps to help ensure the integrity of its oil supply: direct petroleum transfer via Korean tankers and the building of refineries. In 1973, the Ministry of Commerce and Industry decided to replace all foreign ships carrying imported oil with Korean tankers by 1976. In order to have this plan come to fruition within a four-year time frame, the government ordered several giant tankers to be built, and each of them was to be able to carry 280,000 tons of oil. The *raison d'être* of this strategy, for all that, was to significantly axe the country's crude oil transportation costs – particularly at a time when South Korea's rising oil consumption required enormous sums of foreign currency to pay for its imported petroleum. A year before crafting this policy, Seoul had spent about $44 million on freight charges to buy roughly 12,630,374 tons of crude oil in 1972. The transportation expenses seemed to be rather costly when one considers the fact that South Korea's imported petroleum costs at the time totalled $219 million or approximately 20 percent of the country's total imports in 1972.[7]

Korea's oil refining policy was an even older initiative, dating back to 1962, when the ROK's policymakers considered the petroleum refining industry to be crucial to their import-substitution plans. Since the country lacked the necessary technological know-how at the time, the government had to approach foreign companies for aid in the form of joint ventures, offering them a variety of incentives from free land to tax concessions, and from complete control over finance and operations to a guaranteed minimum profit. Until the mid-1970s, South Korea's partners in these joint refining ventures included the Gulf Oil Corporation, Chevron Corporation (Caltex) and Gold Star Resources Corporation, and Union Oil Company.[8] Iran, however, was to be the fourth entity to partner with the ROK, when the latter persuaded its Persian Gulf counterpart to embark on a 50–50 project that would see the NIOC[9] partner with Ssangyong Corporation.[10] It was a $160 million petroleum refining project with an equity capital of $34 million, and the early agreement between the two parties was signed during an official visit to Tehran by South Korean Minister of Commerce and Industry Yie-joon Chang in October 1975. Based in Onsan District and due to be completed at the end of 1977, the joint venture was going to have an oil refining capacity of 3,000,000 tons per year.[11]

In addition to a number of ongoing plans that were germane to having a direct oil supply via petroleum refineries, South Korea's unflinching quest for energy security in the period following the second oil shock focused on three particular strategies. First, the government acknowledged the importance of diversification with respect to the sources of its oil supply and with respect to the combination of energy products it was importing. Not only could this policy significantly increase the security of the ROK's energy supply in the long run, it also had the potential to bring down the nation's energy costs through its active support of competition. Second, Korean companies were encouraged to engage in exploration and production operations in energy-rich regions of the world outside the Persian Gulf – regions which were previously unknown to them. Finally, South Korea could better expand its chances of obtaining long-term energy security through forging closer political as well as economic ties with as many petroleum-producing countries as possible, especially with those considered unfriendly to Seoul. This last strategy hinged upon the successful implementation of Korean technological innovations and its ability to successfully export its products abroad.[12]

While South Korea still needed to rely on the Persian Gulf region for a bulk of its imported petroleum long after implementing the foregoing strategies aimed at attaining energy security, Seoul was still better off in the late 1980s than it was a decade earlier. The direct supply policy enabled Seoul to ship the lion's share of its petroleum imports on the country's own flag-carrying tankers by the end of the 1980s. The joint refining initiatives made it possible for South Korea to single-handedly fulfill all of its domestic refining needs and assume full financial and operational control over the nation's oil refining industry by the early 1990s.[13] The diversification policy led to bilateral energy deals with countries in different parts of the world, most notably Libya and later Russia. In the Persian Gulf, South Korean companies engaged in various exploration and production activities, and the country's long-established oil businesses there extended to other small states across the region, importing a variety of fossil fuels such as liquefied natural gas (LNG) from Qatar and Iran. More importantly, Seoul could maintain a significant energy trade with Tehran throughout the 1980s and beyond, right in the midst of a growing relationship between Iran and North Korea, which had started following the outbreak of the Iran–Iraq War in September 1980.

The Iran–Iraq War

On September 23, 1980, the government in Baghdad led by Saddam Hussein unilaterally tore into pieces a 1975 treaty with Tehran over the Arvandrud Waterway (known as Shatt al-Arab in Iraq) and invaded Iran, thereby starting an internecine war that was to grind on for eight years. As many months of domestic chaos and political instability had considerably enfeebled the military might of the Iranian army, Saddam's long-cherished aspiration and burgeoning desire to become a dominant regional player in lieu of his Iranian counterpart (and a host of other considerations) tempted the Iraqi leader to take the opportunity to conquer Tehran in a few days. An overwhelming majority of Arab countries, among many other nations, soon threw their unequivocal moral, financial and even military support behind Iraq, encouraging Saddam to push ahead and try to achieve his self-serving agenda.[14]

Saudi Arabia's King Khalid phoned Saddam and informed the latter that his country stood by the side of Iraq "in its pan-Arab battle and conflict with the Persians, the enemies of the Arab nation." The pledge of full-fledged support made by the Saudis, tinged with the invocation of a deeply rooted Arab–Iranian enmity, negatively influenced both the direction and duration of the protracted conflict – regardless of the loss of life and collateral damage on both sides.[15]

At the outset of the war, South Korea had enormous stakes in the Persian Gulf region, compelling Seoul to first cautiously evaluate the situation and then take appropriate measures to safeguard its interests there. Among these interests were its people: Thousands of its citizens working in the region, especially in areas adjacent to the Iraq–Iraq border, came under direct fire, and dozens more, who were working in Iraqi and Iranian port cities and even in Tehran and Baghdad themselves, were in immediate danger. More importantly, trade with the region and the security of its oil supply were unexpectedly jeopardized, while all South Korea could afford to do did not go much beyond simply "urging the two feuding parties to lay down their arms and seek a settlement of their outstanding issues by peaceful means."[16] On a more official level, and when pressured by the press, South Korea's foreign ministry declared neutrality toward the two nations in conflict, assuring everyone that Seoul "is objectively watching the war between the two Mideast states without favoring either of the two parties."[17]

On the eve of the war, there were 960 South Koreans working in Iran and about 930 more working in Iraq. And while the South Korean government had already withdrew a significant number of its nationals from Iran following the political turbulence in that country that began in late 1978, Seoul still considered Iran to be a safer place than Iraq for its citizens.[18] In addition to the closure of the Baghdad and Basra airports due to heavy bombardment, the lack of diplomatic relations between Iraq and South Korea proved to be a greater impediment for the Koreans in the region, leaving them completely reliant on the Korean embassy in Kuwait to make urgent evacuation plans for them before they run out of their "stored emergency rice for 40 days." Within a few days, a majority of Korean workers in Iraq moved to Kuwait, but most of those residing in Iran were not asked to leave, because they were not in immediate danger.[19] Meanwhile, the South Korean diplomatic mission in Iran was still working at an ambassadorial level until the turn of events pushed Seoul's embassy in Tehran to function with a *chargé d'affaires* as its senior representative, while the new Iranian government had never assigned an ambassador to South Korea, its embassy in Seoul already operating with only a *chargé d'affaires* at the helm.

Relations with Iran

On the cusp of the regime change in Iran, when political turmoil was engulfing the country, there were over 12,000 South Koreans residing there, of whom more than 3,000 were evacuated by early February 1979.[20] From late 1978 until the outbreak of the Iran–Iraq War in September 1980, therefore, the number of South Korean nationals in Iran shrank from more than 12,000 to less than 1,000,[21] though a significant number of them were still reluctant to leave, and the Korean government had never perceived any imminent danger to their safety.[22] In the realm of politics and diplomacy, the South Korean government vowed to cooperate with the new Iranian regime and even to "expand the existing friendly relations with Iran."[23] The South Korean ambassador in Tehran, Dong-hwi Kim, was assigned the task of informing the new political officials in Iran of his nation's desire to continue working with the Persian Gulf country as it had before – or even more closely, if possible. Kim was able to arrange a meeting with the new Iranian supreme leader, Ruhollah Khomeini, and present him with a message from the South Korean president, Park Chung-hee.

South Korea's diplomatic move soon hit a snag when North Korean ambassador to Tehran, Byong-ok Cha, started a smear campaign against Seoul and its interests in Iran. In a meeting with the influential son of the Iranian leader, Ahmad Khomeini, the North Korean envoy requested an immediate end to South Korea's diplomatic presence in the country and the closure of its embassy in Tehran, alleging that Seoul had been guilty of espionage against Iran and colluded with the United States to rescue the American hostages kept by the Iranian government.[24] Cha later met with the Iranian president, Abolhassan Bani-Sadr, and reiterated the same allegation, asking the latter "to seize the opportunity and close down the South Korean embassy" in Iran.[25] South Korean officials refuted the accusation and during a meeting with the Iranian *chargé d'affaires* in Seoul blamed Pyongyang for attempting to damage their country's interests in Tehran through a "false slur aimed at estranging the Republic of Korea from Iran."[26] While it is not clear how much North Korea actually harmed the ROK's relationship with the new Iranian regime, the issues raised by Pyongyang's ambassador to Tehran were nevertheless highly sensitive at that particular time and had the potential to seriously damage South Korea's image among many up-and-coming Iranian elites at various prominent political and economic institutions throughout the country.

Economically, a number of important contracts and business deals between Iran and South Korea were canceled, and some of the ongoing activities between the two nations were temporarily put on hold. The 50–50 joint refining venture between the NIOC and Ssangyang Corporation was among the projects which the new Iranian government soon abandoned. In June 1980, Iran notified South Korea about a decision to withdraw from the joint project. This announcement made by Iran happened to dovetail neatly with a recent South Korean policy that aimed to nationalize foreign-held equity in joint refining ventures. Once the NIOC agreed to sell its equity to Ssangyang Corporation, the South Korean government provided the latter with the financing it required to gain full control of the entire joint venture.[27] After several meetings and bargaining rounds, the two sides finally reached a compromise according to which Ssangyang Corporation was to pay the NIOC a (rather low) sum of $20 million for its 50 percent stake in the joint project, a project that was initially supposed to consist of a $200 million refinery.[28]

In the wake of the downgrading of diplomatic ties between South Korea and Iran from the ambassadorial level to a chilly *chargé d'affaires* level and the discontinuation of some economic commitments between the two countries in the midst of a bitter conflict involving Iran and Iraq, Seoul still decided to maintain as many connections as it could to Tehran, especially through the purchase of petroleum. South Korea tactically decreased its oil imports from Saudi Arabia and replaced the shortage with an increased supply from Iran. This strategy served to protect Seoul's interests in Tehran in two different ways. First, South Korea was able to keep its foothold in Iran both to assure the reliability of its oil supply and to keep an eye on the goings on in the country, as it was potentially its biggest export market in the entire Middle East – this happened in spite of the fact that the chaotic situation there, which largely stemmed from the ongoing war with Iraq, did not allow it to enjoy full diplomatic relations with the Persian Gulf nation for the time being. Second, the energy trade facilitated South Korea's access to Iran, which in turn allowed it to keep the rising North Korean presence in Tehran in check and, if possible, to counteract Pyongyang's accusation (mentioned above) concerning Seoul's alleged collaboration with the United States.[29]

Relations with Iraq

South Korea enjoyed a straightforward relationship with Iran prior to 1979, when its relationship with Iraq was almost nonexistent. Baghdad's ideological stance and its interactions with Pyongyang were the main cause that lay behind South Korea's various unsuccessful attempts to establish diplomatic ties with Iraq.[30] Despite Baghdad's disinclination to forge a formal relationship with Seoul, South Korea still tried to penetrate Iraq's construction market in the second half of the 1970s. The East Asian country also followed an almost identical strategy in Algeria, Libya and Syria, where the lack of diplomatic relations did not stymie Korean attempts to win construction contracts. In 1978, Iraq awarded South Korea's Hyundai a few small projects in Baghdad in addition to a contract valued at $130 million to build piped-water and sewage infrastructure in Basra, Iraq's second largest city and home to its main port. When the Iran–Iraq War broke out, Hyundai's Basra project had been 80 percent complete. Samsung, another South Korean company, scurried to withdraw its 36 Korean workers from a project in Iraq's Um Qasr harbor.[31] For its part, Hyundai also pulled out the bulk of its laborers from Iraq soon after, but it did not fully shut down its Iraqi projects during the war.

When Iraq cut ties with North Korea in October 1980, accusing Pyongyang of having an allegiance to Tehran, Baghdad was in no rush to embrace Seoul. Iraq was still largely attached to the same ideology that guided the ardent nationalism of the Ba'ath Party and the country's overall pattern of interaction with the outside world. The overthrow of the monarchy in Iran and the ensuing Iran–Iraq War led Baghdad to become even more stubborn in its ideological rhetoric, which then became even more hostile to Iran. A combination of external and internal factors, therefore, prevented Iraq from feeling any urgent need to broaden the scope of its international connections to include South Korea for the time being. Not only did Baghdad benefit from the overwhelming sympathy and support of many Arab and Western countries, Iraq enjoyed tremendous political stability, and it had few financial difficulties, if any, at the time. With a population of 13 million people, Iraq had the necessary infrastructure and sufficient revenues – more than $50 billion from the sale of petroleum – to manage its national economy and fund its war effort for some time to come.[32]

Although Baghdad and Seoul remained reluctant to push for the establishment of a formal diplomatic relationship throughout the Iran–Iraq War, Iraq still wanted to keep its construction market open to South Korean contractors. Whether or not it was an invidious act of retaliation against North Korea, Saddam awarded several construction projects to South Korean companies, particularly Hyundai, which had demonstrated a keen desire to stay in Iraq despite a dangerous state of affairs caused by the war with Iran. Since the war had forced many contractors to flee Iraq, Hyundai was able to win more than 90 percent of the projects awarded to South Korean companies there. Hyundai's Iraqi projects included apartment blocks, a $400 million power plant 60 miles away from Baghdad, and a highway connecting the Syrian and Jordanian borders. Moreover, the two sides cooperated with each other during the bloody and costly war to such an extent that the Iraqi government, unlike that of Saudi Arabia, provided visas to Korean entertainers and hostesses to fly over and perform for Korean nationals; Hyundai, for its part, agreed to allow Iraq to delay its payments throughout the mid-1980s and to pay down its outstanding debts in numerous installments.[33]

In spite of any formal diplomatic relationship, South Korea still benefited from a remarkable trade surplus with Baghdad throughout the Iran–Iraq War. From 1980 to 1988, the East Asian nation's total exports to Iraq totalled more than $1.6 billion, whereas its total imports from the country totalled less than $370 million, a nearly fivefold trade surplus in favor of Seoul. Of this (over) $1.6 billion in exports, more than one quarter of it, or approximately $446 million, can be traced to a single year: 1982. The surprisingly large trade imbalance between Seoul and Baghdad had probably much to do with Hyundai's construction businesses and possible South Korean arms exports to Iraq. South Korea's bilateral economic exchanges with Iraq were now clearly much more beneficial for the East Asian nation than they were a decade earlier, when its total trade balance with Baghdad was less than one tenth of its exports to Iraq alone during the Iran–Iraq War. In a decade, from 1970 to 1979, the ROK's total imports from Iraq had reached $109 million, while the former's total exports to the latter amounted to less than $46 million, a more than twofold trade surplus in favor of Baghdad.[34] The tables had definitely turned.

Military connections

The Iran–Iraq War turned the international arms trade into a bustling business; it saw the two warring states spend billions of dollars on military equipment over the course of the eight-year long conflict. Iraq spent approximately $50 billion and Iran more than $15 billion on the purchase of weapons. From 1980 to 1983, a period of just three years, Iraq bought $15 billion worth of arms, while Iran's imported weapons cost it around $3.7 billion.[35] Weapons suppliers included countries from the two Cold War blocs, some of which (most notably the Soviet Union and China) supplied arms to both Iraq and Iran simultaneously. The profitability of arms sales to Baghdad and Tehran tempted private dealers as well as major states to get into business with the two Middle Eastern states: This was a significant phenomenon through which the Iran–Contra scandal emerged, and it was only the tip of the proverbial iceberg. Between January 1985 and July 1986 alone, the United States Department of Justice subpoenaed more than 70 individuals for trying to smuggle arms into Iran.[36] Since many great powers, including the two superpowers and China, also needed plausible deniability when it came to selling their weapons, they often used a third party as a go-between to peddle their arms to Iraq and Iran.

The United States traded arms with Iran through Israel, which later pulled out of the arrangement during the Iran–Contra affair. China first sold military equipment to Iran through North Korea before Beijing decided to deal with Tehran directly and become one of its major weapons suppliers by the mid-1980s. In the context of superpower geopolitics and the rivalry between the United States and the Soviet Union with regard to supporting the two warring parties, the Soviet Union somehow ended up taking a relatively moderate approach: In the early months of the war, when Iran was in trouble, Moscow shifted its weapons supply in favor of Tehran, but as the war raged on and as Iran started to improve its position, it later decided to sell more arms to Iraq. To make an illegal arms shipment to either party look lawful, misleading measures were occasionally applied by both sides. For instance, a package of military engine parts originally shipped to Britain from the United States could finally end up in Iran after being declared as containing civilian engine parts, being repacked, and then being shipped through Austria and Yugoslavia.[37]

Besides private brokers and major arms producers, there were a number of countries which took the opportunity to both earn some easy cash and improve the quality of their developing weapons industries; they did not much care about which side of the war each Cold War bloc supported or which of the two parties in conflict was wrong or right. These countries included Brazil, Chile, Czechoslovakia, Yugoslavia, Bulgaria, Greece and South Korea. In the period between 1982 and 1986, the heyday of arms sales during the Iran–Iraq

War, South Korea was considered to be the sixth largest weapons exporter in the third world, even outstripping its Chinese and North Korean neighbors. According to the Stockholm International Peace Research Institute (SIPRI), South Korea's arms clientele at that time included Iran, the Philippines and Argentina. Despite selling some low-profile and conventional arms to Iran such as tanks, attack boats and small weapons, the South Korean government still wanted to become one of Tehran's major weapons suppliers. However, Seoul was seriously pressured at that time by both the United States and Saudi Arabia not to cross a red line and disadvantage Iraq.[38]

What is not palpably clear, however, is the intermediary role of South Korea in transferring weapons made by other major suppliers – most notably the Americans – to Iran and possibly Iraq. Once the Iran–Contra scandal fizzled out, South Korea suddenly became part of congressional investigations that were attempting to find out whether the East Asian state had shipped "TOW anti-tank missiles to Iran, either on its own or on behalf of the United States." Moreover, there was a great deal of media scrutiny and "continuing questions and hints of a South Korean connection to the covert arms sales to Iran and a private supply network for the Contra rebels fighting the leftist government of Nicaragua." In late 1986, the then American secretary of state, George Shultz, had asked the South Korean government to stop and turn back an arms shipment to Iran "while still on the high seas." The ship, loaded with weapons, "had left South Korea with orders to go to Europe, but in the mid-course had been told the true destination was Iran."[39] A few years later, Donald Gregg, an American ambassador to South Korea from 1989 to 1993, was designated as a "subject" of a criminal investigation related to the Iran–Contra affair. A CIA agent for over 30 years and a very well-connected official in both the Reagan and Bush (I) administrations, Gregg completely denied his involvement as well as that of the political office under his management.[40] Not only did Gregg survive and serve out his term in office in Seoul, the whole Iran–Contra affair was soon swept under the rug along with the idea that South Korea was possibly involved in clandestine arms shipments to the warring parties, particularly Tehran, over the course of the Iran–Iraq War.[41]

North Korea's golden opportunity: The DPRK's relationship with Iran

Like their South Korean counterparts, the North Koreans first strove to develop better relationships with and numerous connections to Iran, favoring the latter over other countries in the Persian Gulf region. Although Tehran's alliance politics and its main foreign policy pattern during the 1950s and 1960s had curtailed Pyongyang's efforts to develop political ties with Iran, the establishment of a South Korean embassy in Tehran in the second half of the 1960s motivated North Korea more than ever to establish diplomatic ties to the Persian Gulf nation. Despite the existence of a small volume of economic exchanges between Iran and North Korea, it still took a few more years before the two countries finally established formal diplomatic relations in April 1973. To guard against any objections and/or criticisms on the part of the South Korean government (as well as other parties), Iran primarily linked its decision to recognize the DPRK regime to the ongoing discussions between the two Koreas at that particular time.[42] The then Iranian foreign minister, Abbas Ali Khalatbari, clearly hinted at such a correlation by mordantly pointing out that "if there were some sort of relationship between the two Koreas, there would be no reasons for Iran not to have relations with North Korea."[43]

Another probable reason for Tehran's recognition of Pyongyang was the fact that Iran had ongoing diplomatic relations with other communist countries, including many Eastern European nations, the Soviet Union and China – the latter being recognized by Iran in August 1971. All of these communist nations had close relationships with North Korea and were considered at the time to be Pyongyang's top political allies and trading partners. Moreover, the NAM and its championing of the Korean Cause might have had some impact on the Iranian diplomatic move regarding North Korea. As we have seen, Iran was an active member of the NAM right from the start. A series of informal diplomatic initiatives within the movement and the growing influence of North Korea in the NAM, particularly during the early 1970s, therefore likely further convinced the Iranian government to come to terms with the DPRK and accept its diplomatic presence in Tehran.

North Korea soon established its embassy in Tehran in late June 1973[44] and immediately invited the Iranian prime minister, Amir Abbas Hoveyda, to pay an official visit to the DPRK. The invitation, which surprised many in the media, was politely declined by Hoveyda, who was overburdened by his official duties at home and who could therefore not leave the country.[45] Iran still preferred to approach Pyongyang cautiously following its establishment of official ties with the DPRK and manage its relationship with the Asian country through Tehran's embassy in Beijing. Iran and North Korea subsequently signed a number of bilateral agreements related to trade (1973), culture (1974) and an inter-state news agency (1978), and some low-profile officials from Pyongyang, many of whom specialized in economics, visited Tehran before the regime toppled in early 1979. During this period of around six years, the North Korean media usually refrained from openly criticizing Iran's political system or its general handling of its foreign policy, tending instead to take a sanguine, and often neutral, view of different aspects of the ongoing economic developments and positive social changes taking place within Iranian society.[46]

From August 1973 to January 1979, therefore, Iran's relationship with North Korea, both politically and economically, was very limited in scope; closer ties between Tehran and Pyongyang were to materialize after the fall of the Pahlavi regime, when a new political system briskly and naïvely embraced the DPRK in spite of its anti-communist ideology and its "neither the East nor the West" rhetoric. Besides various moves made by the North Korean embassy in Tehran, the DPRK leader, Kim Il-sung, also sent a congratulatory message to the new Iranian leader, which denounced severely the previous political establishment in Iran and announced that "the fascist ruling machines in the days of the imperial regime are destroyed."[47] The DPRK regime and its affiliated media, therefore, capitalized on the ideological affinity between the two nations by issuing forth many of the same slogans as their Iranian counterparts. Soon after, the growing partnership between Iran and North Korea was to be further fortified by the flow of North Korean arms to Tehran upon the outbreak of the Iran–Iraq War, when the reclusive communist country, which had been waiting in the wings, was eager to take advantage of a newly beneficial diplomatic situation.

As a consequence of an expanding bilateral relationship and an increase in behind-the-scenes military deals being signed by Tehran and Pyongyang, many top-level Iranian politicians visited North Korea throughout the 1980s. A top member of the judiciary and dozens of Iranian parliamentarians visited the DPRK[48] before the Speaker of Parliament Akbar Hashemi Rafsanjani and Defense Minister Seyed Mousa Namjoo met Kim Il-sung in Pyongyang in September 1981.[49] Prime Minister Mir-Hossein Mousavi and Defense Minister Mohammad Salimi were the next top Iranian politicians to pay a visit to the DPRK, arriving for a three-day visit in October 1983.[50] In 1985, Rafsanjani once again returned to Pyongyang when he was still the speaker of parliament; his tour was soon to be followed by another top-level visit to the DPRK, that of (then) President Ali Khamenei, who also met the North Korean leader in 1989, though the main purpose and agenda of this meeting were, as usual, not disclosed. In addition to an increase in political and military cooperation between Tehran and Pyongyang during the 1980s, Iran and North Korea further expanded their bilateral agreements and protocols from the previous decade and had them apply to other fields such as fishery (1981), economics, science and trade (1982), sports (1982), and mining and technical aid (1988).

Arms trade with Tehran

The Iran–Iraq War virtually consolidated Pyongyang's position in Tehran and laid the foundations for a long-term relationship between North Korea and Iran, a relationship that still exists to the present day. Although the new government in Iran shared with the DPRK regime some ideological perspectives regarding various global and regional issues, Tehran's engagement with Pyongyang only occurred when the former's demand for military equipment started to increase by leaps and bounds. Not only did Iran have to confront an ambitious enemy that was armed to the teeth and that had received numerous pledges of military assistance, its stock of fully modern weapons was drying up apace and had to be replenished as early as possible. What made things worse was the widespread arms embargo enacted by Western countries in the wake of the infamous hostage crisis. As one of the world's leading arms importers throughout the 1970s, Iran had previously enjoyed easy access to Western-made military equipment; however, on the eve of its war with Iraq, it found itself having difficulty replacing some of this equipment – even through the black market. This dire situation left Iranian officials with little choice but to turn to Pyongyang. North Korea's weapons were backward in comparison to what the West was supplying Iraq; however, they were definitely more affordable. They were also – from a logistical point of view – relatively easy to obtain.

Like a gift from out of the blue, Iran's request for arms was immediately accepted by North Korea. Pyongyang did not hesitate to seize this diplomatic and economic opportunity that was at hand, agreeing to supply Tehran with different types of high-powered weapons. The Iran–Iraq War, in fact, happened to start at a time when the DPRK was in the midst of an economic crisis. North Korea needed to renegotiate much of its foreign debt in 1979, and its situation got even worse during the following year, when Pyongyang defaulted on all of its external loans except those it had received from Japan.[51] Pyongyang, therefore, dispatched its first shipment of military cargo to Iran soon after the war started in September 1980; the DPRK gradually became Tehran's largest arms supplier by the end of 1982, sending the Persian Gulf nation all sorts of equipment from tanks to artillery pieces, mortars and anti-aircraft weapons.[52] It has been estimated by various sources that Iran's arms purchases from North Korea in 1982 alone reached $500 million to $2 billion or around 40 percent of Tehran's total purchases of military equipment for that year – an astonishing sum by any reckoning. This led some pundits to bestow upon the East Asian communist state the dubious title of "comrade 40 percent."[53]

Considering Pyongyang's arms deals with Tehran during the Iran–Iraq War of 1980–1988, a significant issue is the dearth of reliable information and impartial data relating to the volume of military equipment supplied, the types of equipment, the approximate cost of the equipment, the payments made for the equipment, the means of delivering the equipment, and – to top it all off – the original manufacturer(s) of the equipment. Not only were key statistics related to this issue shrouded in secrecy by the various parties involved, North Korea was also asked – and this is even more important – to serve as a conduit by which both China and the Soviet Union could send military aid to Iran in the initial stages of the war. China's main arms factories, for example, were located close to the North Korean frontier, and Beijing first exported combat aircraft and other weapons to Iran through the DPRK at the outset of the Iran–Iraq War. China also played an instrumental role in the war because it permitted Iranian planes to wend their way through its airspace on their way to and from North Korea. China subsequently managed to ship arms to Iran directly and become Tehran's most important supplier of military equipment by the mid-1980s.[54]

Rupturing relations with Iraq

North Korea's relationship with Iraq predates its relationship with Iran by about a decade and a half. And while Pyongyang could establish official ties with Iran under the Pahlavi monarchy in 1973, it was the very fall of that monarchy in Iraq that had already paved the way for North Korea's approach to Baghdad in the late 1950s. When the regime of King Faisal was toppled in Iraq in July 1958, the DPRK swiftly moved to extend its recognition to the new republican regime a month later. The two countries held several bilateral meetings in late 1959 and early 1960, vowing to establish closer political and economic ties.[55] After several years of maintaining tenuous contacts and exchanging messages mostly through official channels, a North Korean trade delegation visited Iraq in December 1965 and concluded an agreement with Baghdad according to which the DPRK could export to Iraq various items such as steel and metal products, glassware, and fountain pens. The two parties soon agreed to raise their relationship to the consul-general level in July 1966, when Ryang-wuk Kang, vice-president of the Presidium of the Supreme People's Assembly of the DPRK, visited Baghdad and met with the Iraqi president, Abdul Rahman Mohammed Aref.[56] North Korea subsequently set up its consulate general in Baghdad in October 1966,[57] but the relationship between the two sides did not improve beyond that point until another regime change took place in Iraq in 1968.

Iraq's second military *coup d'état* in a decade led to the ascendancy of General Ahmad Hassan al-Bakr, under whom the relationship between Baghdad and Pyongyang reached its acme. Once the nationalist Ba'ath Party led by al-Bakr seized power in 1968, the ruling Korean Workers' Party (KWP) of the DPRK wasted no time in congratulating the new leadership in Iraq, paving the way for the two sides to establish full-fledged diplomatic ties in the same year. During several meetings between political, economic and military officials from the two countries over a period of ten years, the ideological commonalities shared by the KWP and the Ba'ath Party were given particular stress – for example, their positions against the United States and Israel, and their desires to be a leading power in their respective regions: Kim Il-sung wanted to be regarded as "the legitimate leader of all 40 million Koreans," and Iraq strove to be the quintessential representative of "all Arabs."[58] In addition to the issuance of various political *communiqués* and the signing of numerous economic accords, including the export of Iraq's oil and petrochemical products to North Korea and Pyongyang's corresponding shipment of agricultural equipment and industrial goods to Baghdad,[59] the two countries persistently promoted each other's viewpoints in their own respective media outlets, especially the newspapers affiliated with the Ba'ath Party and the KWP, respectively.

When Saddam Hussein succeeded Ahmad Hassan al-Bakr in July 1979, the relationship between Iraq and North Korea started to decline (but it did not deteriorate straight away), as Pyongyang was starting to tilt toward the new regime in Tehran, which came to power in February of that year. The North Korean media still continued their usually favorable coverage of Iraqi developments, especially the anniversary of the regime change in Baghdad, which was celebrated with great fanfare year after year.[60] At the same time, however,

Saddam was suspicious of a sudden shift in Pyongyang's approach to Tehran; his patience was growing thin with the DPRK's new fondness for the new Iranian government which he disliked right from the moment it took power – though he did not much like the previous regime either, taking delight in its downfall. The Iran–Iraq War practically put the last nail in the coffin, as it were. Pyongyang's image was forever tarnished in Baghdad when North Korea supplied arms to Tehran, an act which led Saddam to consider the move not as a negligible lapse of judgment but an unforgivable mistake and a hostile act against his country. Less than three weeks after the outbreak of the war with Iran, Baghdad severed all ties with Pyongyang, shut down its embassy in the DPRK, and ordered, on October 11, 1980, the entire corps of North Korean diplomatic mission to leave Iraq within 72 hours.[61]

Meanwhile, North Korea did not remain immune from the wrath of Saddam's regime during the course of the Iran–Iraq War. On September 19, 1985, the North Korean tanker *Song Bong*, the DPRK's first and only oil tanker, became the target of an Iraqi Exocet missile strike while it was being loaded at the Iranian island of Kharg. The Iraqi attack was so powerful that the North Korean tanker sank immediately, leaving behind the dubious reputation of being the only very large crude carrier (VLCC) to submerge upon being hit. In addition to the material cost to the DPRK, there was the human cost: Two of the *Song Bong*'s crew were killed right after the searing attack.[62] Compared to the isolated case of the DPRK-registered tanker, at least seven South Korean commercial ships came under direct attack throughout the Iran–Iraq War beginning with the bulk carrier *Sanbow Banner* which was buffeted by a similar Exocet missile strike in the Khowr-e Musa Channel on August 9, 1982, leaving one crew member dead and eight crew members missing. Moreover, South Korea saw the highest number of ship incidents among its East Asian neighbors during the war. Japan, with a much larger volume of trade with the Persian Gulf region, had five of its merchant vessels attacked, Hong Kong had two of its vessels targeted, China had one ship assaulted, and Taiwan was fortunate not have any of its ships come under attack.[63]

Relations with other Persian Gulf states

From the beginning, North Korea's approach to Persian Gulf countries epitomized the general pattern of its interactions with the broader Middle East region. When Pyongyang first decided to build connections to the region in the mid-1950s, it immediately sought relations with the Middle East's socialist and radical regimes. The latter shared with the DPRK certain political and ideological views concerning both the region and the world. North Korea received favorable responses from the governments of Egypt, Syria, Algeria, Yemen and Iraq.[64] However, with the exception of Baghdad, there was no other regime in the Persian Gulf region that both openly and wholly embraced the *Weltanschauung* of the KWP ruling in Pyongyang. As far as Tehran was concerned, its diplomatic friendship was sought after by the DPRK in 1973 because of its proactive policy within the NAM and its rather independent position toward the bloc of communist states – not because it shared specific ideological positions with the KWP. Before the turn of events in Iran in the late 1970s, therefore, North Korea's economic requirements and commercial interests played a major role in the DPRK's attention to Persian Gulf countries, particularly Kuwait and Saudi Arabia – though it should be noted that Pyongyang's early approach to both Iraq and Iran was not entirely devoid of economic motivation.

One of the first North Korean trade delegations to the Persian Gulf region was to Kuwait in early 1966, and it tried to convince the Arab nation to accept some of the DPRK's exports, including steel products, cement, porcelain and plate glass.[65] In 1968, the two countries reached an agreement to establish bilateral trade relations to further improve their "friendship and cooperation." To make the most out of such an economic arrangement, and to potentially score a few political points as well, North Korea simultaneously played up the importance of Kuwait's independence and its ostensible solidarity with the Palestinian People. These two subjects were possibly the only two issues that the DPRK regime could highlight in order to show how "the Korean and Kuwaiti peoples are closely linked … although Korea and Kuwait are far away from each other geographically."[66] Pyongyang's economic relations with Kuwait subsequently increased during the 1970s and 1980s, paving the way for a number of visits to the Arab country by low-profile North Korean officials; however, the small and reclusive communist state still failed to set up official diplomatic ties.

In the 1970s and 1980s, North Korea additionally developed a remarkable economic relationship with Saudi Arabia despite the existence of substantial political differences between them as shown by a dearth of Saudi-related news coverage in the DPRK at the time (North Korea was also linked to a few isolated cases of commercial interaction with the UAE, e.g. the importation of oil). Coupled with a sharp rise in the Saudis' desire for imported goods and a subsequent growth of imports into the kingdom, the North Korean trade with Saudi Arabia turned out to be relatively one-sided in favor of Pyongyang. In 1978 and 1979, for instance, North Korea recorded a whopping $200 million trade surplus with Saudi Arabia, a sum which was considered to be quite a hefty amount of cash for Pyongyang at that time.[67] However, these disjointed exchanges and sporadic economic accomplishments with Kuwait and Saudi Arabia were not enough to satisfy Pyongyang, which was most definitely seeking stable, long-term economic benefits from its trade with these countries. Such trade certainly paled in comparison to its commercial exchanges with Iraq before 1980 and Iran after 1979.

A new economic dynamism: Toward a better standard of living in South Korea

Almost two decades of incessant economic growth and industrialization significantly contributed to South Korea's international standing as well as to the restructuring of its internal equilibrium by the mid-1980s. The ROK's exports rose to more than $20 billion, while its per capita GNP increased to more than $2,000 from less than $100 in the early 1960s. Although South Korea still remained one of the world's largest debtors, a number of ongoing economic initiatives were slowly remedying this situation: In just five years, the ROK would become more economically appealing to the world. The country's economic focus began to shift away from investments in heavy industry in the 1970s and lean toward the development of high-tech companies in the 1980s. Alongside this important change was an ongoing process of liberalization which saw government loosen up its indisputable control over the management of industrial activities, ceding some of its power in this regard to the country's top *chaebol*. The Korean economy, moreover, needed to rely more on tariffs instead of quotas as a means of protectionism and spend more on marketing and brand promotion to better achieve its macroeconomic goals.[68]

In the second half of the 1980s, the fortuitous "three low phenomena" (low interest rates, low foreign exchange rates [especially of the US dollar against the Japanese yen], and low oil prices) further boosted the growth of the Korean economy – even though these three conditions would peter out by the end of the decade. These phenomena, also known as the "three blessings" and the "three tides," improved the comparative advantage of a weak won for Korean exports, enabling the country to both achieve a trade surplus and become one of the fastest-growing economies in the world.[69] And while South Korea was emerging as an economic power and drawing more attention to itself in this regard, its tale of industrialization and economic growth, in line with the similar cases of Taiwan, Singapore and (previously) Japan, persuaded many in other parts of the world, including various Arab leaders, to curiously look for "potential secrets" behind the East Asian model of development. Academics began to crank out a great deal of literature on this topic, and political officials developed contacts with their counterparts across Asia, aiming "to learn about the secret of this East Asian success quite closely."[70]

The Korean economy's success in garnering international attention had various political and economic ramifications for the ROK's internal stability: The relationship between the state and the general public, the employment rate, and Koreans' standard of living all became hotly contested issues. In tandem with the democratization process, which forced the government to loosen its adamantine grip on various political and economic activities (as was just mentioned above), an improvement in economic conditions at home led to a subsequent surge in both employment and real wages. Not only were South Koreans now getting higher wages, they were also converting a larger portion of their income into savings, stashing away 32 percent of their income in 1987 and having the second-highest savings-to-earnings ratio in the world (behind the Taiwanese).[71] As it so happened, this significant improvement in the economic circumstances of South Koreans – which also saw an increase in their financial security in comparison to the recent past – coincided with a sudden slump in petroleum prices. Both of these phenomena had an immediate impact on South Korea's construction businesses, which saw the number of their workers in the Persian Gulf region start to dwindle.

A hard time for contractors

In 1986, petroleum prices plummeted to less than $13 per barrel, and their subsequent fluctuations remained in the $15–$20 range for some time. Although fluctuating oil prices was not a new development and although petroleum prices had already witnessed a dramatic variation – ranging from about $2 per barrel in 1973 to over $36 per barrel in 1980 – the decrease that occurred in 1986 nevertheless came as quite a surprise and had serious implications for the economic policies of oil producers in the Persian Gulf region, especially with regard to their infrastructure projects. Iran was still fighting a costly war with Iraq when its oil incomes nosedived from about $20 billion in the early 1980s to less than $6.5 billion in 1986.[72] The shattering impact of a fall in petroleum revenues for Saudi Arabia, the largest construction market for South Koreans, was quite palpable as well: Saudi oil incomes tumbled from more than $110 billion in 1981 to around $17 billion in 1986.[73] As Saudi Arabia encountered serious fiscal problems, it had to resort to a number of measures to help it cope with the crisis – measures which included a sharp cut in the planned budgets for various development programs and infrastructure projects.[74]

The period from 1973 to 1985 was far and away the most beneficial one for South Korean construction businesses in the Persian Gulf region, attracting over a million temporary workers and contributing tens of billions of dollars to the Korean economy in one way or another.[75] When construction activities in the region reached their apogee in 1982, they accounted for more than 6.5 percent of the South Korean GNP. The construction industry also accounted for more than 40 percent of South Korea's merchandise exports to the region from 1974 to 1981.[76] The bustling construction market in the Persian Gulf started to diminish in 1983, and its absolute decline began in early 1986, when falling oil prices took their toll on development projects across the region. The number of South Korean workers subsequently decreased from more than 170,000 in 1982 to less than 60,000 in 1986 – though one must also take into consideration the fact that working conditions were significantly improving in the ROK (e.g. more job opportunities and increased wages). The number of Korean companies in the region and the total value of the contracts they signed both decreased as well.[77]

A reversal of fortunes in the Persian Gulf made some Korean contractors go bankrupt, while others were forced to immediately withdraw from the region. Meanwhile, those companies which still managed to survive had to adapt to changing circumstances and develop new strategies to support their long-term presence in the region. They particularly needed to invest in innovative technologies and capital-intensive equipment in order to increase their comparative advantage over their international rivals as well as newly emerging local and regional competitors. Since South Korean companies could no longer overwhelmingly rely on their own low-cost, disciplined workforce, they had to get used to acquiring labor from alternative sources, which included local laborers and workers from South Asian and Southeast Asian countries. This was an important matter simply because new guest workers from South Asian countries, including Indians, Pakistanis, Bangladeshis and Sri Lankans, were increasingly changing the demographic pattern of construction workers, especially in the small states of the Persian Gulf.[78] Finally, the region's construction business never dried up after 1986: It merely waxed and waned largely in lockstep with oil revenues; South Korean contractors had no option but to adjust to this new reality.[79]

Changing trade patterns

The outbreak of the Iran–Iraq War in September 1980 was the first and largest physical setback to South Korea's commercial operations in the otherwise placid waters of the Persian Gulf. As the conflict visited severe damage upon both Iran and Iraq's oil production and transportation facilities, the war at first caused a petroleum shortage of about 3.9 million bpd in the world's energy markets. Since other major producers, especially Saudi Arabia, increased their supply, a shortfall in the petroleum supply neither caused another oil shock nor led to a significant hike in global oil prices.[80] Despite the fact that the Iran–Iraq War did not have a corrosive impact on South Korean energy security in the long term, the internecine conflict still had other repercussions for the East Asian nation. Less security and more uncertainty in two of three largest states in the region; the mobilization of human and financial resources for military purposes; the preferential allocation of import quotas for foods and other essential goods rather than for unnecessary manufactured products and/ or luxury items; and an almost complete stop to extensive construction projects and large-scale development programs all took their toll on South Korea's overall economic interactions with the Persian Gulf region – and especially with Iran.

The war in Iran and Iraq, with its detrimental effects on oil production, played right into the hands of Saudi Arabia, giving a considerable boost to its thriving construction industry and its bustling trade with many other nations, particularly the East Asian countries of Japan, South Korea and Taiwan.[81] In 1980, South Korea was importing 93 percent of its oil from Saudi Arabia and Kuwait, while the two Arab countries were receiving merely 2.2 percent of Seoul's total exports and the East Asian nation could not do anything to alleviate this trade imbalance. Later, South Korea made an attempt to scale back its overdependency on Saudi Arabia for its energy imports, decreasing the supply of Saudi oil from more than 60 percent in 1980 to about 18 percent in 1984.[82] Additionally, when the construction business of the Saudis reached its acme in 1982 and the volume of South Korean exports to the Persian Gulf country increased as well, Saudi Arabia accounted for 7 percent of Seoul's total foreign trade. South Korea even managed to bring down its trade deficit with Saudi Arabia by 80 percent in the first half of 1983. The East Asian nation, moreover, moved to become Saudi Arabia's third largest trading partner behind Japan and the United States.[83]

Japan's exports to Saudi Arabia totalled more than $6.5 billion, making the Saudis the second largest trading partner for the Japanese after the Americans but way ahead of the Germans, which received $5 billion worth of Japanese exports at the time.[84] In the same way, the Persian Gulf region became a crucial target for South Korea's foreign trade when Saudi Arabia and Kuwait were positioned as Seoul's third and fourth largest trading partners after the United States and Japan in 1983. For over a decade, South Korea had striven to diversify its export markets with a new focus on a vast swath of the Middle East region. The ROK achieved great success when American and Japanese markets only accounted for 55.6 percent of its exports in 1986 down from 75.6 percent in 1970. For its part, the Middle East accounted for 12 percent of South Korea's exports from 1972 to 1977, a chunk of which can be attributed to the Persian Gulf. However, the region's share of Seoul's overall exports shrank to only 5.2 percent in 1986 mainly due to the outbreak of the Iran–Iraq War, the fall of oil prices, and the collapse of the erstwhile booming regional construction industry.[85]

In short, while South Korea was gradually able to decrease its overall trade deficit with the Persian Gulf up until the mid-1980s, the ROK saw it increase once again by the end of the decade. In 1980, South Korea's total exports to the entire Persian Gulf region amounted to about $2 billion and its total imports from the region amounted to $5.7 billion, yielding an approximate $3.7 billion trade deficit. This huge deficit went down to less than $1.4 billion in 1985, when South Korea's total exports to all Persian Gulf countries amounted to $2.2 billion and its total imports amounted to about $3.6 billion. The difference once again shot up to more than $2.4 billion in 1989, when Seoul's total imports from the Persian Gulf reached $4.3 billion but its total exports to the region amounted to approximately $1.8 billion. Moreover, the share of the Persian Gulf region in South Korea's total global trade underwent considerable changes throughout the decade. While the Gulf accounted for a staggering 25 percent of South Korea's total global imports in 1980, its share decreased to 11.4 percent in 1985 and less than 7 percent in 1989. In 1980, the Persian Gulf region absorbed 12 percent of the East Asian country's total exports, but its share contracted to only 7.4 percent in 1985 and to less than 3 percent in 1989.[86]

Meanwhile, there happened to be some variation in South Korea's major trading patterns in the region because of its dealings with some of the smaller members of the GCC. The GCC was a political as well as an economic body which came into existence in 1981 primarily in order to counter threats, imagined or otherwise, to its members' security posed by Iran. Take, for example, the UAE and Oman, which became South Korea's second and third largest import partners, respectively, after Iran in the Persian Gulf region during the mid-1980s. In 1989, the UAE stood as the ROK's second largest export market and third largest import partner in the region, while Oman surprisingly became South Korea's top import partner ahead of Saudi Arabia – in the 1970s, the combined share of both the UAE and Oman of the East Asian country's total trade with the Persian Gulf was negligible. South Korea enjoyed once again a far more favorable trade pattern with Iran in comparison to its other Persian Gulf partners simply because Seoul's two-way economic connections to Tehran experienced, by and large, less trade deficit and occasionally even surplus in favor of the former. Unlike its trading relationship with Iran, South Korea's bilateral trade with most of the GCC countries resulted in trade deficits most of the time, if not all the time: It was almost as if achieving a satisfactory balance of trade with these Arab states had become a perpetual wild goose chase.[87]

Notes

1 For playing a direct role in suppressing the Gwangju Uprising, Chun Doo-hwan and a number of his military colleagues were arrested in December 1995 and put on trial in 1996. Chun received a life sentence, but he was dubiously pardoned later.

2 Lowell S. Feld, "Oil Markets in Crisis: Major Oil Supply Disruptions since 1973," in Siamack Shojai (ed.), *The New Global Oil Market: Understanding Energy Issues in the World Economy* (Westport, CT: Praeger, 1995), pp. 103–116.

3 Bruce Cumings, "The Origins and Development of the Northeast Asian Political Economy: Industrial Sectors, Product Cycles, and Political Consequences," in Frederic C. Deyo (ed.), *The Political Economy of the New Asian Industrialism* (Ithaca: Cornell University Press, 1987), pp. 44–83.

4 Thomas Stern, "Korean Economic and Political Priorities in the Management of Energy Liabilities," in Ronald C. Keith (ed.), *Energy, Security and Economic Development in East Asia* (New York: St. Martin's Press, 1986), pp. 138–166.

5 Stern.

6 Stern.

7 "Oil Imports Planned by ROK Ships by '76," *Korea Times*, April 19, 1973, p. 4.

8 Mardon.

9 Among the factors which probably lured the NIOC into the deal was the fact that Ssangyong Corporation had already become one of South Korea's largest oil consumers in the private sector as well as a major company in some other areas such as cement manufacturing, shipping and commercial operations.

10 A decade after signing the NIOC–Ssangyong Corporation joint venture, Seoul entered into another joint refining initiative between British Petroleum (BP) and Kukdong Corporation in 1986. This time, BP only held a 40 percent equity stake; the remaining 60 percent equity stake was held by Kukdong Corporation.

11 "Korea, Iran to Build $160 Mil Oil Refinery," *Korea Times*, October 14, 1975, p. 1.

12 Stern.

13 Mardon.

14 Ibrahim Anvari Tehrani, "Iraqi Attitudes and Interpretation of the 1975 Agreement," in Farhang Rajaee (ed.), *The Iran–Iraq War: The Politics of Aggression* (Gainesville, FL: The University Press of Florida, 1993), pp. 11–23.

15 "Saudi Supports Iraq in War with Iranians," *Reuters*, September 26, 1980.

16 "Persian Gulf Crisis," *Korea Times*, September 25, 1980, p. 2.
17 "Korea Impartial on Iran–Iraq War," *Korea Herald*, October 1, 1980, p. 1.
18 "All Koreans Said Safe," *Korea Times*, September 25, 1980, p. 1.
19 "Koreans in Iraq Move to Kuwait," *Korea Times*, September 27, 1980, p. 1.
20 "Evacuation from Iran Expedited," *Korea Times*, February 4, 1979, p. 1.
21 Many of the workers later returned back as the number of South Korean laborers in Iran crept up to more than 3,600 in 1985 (roughly equivalent to the number in April 1977) before it ratcheted down again to about 2,000 in 1987. Despite such fluctuations, over 25,000 South Koreans worked in Iran during just a decade between 1975 and 1985.
22 "Korean Workers Safe in Iran, Consul Says," *Korea Times*, January 6, 1979, p. 1.
23 "ROK–Iran Ties Desired to Remain Unchanged," *Korea Times*, January 18, 1979, p. 1.
24 "Iran Response to N. Korean Demands Cool," *Korea Times*, October 26, 1980, p. 1.
25 In tandem with the campaign of Pyongyang's envoy, North Korean media also ran a series of demeaning materials against South Korea's interests in Tehran, focusing particularly on Seoul's cooperation with some American policies against Iran in the aftermath of the hostage crisis. A case in point is a piece published by the *Pyongyang Times*, which criticized Seoul trenchantly, pointing out that "no country in the world acts so foolishly as to sacrifice itself by partaking in the aggressive policy of others, turning away from the interest and dignity of its people. The South Korean authorities, however, are unhesitatingly committing such a despicable act as to respond to the US 'sanctions,' recalling their ambassador from Iran and disgracefully behaving themselves in subservience to the United States. In this way, they are comporting themselves as an enemy of the Iranian people and the people of the third world as the former dictator (Park Chung-hee) did." See "No Scheming Can Subdue Iranian People," *Pyongyang Times*, April 26, 1980, p. 4.
26 "Alleged ROK–U.S. Collusion: N.K. Iran Slur 'Unfounded'," *Korea Herald*, October 16, 1980, p. 1.
27 Mardon.
28 The Financial Times, *Financial Times Oil and Gas International Year Book* (London: Longman, 1983), p. 481.
29 Joseph A. Yager, *The Energy Balance in Northeast Asia* (Washington, D.C.: Brookings Institution, 1984), p. 73.
30 Reich, p. 323.
31 "Iran–Iraq War: All Korean Workers Safe," *Korea Times*, September 26, 1980, p. 8.
32 Roberts, p. 158.
33 Kirk, pp. 90–91.
34 Korean Statistical Information Service.
35 In comparison to the arms sales by both Iraq and Iran in this period, South Korea's total purchases of American weapons and parts reached around $800 million annually by 1984, while its GNP was more than $76 billion. See Ralph N. Clough, *Embattled Korea: The Rivalry for International Support* (Boulder, CO: Westview Press, 1987), p. 175.
36 Michael Brzoska, "Profiteering on the Iran–Iraq War," *Bulletin of the Atomic Scientists*, Vol. 43, No. 5 (1987), pp. 42–45.
37 Brzoska.
38 William D. Hartung, "U.S.–Korea Jet Deal Boosts Arms Trade," *Bulletin of the Atomic Scientists*, Vol. 46, No. 9 (1990), pp. 18–24.
39 Alison Mitchell, "Officials: Shultz Halted Arms S. Korea Sent Iran," *Newsday*, January 24, 1987.

40 "U.S. Ambassador to South Korea under Scrutiny of Iran–Contra Probe," *Associated Press*, July 31, 1991.

41 Many other things about the Iran–Contra scandal are still shrouded in secrecy, including the ignominious fate of some big actors from the private sector who might have played a role in one way or another. A number of such people ended up fleeing to an East Asian country like South Korea to lick their wounds and hide from a propitious life ruined by the Iran–Contra affair. One such reported case was the story of an Iranian–American private dealer, Albert A. Hakim, who lost a great fortune for his failed partnership in the crime and who later lived and died in South Korea. It is, however, difficult to further track Hakim's exact role in the scandalous affair or even establish the plausibility of his story in the first place. For a more detailed narrative concerning Hakim's account of the affair and his role in it, see Robert Neff, "Korea and the Iran–Contra Affair 1&2," *Oh My News*, November 23 and December 3, 2007.

42 Contrary to the Iranian point of view, the South Korean government expressed its deep regret over Tehran's decision to extend diplomatic recognition to Pyongyang, considering the move counterproductive to the wishes of Koreans. In a letter to Khalatbari, South Korean Foreign Minister Chong-kyu Kim criticized the Iranian policy, stating that "the Iranian government has taken a step against the wishes of the people and government of the ROK … the Iranian recognition of North Korea not only runs counter to the endeavors of the Korean People to realize a long-cherished aspiration for a national reunification, but also endangers the successful progress of the south–north dialogue by disturbing the most delicate political–military balance existing between the south and north on the basis of which the dialogue itself was possible." See *Wegyo Munseo* [Diplomatic Archives], 2003.

43 "Taghirate jadid dar siyasate kharejiye Iran," ["New Changes in Iran's Foreign Policy"] *Ettelaat*, January 22, 1973.

44 "Ijad sefaratkhaneh koreye shomali dar Tehran," ["North Korean Embassy Established in Tehran"] *Ettelaat*, July 1, 1973.

45 "Premier Will not Visit North Korea," *The Echo of Iran*, Vol. 21, No. 155, July 16, 1973.

46 "Iran in the Quick Process of Transformation," *Pyongyang Times*, October 29, 1977, p. 4.

47 "New Epoch in the History of Iranian People," *Pyongyang Times*, April 14, 1979, p. 4.

48 "President Kim Il Sung Receives Iranian MP and His Party," *Pyongyang Times*, June 27, 1981, p. 1.

49 "President Kim Il Sung Meets Iranian Parliamentary Del.," *Pyongyang Times*, September 26, 1981, p. 1.

50 "Iranian Prime Minister Arrives in North Korea," *Reuters*, October 24, 1983.

51 IBP USA, *North Korea: Energy Policy, Laws and Regulations Handbook, Volume 1: Strategic Information and Development* (Washington, D.C.: International Business Publications, 2011), p. 31.

52 Richard Halloran, "North Korea Said to Be Arming Iran," *New York Times*, December 19, 1982, p. 1.

53 Husain Haqqani, "Comrade 40%: Pyongyang's Arms for Iran," *Arabia-The Islamic World Review*, No. 30, February 1984, p. 17.

54 John W. Garver, *China and Iran: Ancient Partners in a Post-Imperial World* (Seattle: University of Washington Press, 2006), pp. 170–171.

55 Gills, p. 65.

56 "Consul-General Relations Agreed with Iraq," *Pyongyang Times*, July 28, 1966, p. 1.

57 "DPRK Consulate General Opens in Iraq," *Pyongyang Times*, October 27, 1966, p. 1.

58 To further please their Iraqi counterparts and thereby benefit from potential gains, North Koreans were not afraid of backing the wrong horse, throwing their

diplomatic weight behind Baghdad regarding some contentious issues. For instance, during a meeting between Ahmad Hassan al-Bakr, secretary-general of the Ba'ath Party and president of the republic, and a North Korean delegation led by Sung-chull Pak, member of the Politbureau and Central Committee of the KWP and second deputy prime minister, in Baghdad in May 1971, the DPRK recklessly sided with an Iraqi irredentist claim against neighboring Iran, expressing "full understanding and support for Iraq's attitude in holding on to its absolute right to full sovereignty on national waters and territories." See *Wegyo Munseo* [Diplomatic Archives], 2001.

59 See "Joint Announcement on Visit of Government Economic Delegation of Republic of Iraq to DPRK Issued," *Pyongyang Times*, November 6, 1971, p. 6; "Reception of Government Military Delegation of Republic of Iraq," *Pyongyang Times*, May 6, 1972, p. 3; "Government Delegation of Republic of Iraq Visits DPRK," *Pyongyang Times*, July 19, 1975, p. 2; and "Korean Party and Gov't Del. Visit Iraq and Syria," *Pyongyang Times*, August 5, 1978, p. 2.

60 "Iraqi People Greet their Fete Days," *Pyongyang Times*, July 12, 1980, p. 4.

61 "Iraq Breaks Diplomatic Ties with N. Korea, Syria, Libya," *Reuters*, October 11, 1980.

62 Martin S. Navias and E.R. Hooton, *Tanker Wars: The Assault on Merchant Shipping during the Iran–Iraq Conflict, 1980–1988* (New York: I.B. Tauris & Co. Ltd., 1996), pp. 107–108.

63 Navias and Hooton, pp. 205–214.

64 The DPRK established diplomatic relationships with Algeria, Egypt and North Yemen in 1963, with Syria in 1966, and with both South Yemen and Iraq in 1968.

65 "Korean Trade Del. Back from Arab Nations," *Pyongyang Times*, February 24, 1966, p. 1.

66 See, for instance, "Condolences to Kuwait President," *Pyongyang Times*, December 2, 1965, p. 1; "Kuwaiti National Day," *Pyongyang Times*, March 2, 1967, p. 2; "Greetings to 8th Anniv. of Kuwait's Independence," *Pyongyang Times*, March 3, 1969, p. 12; "Tenth Anniversary of Kuwait's Independence," *Pyongyang Times*, February 27, 1971, p. 4; "Congratulations to Kuwaiti People on their National Holiday," *Pyongyang Times*, February 26, 1977, p. 4; and "Kuwait on its Fete Day," *Pyongyang Times*, February 28, 1981, p. 4.

67 *China Newsletter*, Volumes 49–65 (Tokyo: Nihon Boeki Shinkokai, 1984), p. 20.

68 Sanjaya Lall, "Industrial Development and Technology," in D. Kim and T. Kong (eds.), *The Korean Peninsula in Transition* (London: Macmillan Press, 1997), pp. 13–35.

69 Brian Bridges, *Korea after the Crash: The Politics of Economic Recovery* (London and New York: Routledge, 2001), p. 22.

70 Mustapha Al-Sayyid, "International and Regional Environments and State Transformation in Some Arab Countries," in Hassan Hakimian and Ziba Moshaver (eds.), *The State and Global Change: The Political Economy of Transition in the Middle East and North Africa* (Richmond, UK: Curzon Press, 2001), pp. 156–177.

71 Porter, p. 467.

72 Roberts, p. 165.

73 Kiren A. Chaudhry, *The Price of Wealth: Economies and Institutions in the Middle East* (Ithaca: Cornell University Press, 1997), p. 269.

74 Chaudhry, p. 34.

75 It has been estimated, by various sources, that the overall contribution of the period 1973–1985 might be more than $40 billion but less than $80 billion.

76 John Lie, *Han Unbound: The Political Economy of South Korea* (Stanford: Stanford University Press, 1998), p. 88.

77 Hapdong News Agency, *Korea Annual 1987* (Seoul: Hapdong News Agency, 1987), p. 215.

78 Robert E. Looney, *Manpower Policies and Development in the Persian Gulf Region* (Westport, CT: Praeger, 1994), p. 97.

79 At the same time, South Korean contractors greatly benefited from a number of lucrative contracts in other parts of the Middle East, particularly from Libya, in the 1980s and thereafter. South Korea's Dong-Ah Construction Company signed contracts worth billions of dollars to participate in different phases of Libya's flagship infrastructure program, the Great Man-Made River (GMR) project. In 1986, the number of contractors and workers from South Korea in Libya also exceeded the number of those from North Korea, the former pressing the Libyan government to grant tourist visas to South Korean nationals for the first time. Like a number of other destinations such as Iraq, this visa category was also a convenient cloak to take Korean entertainers and hostesses to a given country in order to cater to the needs of the contractors and their workers. See "Libya to Grant 30-Day Tourist Visas to Koreans," *Korea Times*, October 31, 1986, p. 2.

80 Feld.

81 For instance, Saudi Arabia became Taiwan's chief petroleum supplier and the only nation among the tiny East Asian country's top ten trading partners which still maintained full diplomatic relations with Taipei. Saudi Arabia did not hold bilateral connections to China, as Riyadh established official diplomatic relations with Beijing only in July 1990. See Geldenhuys, p. 294.

82 Stern.

83 Rodney J.A. Wilson, "Japan's Exports to the Middle East: Directional and Commodity Trends and Price Behavior," *Middle East Journal*, Vol. 38, No. 3 (1984), pp. 454–473.

84 Wilson.

85 Metraux.

86 Korean Statistical Information Service.

87 Korean Statistical Information Service.

4 Business as usual in an era of transition and uncertainty

A transitional period and a new political environment

The late 1980s was an epoch-making period and an era of unprecedented economic and political developments in South Korea. It had significant implications for the country's domestic outlook as well as for its broader interactions with the outside world. The ROK's per capita GNP had increased from roughly $87 in 1962 to $1,500 in 1980 and to more than $3,000 in 1987.[1] With total exports of $57 billion in 1988, the East Asian country was no longer considered to have a low-wage economy, as average family income had shot up to somewhere between $550 and $650 per annum a year earlier.[2] This economic growth continued apace throughout the following years into the early 1990s, enabling South Koreans to see their fortunes double in less than half a decade. In 1991, South Korea's per capita GNP had increased to approximately $6,500, the unemployment rate was low, domestic consumption had risen – with Koreans buying more luxury goods – and a larger number of people developed a taste for leisure activities and foreign travel. Moreover, the percentage of South Korea's urban population had already shot up from 28 percent in 1960 to more than 74 percent in 1990, giving a tremendous boost to the foregoing trends among a sprouting crowd of *nouveaux riches*, many of whom had already begun to reside in Seoul and its suburbs.[3]

South Korea's political establishment, however, had not developed in lock-step with the rapid economic changes the country had undergone since the early 1960s. A lack of political freedom and the suppression of civil rights coupled with widening disparities in wages and employment opportunities thrust the country into political chaos in 1987, forcing the military to gradually relinquish its control over the economy as well as the governmental apparatus to a new generation of Korean politicians and managers whose rule and authority were to no longer be considered illegitimate – even if they still followed some policies and methods which had long been applied during the military dictatorship. The presidential election in December 1987 and the follow-up general election for the National Assembly in April 1988 ushered in the beginning of what has been called the "democratization process" in South Korea. It was the right time for the new leadership to present South Korea's achievements to a global audience that was paying a great deal of attention to the country during the 1988 Olympic Games in Seoul.[4] In addition to the implementation of a series of measures related to civil and political rights, the new government, led by Roh Tae-woo, also needed to find a way to enhance the competitiveness of the South Korean economy through starting up various privatization programs and introducing free-enterprise mechanisms.[5]

A combination of both economic and political accomplishments, capped off at exactly the right time by Seoul's Olympic Games of 1988, paved the way for South Korea's internationalization. Within just three decades, South Korea had somehow leapfrogged from an economic status akin to that of Egypt and the Philippines in 1962 to a new, much higher economic status in 1992: The Korean state had a per capita income that was more than ten times those of the aforementioned countries.[6] Its international standing had improved even more dramatically; the ROK went from having an unstable economy and an insolvent political apparatus in the early 1960s to a thriving industrial power and a major global trading partner in the early 1990s. The commencement of South Korea's internationalization also dovetailed neatly with a number of other important developments, including the end of the Iran–Iraq War in the Persian Gulf region and the cessation of the Cold War as a pressing geopolitical concern. And while each of these developments could present itself as a litmus test for South Korea's internationalization and its presence beyond East Asia, it was the country's previous improvements which made it possible for it to now take advantage of such events to better its political standing in and enhance its economic connections to the world at large.

The end of the Iran–Iraq War

On July 18, 1988, when Tehran unconditionally accepted UN Resolution 598, which had been adopted by the Security Council almost one year earlier, Iran and Iraq formally put an end to a protracted and internecine conflict that had cost both of them no less than $1 trillion. The Iranian move had an immediate impact on the South Korean stock market, as the KOSPI was buoyed by a record 23 points and share prices of major Korean construction companies such as Hyundai Engineering and Construction Company and Daelim Industrial Company went up on a daily basis for over a week. In fact, Korean and Japanese contractors had long waited for a ceasefire between Iran and Iraq, and some of their companies had even maintained offices in Tehran and Baghdad throughout the war, so that they could resume their work once the conflict came to an end. Japan and South Korea now entered into a contentious rivalry, each country wanting to get a larger share of the reconstruction contracts in Iran and Iraq. In fact, both states predicted they would generate billions of dollars in construction earnings over the years to come. The Koreans in particular claimed that they were more entitled to the lion's share of the contracts than their rivals, arguing that they had "a better knowledge of those countries than other countries that did not work during the war ... Iran and Iraq are grateful for Korean loyalty."[7]

Meanwhile, the conclusion of the war paved the way for a rapprochement in diplomatic relations between Seoul and Tehran. It should be noted that a high-ranking South Korean foreign ministry official had already visited Iran more than a year before to lobby for such a rapprochement. An advancement in their bilateral relations proceeded apace when the deputy foreign minister of Iran, Javad Mansouri, visited Seoul in January 1989 to hold talks with a number of South Korea's top officials, including the prime minister. In a meeting with the South Korean foreign minister, Ho-joong Choi, the two countries decided to dispatch ambassadors to their respective capitals to run each other's diplomatic missions, both of which had been managed by a *chargé d'affaires* since 1981. Mansouri also revealed that Tehran was soon to go ahead with dozens of infrastructure and development projects, informing his host country that "Korean firms as well as firms of several other countries may participate in the reconstruction projects according to their own capabilities."[8]

Mansouri's trip to South Korea, however, occurred at a crucial time in Iranian history: Iran was at loggerheads with Western nations, particularly European countries, over the political drama that followed the publication of *The Satanic Verses* by British–Indian novelist Salman Rushdie in 1988. Tehran's relations with European countries reached its nadir when the 12 Common Market nations decided to recall their ambassadors from Iran on February 20, 1989, for more than a month to protest a religious decree made by the Ayatollah, which sought to end Rushdie's life.[9] Iran soon reciprocated, but the political standoff essentially minimized its economic interactions with the West for quite a while, forcing Tehran to further set in motion its diplomacy toward non-Western nations, particularly those in Asia. Iran still adamantly stuck to its ideological principles while dealing with non-Western countries during this tough time, and such a stance was made clear when Mansouri told the South Koreans in Seoul that "political consideration will be also an important criterion in the screening, and the Iranian government won't let any country with a goal of 'hegemonistic roles' in other countries to participate in the projects."[10]

A couple of months later, the Iranian minister of oil, Gholamreza Aghazadeh, led a high-ranking delegation from various ministries and economic bodies to South Korea. During his visit in July 1989 – the first trip to Seoul by an Iranian cabinet minister since the two nations upgraded their diplomatic relations to the ambassadorial level – the two countries agreed to restart the annual meetings of Iran–Korea Joint Economic Commissions, which had been suspended since 1979.[11] Apart from negotiations over a number of construction and trading contracts, the oil minister also indicated that "Iran is interested in supplying its crude oil to other Korean refineries in as favorable terms as they do now for Ssangyong Oil Refining Co." Moreover, Aghazadeh hinted about the possibility of South Korean participation in a massive petrochemical project in southern Iran which had been abandoned by Japan owing to the outbreak of the Iran–Iraq War.[12] The $3.6 billion project, known as the "Iran–Japan Petrochemical Complex" (IJPC), was located in a coastal city of southern Iran and was 73 percent complete when the war broke out. Once the war came to a halt, the Japanese partner, Mitsui, decided to permanently abandon the partnership, arguing that the Iranian project was no longer economically feasible.

Iran initially turned down an offer made by Mitsui to pay a $1.25 billion settlement and leave the partnership for good, but Tehran later decided to negotiate with South Korea and see whether they could provide a replacement for the Japanese company.[13] The South Koreans were, however, rather wary about taking on a project that the Japanese had already started and were now quitting for apparent economic reasons. The ROK declined. Disappointed with the responses it received from the two East Asian countries, the Iranian government later decided to complete the petrochemical project in cooperation with European companies (as well as local Iranian companies). What had motivated Iran to ask South Korea for help with this project (in place of Japan's Mitsui) in the first place was the fact that its companies had the technological know-how to do the work and the fact that they had previously implemented, rather successfully, a number of Iranian projects under wartime conditions. At the time of Aghazadeh's visit to Seoul, there were 2,000 South Koreans working in Iran, and the annual bilateral trade between the two countries had reached approximately $2 billion, including $700 million in direct trade.[14] This was more than three times Iran's $600 million in two-way trade with China, though Beijing was gradually gearing up to play a larger role in Iranian reconstruction projects, as Tehran was now inclined to expand its commercial interactions with East Asia.[15]

Additionally, the conclusion of the Iran–Iraq War was favorable to South Korea's long-cherished policy of engaging Iraq, as both countries had maintained bilateral relations only at the consular level since 1981. In July 1989, South Korean Foreign Minister Ho-joong Choi paid a three-day official visit to Iraq during which Seoul and Baghdad raised their diplomatic relations to the ambassadorial level.[16] Choi's trip, the first such move made by a South Korean foreign minister, still largely focused on the possible involvement of Korean companies in postwar reconstruction projects in Iraq that were estimated to reach a total of $30 billion.[17] Although Iraq could rely on its gargantuan oil reserves to underwrite the reconstruction projects, Baghdad had already been saddled with what some called "an oil revenue straitjacket" in which the country's previous export capacity had been restricted and its future petroleum exports were to face either an OPEC-implemented quota or an oil glut. Accounting for at least 95 percent of Baghdad's export income, Iraq's oil revenue was approximately $12 billion in 1988 and was expected to reach no more than $15 billion in the following year.[18] Not only did Iraq refuse to even entertain the idea of repaying its debts, at least its debts owed to non-Arab countries ($30–$35 billion), it lost its chance to have South Korean companies come help rebuild the country when Saddam decided to march into Kuwait. In what was widely considered to be a reckless move, Saddam caused yet another disastrous conflict, which saw the ensuing implementation of a sanctions regime. These sanctions targeted against Iraq's economy were relatively easy for the West to enforce largely because of the end of the Cold War and the virtual removal of the Soviet Union, Baghdad's erstwhile ally, from world politics.

The end of the Cold War

The disintegration of the Soviet Union and the collapse of communist regimes in its satellite states of Eastern Europe and Central Asia put an official end to the Cold War and the political rhetoric associated with it from the world arena. But the cessation of Cold War discourse from international relations was to mean a lot more to South Korea. In fact, the partition of the Korean Peninsula, epitomized by the creation of the ROK in the south and the DPRK in the north, and the follow-up outbreak of the Korean War were all the results of the emerging Cold War in the late 1940s and the early 1950s. For the South Koreans, the pangs of the Cold War's birth did not subside, as their country was to become a crucial part of a *cordon sanitaire* carved out by the West to contain the advancement of a sprouting communism in continental Asia and in Northeast Asia in particular. Moreover, Seoul's general pattern of regional as well as international interactions needed to move *pari passu* with its anti-communist orientation so that the ROK forged congenial connections to Japan, Taiwan and Thailand at the cost of forging similar ties with the Soviet Union, China and North Korea.[19]

In comparison to its perplexing and tortuous beginning, the end of the Cold War was a real relief for many nations around the world – while it turned out to be only a bittersweet occurrence for South Koreans regardless of the bitter history of their brethren in the northern part of the Korean Peninsula. Contrary to what many expected, the post–Cold War era still conjured up unpleasant memories of previous decades simply because the long-cherished goal of unification failed to materialize. The Korean Peninsula technically remained at war, and leniency of any sort toward the North Korean regime was seen as a red line of sorts with respect to the ROK's national security. In many other ways, however, the period following the Cold War's conclusion seemed to be a harbinger of a promising future. China, its giant neighbor, was at one time a frightening foe, but gradually became a pivotal economic partner; its security threat to Seoul was perceived by Koreans as being quite low. More importantly, South Korea stepped into the post–Cold War world when it was mature enough economically, politically and militarily. Further boosted by membership in the UN, such a colorful background significantly increased the ROK's chances of better coping with new challenges and of benefiting from new regional and global opportunities.[20]

The end of the Cold War, for all that, had its own implications for South Korean foreign policy toward the Persian Gulf, and, in general terms, the

Middle East region. The East Asian country patched up its relationship with Israel and even recognized the Palestinian Liberation Organization (PLO) as the sole legitimate representative of the Palestinian People. Korean companies gradually yet quietly engaged in significant commercial activities with Israel, and the Oslo Peace Process gave the Korean government the leverage it needed to no longer be bogged down by its relationship with Israel when dealing with Arab countries, especially the GCC states.[21] In the Persian Gulf region, Seoul's political and economic relations with the GCC member states further developed for the better, but its relationship with Iran did not expand beyond a certain point and often encountered onerous hurdles that needed to be overcome. The so-called "dual containment policy," that is, the keeping of both Iran and Iraq on tenterhooks through political isolation and economic restrictions, was one such hurdle, and it partially restrained Seoul's economic interactions with Tehran, despite the potential for a highly profitable economic partnership.[22] Compared to its lackluster but respiteless relationship with Iran, South Korea's relations with Iraq in 1989 turned out to be very short-lived because Saddam's invasion of Kuwait rewound Seoul's bilateral relations with Baghdad to the level they were at about a decade earlier.

A crisis of a different stripe: The invasion of Kuwait, 1990–1991

Saddam Hussein's invasion of Kuwait in August 1990 triggered an upheaval with political and economic implications not only for the Persian Gulf region but for the world as well. The episode that followed the annexation of Kuwait as Iraq's nineteenth province thoroughly exploded the spurious notion that power politics and market mechanisms – especially as they relate to international commerce in general and the energy trade in particular – were mutually exclusive phenomena. As far as the world's commercial interests in the Persian Gulf were concerned, the rapid reaction and bloody response to Saddam's seizure of his tiny Arab neighbor accentuated the link between international politics and the world economy because "market exchange, and especially long-distance trade, cannot exist without rules imposed from somewhere."[23] As a major trading nation and a country heavily dependent on unremitting commercial connections to the Persian Gulf region, Japan, for instance, was eventually pressured into contributing $13 billion to fund the international effort to remove Saddam's forces from Kuwait – although Tokyo was later told by the people in charge of Operation Desert Storm that its financial contribution was "too little too late."[24] The Japanese perception of their haunting humiliation was soon reified when the country's foreign minister, Taro Nakayama, was not invited to the coalition's victory celebrations in Washington, D.C. To further add insult to injury, Japan was intentionally removed from the list of countries that the Kuwaiti government set out to thank in a paid advertisement published by the *New York Times* after the Al-Sabah family had been restored to power.[25]

Meanwhile, a number of international observers were quick to notice the similarity between the Persian Gulf crisis and the history of South Korea's creation. For such people, the invasion of Kuwait by Iraq, as the first major challenge in international politics following the end of the Cold War, somehow resembled the prelude to the Korean War, which itself was the first major global crisis at the beginning of the Cold War. The secular Saddam could easily be seen as the communist Kim Il-sung, and the former's invasion of Kuwait, which many feared would ultimately promote religious fanaticism, can easily be seen as the latter's intention of fostering communism throughout the Korean Peninsula by invading the ROK.[26] To other pundits, who viewed this argument as spurious, drawing a connection between how the two conflicts ended seemed to be a more plausible comparison. It was, in retrospect, the first time since the Korean War that the world acted collectively to punish an act of international aggression – this time in the name of "collective security" sanctioned by the UN. Such a sanguine yet myopic view about the whole episode asserted, after all, that the UN-authorized collective measure against Saddam's Iraq was going to send a powerful message to potential aggressors to think twice before deciding to invade a sovereign nation.[27]

Regardless of how one chooses to compare the two situations, the occupation of Kuwait had considerable repercussions for South Korea's domestic policy as well as its foreign policy. In addition to some trepidation about the supply of oil from the Persian Gulf, many in the ROK worried that a prolonged conflict following the capture of Kuwait could cut South Korean GNP growth by 1.5 percent. Coupled with the negative impacts that such a conflict would have on the ROK's monetary and fiscal policies, the whole crisis seemed like it was bound to severely slow down the progress of the Korean economy in one way or another.[28] In the Persian Gulf region, there were a number of Korean companies working on various projects both in Iraq and in Kuwait; the sudden turn of events not only jeopardized the safety of Korean citizens in the region, it also put at risk nearly $1.3 billion in unpaid debts that Korean contractors were expecting to receive.[29] In addition, South Korea was unexpectedly pressured by the United States into making a financial contribution to and playing a logistical role in the joint military operation against Saddam. How, then, did the South Korean government of Roh Tae-woo handle this situation?

South Korea's response to the Gulf War

Once Iraqi forces seized Kuwait, the South Korean government immediately formed an emergency task force to deal with the economic fallout. Chaired by Deputy Prime Minister Seung-yun Lee, the ad hoc body included the foreign, finance, trade industry, construction, energy resources and environment ministers plus the chief presidential aide for economic affairs. The task force adopted a series of energy-saving measures which were to affect oil prices (and hence gas prices), TV broadcasting times, electronic advertisements (e.g. neon signs), street lights, and stores' opening hours. Such austerity measures were designed to increase in intensity and duration should the Persian Gulf crisis go on longer than expected. Although South Koreans had already borne the brunt of such irritating practices during the oil shocks of 1973–1974 and 1979–1980, those inconvenient measures still helped the country lower electricity consumption by 3 percent and private gas consumption by 12 percent as late as February 1991. The overall state of the South Korean economy, nevertheless, remained relatively healthy, as its growth rate only experienced a minor setback, falling from 9 percent in 1990 to 7 percent in 1991.[30]

With regard to the war zone, the Korean government strove to evacuate 1,300 Korean workers from Kuwait and Iraq, and it even initially advised another 6,000 of its nationals working in five neighboring Arab countries (Saudi Arabia, Bahrain, Qatar, the UAE and Jordan) to leave the region as soon as possible. The Iranian and Saudi border crossings were considered to be the safest locations from which to extract Korean workers from Iraq and Kuwait, respectively.[31] During the evacuation process, Iraqi officials were particularly cooperative, providing assistance to South Korea's embassy and helping its personnel leave the country as fast and as safely as possible. South Koreans themselves were amazed when they heard directly from their ambassador to Baghdad, Bong-eheun Choi, who was called home in January 1991, that "Iraqi officials helped us a lot in evacuating our workers from the country." Ambassador Choi's buoyant narrative of Iraqi cooperation was conveyed to the South Korean press at a time when the ROK had already implemented a series of measures that were rather inimical to Baghdad: It had decided to participate in an oil embargo against Iraq and promised financial, logistical and moral support for the American-led operation against Saddam's forces.[32]

South Korea's sanctions against Iraq, which arose as a result of significant pressure from the Americans and which were formally announced on August 9, 1990, involved both an energy embargo and a trade ban. Before Saddam invaded Kuwait, South Korea was importing 7.6 percent of its crude oil from Kuwait and about 4.2 percent from Iraq, a total of less than 12 percent from the two countries combined. In addition to crude oil, Kuwait was also supplying around one fifth of Seoul's liquefied petroleum gas (LPG).[33] While South Korea could replace these two import items from other countries without serious difficulty, the resulting loss of construction earnings and income from manufactured exports, especially those to Kuwait, would have to be shouldered. One particular step related to energy imports was that the South Korean government encouraged refineries to court non–Middle Eastern oil exporters such as Mexico, Venezuela and Indonesia in order to ensure the country would have continuous access to crude oil should the Persian Gulf crisis turn into a prolonged conflict. As the crisis came to a head in January 1991, Korean Air, the ROK's main national carrier, decided to temporarily suspend its flights to the Middle East – in accordance with a coordinated move that was already being practiced by most foreign airlines.[34]

As far as South Korea's material contribution to Operation Desert Storm is concerned, the Americans[35] initially asked Seoul to provide $450 million, and the ROK ended up agreeing to contribute $220 million.[36] The South Koreans were later asked to donate an additional amount of $280 million, which would see their total contribution to Desert Storm reach $500 million.[37] This half-a-billion-dollar offering, or just 3.8 percent of Japan's $13 billion contribution, was to be divided up to fund the following: direct financial aid, transportation fees, commodity fees (e.g. rice), and other non-food materials. Korean Air was tasked with the mission of transporting American troops from the United States to their designated stations in the Persian Gulf, mostly located on Saudi soil.[38] South Korea's logistical contribution also included the dispatch of a 154-person team of combat medics, five C-130 aircraft, and about 156 ground support personnel.[39] The air force transport unit was flown to a base in the UAE, while the members of the medical team were stationed in eastern Saudi Arabia, where the Saudi government[40] provided them with the medicines and other materials they required in order to function as kind of a mobile army surgical hospital that could serve coalition troops.[41]

Meanwhile, the ROK's involvement was reported domestically in a rather controversial manner. News outlets reported that the United States requested South Korea to send combat troops to join the multinational coalition forces to fight Iraq. In mid-January 1991, a number of South Korean newspapers, such as the *Chosun Ilbo* and the *Dong-A*, revealed that this US call for Korean combat personnel was possibly transmitted through unofficial channels, but both the South Korean foreign ministry and the American embassy in Seoul described these reports as inaccurate.[42] As it happened, South Korea was already in the midst of a dispute with Tokyo over the possible dispatching of the Japanese Self-Defense Forces (SDF) to the Persian Gulf region. South Korea was adamantly opposed to the idea of the SDF being sent to carry out an overseas mission, and its foreign minister, Ho-joong Choi, called such a move "the starting point of the remilitarization of Japan." The fierce opposition to the potential Japanese move, however, could also be seen as a red herring because the South Koreans were worried that the dispatch of the Japanese SDF could further encourage the Americans to pressure Seoul into sending combat troops to the US-led military operation.[43] The South Korean Parliament and South Korean public opinion were both adamantly antagonistic to such an eventuality, warning both sides that "we no longer have the authoritarian government that could decide things without consulting the people. If the US government is thinking that it can rely on the Korean government deciding things unilaterally, it is wrong."[44]

An important ramification of invasion of Kuwait for South Korea's Persian Gulf policy was the very terminology used by the East Asian country's press and media to refer to the region. In January 1991, the South Korean foreign ministry announced out of the blue that the government decided to abandon the use of the term "Persian Gulf" once and for all. The ministry recommended that the South Korean press and media refer to the region simply as "the Gulf" and to the ongoing crisis as the "war in the Gulf." Without regard for the etymology of the geographic term and a globally-acknowledged historical record, the main argument raised by the foreign ministry in order to justify its proposed change in nomenclature was that "the Gulf" was a neutral and safe replacement for other names used by both Persian Gulf states and by countries outside the region.[45] While it is not clear what really prompted the government to opt for such a name change, it was the first time that the South Koreans needed to directly refer to the region with respect to the Iraqi invasion of Kuwait. Like Japan, South Korea had almost always used "the Middle East" to refer to anything that pertained to the countries of that region, a practice which was to continue once the military operation against Saddam's Iraq had finished and once the press and the general public were no longer overly concerned that a regional conflict would threaten the ROK's energy supply or its commercial trade routes running through the Persian Gulf waterway.

North Korea's attachment to Tehran

The conclusion of the Iran–Iraq War did not put an end to Iran's ties with North Korea, as the two countries managed to further develop their wartime relationship well into the 1990s and beyond. Throughout the war, Iran had handled its Pyongyang embassy through an ambassador, whereas it handled its embassy in Seoul through a *chargé d'affaires* (having previously downgraded its relations with the ROK) until early 1989. However, once Tehran had upgraded its diplomatic ties with the ROK, Iranian officials vowed to pursue what they called a policy of "equal distance" toward Seoul and Pyongyang, holding that they "have had satisfactory relations with both Koreas and will try to continue the relations."[46] Tehran was making an effort to maintain relations with both parties without getting involved in perplexing political grievances. However, incompatible ideological differences had existed between Seoul and Pyongyang for decades. Far from being an "equal-distance" policy, the Iranian initiative turned out to espouse some sort of "equal-advance" approach that aimed to achieve Tehran's diplomatic goals in both South Korea and North Korea without having to reckon with the intricacies involved in dealing with the ideological impasse between the two states.

In the period following the Iran–Iraq War, military cooperation and defense connections still remained the linchpin of Tehran's interactions with Pyongyang. The two countries had previously signed a half-a-billion-dollar missile technology development deal in 1987 which was to come to fruition, and expand even further, after the war. In order to better coordinate their bilateral interactions related to various military and political areas, Tehran and Pyongyang cautiously and quietly set up a joint defense commission in December 1989. As part of such a process, a good number of Pyongyang-made missiles, short-range ballistic missiles in particular, found their way into Iran at a time when arms sales constituted a significant portion of the DPRK's exports.[47] Moreover, the North Koreans also repeatedly invited Iranian officials to come observe their own military operations in order to convince their counterparts of the DPRK's technological know-how and military capability. Such a cordial display of friendship by the North Koreans led to the presence of a number of Iranian military and civilian observers at Pyongyang's launch of its putative Taepodong intercontinental ballistic missile (ICBM) in 1998 as well as at the follow-up nuclear tests.[48]

Military cooperation between Iran and North Korea at times often involved the use of third parties, a fact that made other nations with interests in the Middle East somewhat anxious about the extent and scope of Pyongyang's relationship with Tehran. For example, China was involved when the DPRK first started selling arms to Iran, and Pakistan too would later have a third-party role to play – and its participation in the arms trade would become more controversial later on. During the Iran–Iraq War, the arms embargo against Tehran turned Pakistan into a convenient corridor through which North Korea could transport arms to the Persian Gulf nation. After the war, rumors arose that the three nations were cooperating with one other on the development of nuclear weapons even though there was no concrete evidence to support such a claim. The Israelis were particularly anxious about such a possibility, and they did everything in their power to try and uncover a nuclear link between Pyongyang and Tehran. And in spite of the DPRK's hostile political rhetoric toward Israel, Tel Aviv did not hesitate to have representatives sit face-to-face with the communist state's officials and urge them not to engage in any clandestine work (let alone work out in the open) with the Iranians. For example, the Israeli foreign ministry's vice-director-general, Eytan Bentsur, arranged a meeting with a ranking official from the KWP in Beijing in June 1993 in order to ask the DPRK regime to halt its missile sales to Iran.[49]

Meanwhile, non-military areas of cooperation between Iran and North Korea received a great deal of attention right after the Iran–Iraq War. Pyongyang asked Tehran to provide technical assistance for the DPRK's oil exploration endeavors on its western continental shelf.[50] In 1993, the fifth Pyongyang–Tehran joint economic commission, hosted by North Korea, served as a sign of their mutual intention to swiftly expand their cooperation beyond the military realm. At this time, the DPRK had every reason to want to increase its economic dealings with Iran – specifically as a source for its energy supply – because the communist nation had been suffering from energy shortages caused by its having limited or (on occasion) no access, in the years following the collapse of the Soviet Union, to the oil that it was accustomed to receiving from Moscow. Following the fall of the eastern bloc and the disappearance of many socialist allies, therefore, the continuation of bilateral relations with Tehran provided Pyongyang with a great opportunity to receive, at times, up to 40 percent of its badly needed oil requirements in return for technical assistance and various other non-economic services.[51]

It's not that the Russians had run out of oil once the Soviet Union collapsed, but rather that they were now asking Pyongyang to pay cash for their oil supply, a demand which the Chinese soon acceded to in early 1993, forcing the DPRK to bring down its total oil consumption by 30 percent.[52] Energy shortages and the disruption of foreign aid coupled with economic misman-agement and the advent of natural disasters (especially floods) caused the communist state's economy to contract by more than 50 percent in the period between 1992 and 1996.[53] In the midst of this chronic economic crisis,[54] the DPRK's commercial connections to Tehran did provide the country with several benefits: They enabled Pyongyang to both earn cash and use a form of barter to receive goods, the latter being a method which had long accounted for a bulk of North Korea's foreign commerce. By the second half of the 1990s, Iran became North Korea's fourth largest export market after Japan, South Korea and China. In fact, Iran was Pyongyang's largest export desti-nation outside of Northeast Asia, beating out Germany, which was Pyongyang's fifth largest export partner. Iran also became the DPRK's fourth largest import partner after China, Russia and Japan.[55]

A new economic shift: Investment abroad

Foreign investment, especially foreign direct investment (FDI), has long been one of the most contentious issues in the international political economy (IPE) field. More specifically, the nature of the impact of foreign investment on the economic development and industrialization of developing countries has generated a great deal of debate. Economists have been ardent advocates and gung-ho proponents of the positive implications that stem from foreign investment, while international relations (IR) specialists and political scientists have often been more concerned with the other ramifications foreign invest-ment can have on a developing nation, which consist of unwanted impacts on sovereignty, legal jurisdiction and cultural mores.[56] Because developing coun-tries' economic situations and degrees of sociopolitical stability have been all over the map, these two contrasting perspectives have usually waxed and waned accordingly – but they have never managed to completely disappear from the conversation. However, thanks largely to the economic achievements of East Asian nations in the past few decades, investors from these countries have benefited from pointing to their own success stories as concrete evidence of how foreign investment might help fill in the economic gaps left by insufficient domestic capital and become a key engine for growth.[57]

Until the establishment of diplomatic relations between Seoul and Tokyo in 1965, South Korea itself had hardly received any amount of foreign investment. It was only in the late 1960s that the ROK started to receive a significant amount of foreign investment: This was when South Korea first started to make equity investments abroad in order to broaden its commercial horizons and accelerate the growth of its economy, which was undergoing the process of industrialization at the time. As the Korean economy further developed and gained more technological and financial sophistication, investment in foreign countries became both economically alluring and strategically unavoid-able – successive Korean governments, for their part, persuaded companies to invest abroad, providing them with various financial incentives in order to do so, including tax deductions, investment insurance and favorable loans through such institutions as the Export–Import Bank of Korea, the Korean Mining Promotion Corporation (KMPC) and the Oil Development Fund.[58]

Like any other foreign investors, South Koreans initially looked to place their capital in countries that enjoyed a high degree of political stability and that were full of economic opportunities. They went to North America, Australia and Southeast Asia, investing mainly in natural resources that were in high demand at home, including coal, iron ore, lumber, and (later) oil and gas. Following the oil shock of 1979–1980, the Middle East, particularly the Persian Gulf region, gradually tried to attract South Korean investment, especially in petroleum and natural gas projects. Upon the establishment of political ties with Beijing in the early 1990s, moreover, South Korean companies made major inroads into the Chinese market; other parts of the world, however, like Latin America and Africa, were still only winning smaller amounts of South Korean capital. It was only in the second half of the 2000s that South Korea made a serious attempt to overcome its long-term regional imbalance and channel some of its investment capital into a number of African countries endowed with ample amounts of natural resources.[59]

Investment in the Persian Gulf

South Korean companies entered the Persian Gulf region as early as 1973, and almost all of them took on construction projects for many years. But construction was not really the most attractive target for foreign investment simply because genuine investment was generally considered to be all about "hard capital" and harnessing the latest technologies. So, instead of pouring in their spare capital into various projects, the East Asian country's ravenous contractors moved into the energy-rich region to make money, and their intermediate to pre-advanced level of technological know-how forced them to take on labor-intensive projects or to work as subcontractors for Western and Japanese companies. The dominant structure of local economies and the main pattern of international trade in most Persian Gulf states, therefore, dictated that foreign investment was to focus primarily on the exploration and development phases of natural resource production – oil and gas being the most sought after natural resources. Still, even when it came to the areas of exploration and development, Western enterprises, and to some extent their Japanese counterparts, had already established a strong foothold, which put South Korean enterprises at an immediate and sizeable disadvantage when it came to winning lucrative contracts.

One important characteristic of South Korea's investment relationship with the region, especially with the GCC countries, was that the South Koreans themselves received at times a considerable tranche of the superfluous funds invested by both public and private sectors from the Persian Gulf. For instance, the state-owned Saudi Arabian Oil Company, Aramco, invested some $470 million to set up a joint refining company with South Korea's Ssangyong Corporation in 1991. It was Saudi Arabia's second major oil venture abroad after the Saudis created Star Enterprise in 1988 as a US joint refining venture with Texaco Inc.[60] Among private investors, one typical case was a Saudi Arabian billionaire named Prince Walid bin Talal, who invested at least $200 million in 1997 and 1998, buying convertible bonds from the Daewoo Corporation worth $100 million and an equivalent amount to that from the Hyundai Motor Company.[61] Another case was Kuwait which invested in South Korea much more than the aggregated capital the South Koreans were willing to pour into the tiny Persian Gulf nation. Over a period of two-and-half decades from 1979 till 2004, the Kuwaitis invested approximately $37.7 million in South Korea, while their South Korean counterparts invested only a tenth of that amount in Kuwait, that is, approximately $3.2 million.[62]

Teeming with petroleum and petrodollars, Kuwait, of course, kept the South Koreans at the negotiating table for many years, seeking some sort of investment guarantee treaty. The two parties signed an initial agreement in 1998 before finally establishing a formal treaty in 2004. This treaty paved the way for further South Korean investment in the Kuwaiti free-trade zone and the avoidance of double taxation.[63] To further stimulate its investment relationships with the GCC states, South Korea also signed an investment protection agreement with Oman in October 2003.[64] A couple of years prior to the signing of this agreement, a consortium of five major South Korean companies had bought a 5 percent stake in a $2 billion Omani LNG project in February 1997. The South Korean side, Korea LNG, was formed by Korea Gas Corporation, Hyundai, Samsung, Daewoo and Yukong, among others. The Omani government owned a 50 percent stake in the project, while a 30 percent stake belonged to Shell, the Anglo-Dutch oil corporation which had originally discovered gas reserves in central Oman. Although the project was to come on line sometime in early 2000, it was the first time that South Korean companies were permitted to invest in an LNG project at an early stage.[65]

The ROK's investments in Iran

In contrast with all GCC states, post-1980 Iran had a completely different set of political and economic conditions for foreign investors to consider. The Iran–Iraq War not only ruined many important projects undertaken and/or supported by foreign investors, it also significantly damaged the country's reputation as a safe haven for foreign capital. But a lack of stability was not the sole stumbling block preventing foreign investors from taking their capital and injecting it into Iranian industries: The end of bloody conflict with Iraq did not see the country turn back into a safe haven for international investors overnight. The crux of the problem was the political unwillingness on the part of the Iranian government to develop and industrialize apace so as to be able to meet investor preconditions. Moreover, the ramifications of this political disinclination to enable foreign investment were exacerbated by the constant presence of Western sanctions against Iran. These sanctions acted to deter international investors who had still been prepared to inject their capital and provide their technical know-how in spite of the foot-dragging displayed by the Iranian government.

A combination of the foregoing factors was responsible for Iran's failure to inject enough financial and technological capital into its oil industry, a mainstay of government revenues and foreign currency. While Saudi Arabia, for example, became the largest oil producer in the world by 1992, Iran was still striving to maintain its oil production at about 60 percent of Shah-era levels in the mid-1990s. This situation largely stemmed from Iran's failure to invest adequately in the development and maintenance of its oil fields, as well as its ineptitude when it came to keeping its oil sector – one of the most vital sectors of its economy – up to date.[66] Iran's energy industry was also negatively affected by other factors, including fluctuations in oil prices, unfavorable marketing and transportation prospects, and uncooperative international insurance companies. An example of this last factor – albeit with a government and government-backed institution taking the place of a private company – is South Korea's Export–Import Bank's decision to deny Iran's request for a $360 million loan to purchase five oil tankers from Daewoo Shipbuilding Company in 1993 because of the Persian Gulf nation's poor credit rating. Seoul refused to provide long-term export insurance, as Tehran was over $5 billion in arrears on its short-term letters of credit, which it had obtained in 1990–1991.[67]

In spite of these obstacles, South Korea still managed to invest in a number of energy and other industrial projects throughout the 1990s and beyond, and it was able to actively benefit from Iran's booming construction sector in the period following the Iran–Iraq War. Some of the investment projects undertaken by South Korean companies, either by themselves or in cooperation with other international investors, included the Bafgh–Bandar Abbas railroad, the Tehran Metro program, the Kangan gas refinery plan, and several other offshore oil and gas projects near Iran's Persian Gulf islands. In these types of projects, South Korean companies found themselves in serious competition with newly emergent Chinese investors. Although the Iranian government had shown its desire to attract more South Korean investors in order to replace the dwindling number of Japanese investors in the country, the Chinese were also vying for investment projects in the Persian Gulf region, offering temptingly low prices as well as convincing technical standards. In some other sectors, like auto manufacturing, South Korean companies enjoyed a considerable edge, while their Chinese rivals still needed many years to catch up. One such auto manufacturing project arose from a deal that was made between South Korea's Daewoo Business Group and Iran's Kerman Automotive Industries Co. (KAIC) in Seoul in 1993 to set up a joint assembly line in Iran's Kerman Province.[68]

Further involvement: Unceasing construction business

The Iraqi reconstruction effort following the end of the Iran–Iraq War turned out to be short-lived, since Saddam's invasion of Kuwait effectively halted building projects in the two countries. During the Kuwaiti crisis, however, South Korea's Hyundai still kept a number of its people in Iraq, so that it would be ready to continue its projects once the conflict was over. In the aftermath of the crisis, the Iraqi government also expressed its desire to assign Korean contractors to some of its reconstruction projects, though Iraq's financial strains, exacerbated particularly by the sanctions regime, meant that such projects would not pay particularly well – a fact that South Korean companies were aware of.[69] Compared to the opportunities presented to them in Iraq, the opportunities presented to South Korean companies in Kuwait, once Saddam's troops had left the country, were far more lucrative. The Kuwaiti government immediately launched a widespread recovery and renovation operation, giving a second chance to some major South Korean companies, such as Hyundai and Samsung, to participate in many construction projects aimed at building and/or repairing roads, bridges and power plants.[70] By the end of 1993, Kuwait had awarded foreign construction companies, including South Korean firms, contracts worth $2 billion for the reconstruction of much of its infrastructure.[71]

In Iran, major reconstruction programs and new infrastructure projects were expanded throughout the 1990s and 2000s, but their pace and scope often waxed and waned – at least in part – because successive reformist and conservative Iranian governments often had different socioeconomic priorities. The participation of South Korean contractors in Iranian projects increased later on when the two countries signed a memorandum of understanding in May 2001 in order to promote bilateral cooperation in the construction sector. By that time, 19 Korean companies had partaken in about 60 projects valued at approximately $4.4 billion since 1975, when Hyundai Construction had won a contract to erect a shipyard for the Iranian navy.[72] Even if their construction earnings from Iran were not as high as those from Saudi Arabia, South Korean companies, especially those engaged in diverse business activities, still strove to maintain their presence in the Persian Gulf country, as it is endowed with a larger consumption market and a much more appealing cultural and physical climate than the GCC countries.

Meanwhile, South Korea's giant contractors made inroads into the construction markets of other GCC states such as Oman, the UAE and Qatar. In 1999, the construction division of Daewoo Corporation was awarded, for the first time, an Omani contract to build a 7 km dyke along its northeast coast, paving the way for other South Korean contractors to subsequently take on Omani infrastructure and development projects.[73] But the neighboring UAE presented more up-and-coming businesses (including South Korean firms) with far more lucrative construction contracts. The UAE's construction boom symbolized by the Burj Khalifa, its tallest structure which was located in

Dubai and in whose construction Samsung had played a major role, engaged financial, technological and human resources from various countries, including South Korea, for many years. Moreover, the uninterrupted oil exports and the considerably small populations of GCC countries made these states less vulnerable to the economic misfortunes often experienced by Iran and Iraq, so that they could keep pumping tens of billions of dollars (petrodollars) into construction projects – even in the 2000s, when the world was in the midst of a recession.

A new pattern of energy imports

In the decade from 1985 to 1995, South Korea's oil consumption quadrupled at an average rate of about 13.5 percent a year. Such a high demand for petroleum forced the ROK to spend 18 percent of its export revenues to pay its oil bill in 1991 – and the cost of petroleum increased further still when the per capita consumption of oil shot up to approximately 16.5 barrels by the mid-1990s.[74] Such a dramatic spike was largely caused by a glut of cheap oil in international markets; a hike in energy-based industrial outputs; and an ever-expanding transportation industry in South Korea that was symbolized by an ever-increasing number of personal vehicles. In spite of a myriad of measures that had been taken for the sake of economic diversification in the period following the second oil shock, the Persian Gulf remained, as it always had been, the chief source for South Korea's oil imports – even though the region's major suppliers were not always providing similar outputs. Saudi Arabia, for instance, provided around 15 percent of South Korea's total oil imports in 1987, but only 5 percent in 1989. Its share would then increase to about 35 percent, or approximately $5 billion, in 1997 on the cusp of that year's (now infamous) financial crisis in Asia.[75]

After a number of joint energy ventures and a significant amount of petrochemical projects with Saudi Arabia in the 1990s, the Korean National Oil Corporation (KNOC) signed an agreement with the Kuwait Petroleum Corporation (KPC) in October 2006, according to which South Korea could store 2 million barrels of Kuwaiti crude oil on its soil. Although this was the first such agreement between the two countries, the KNOC had previously concluded crude storage deals with Norway's Statoil, France's Total, China's Chinaoil, Algeria's Sonatrach, and the Abu Dhabi National Oil Company (ADNOC). The main advantage of such energy accords was that South Korea could enjoy a preemptive right to use the stored crude in emergency situations. It was the impacts of the two oil shocks that encouraged the South Korean government to gradually improve its reserve capacity of crude oil to 27 million barrels by 2006 and to 40 million barrels by 2010.[76] Less than a year before the signing of the storage deal, South Korea's SK Engineering & Construction had walked away with a largely rewarding $1.22 billion Kuwaiti contract, considered to be the largest in Kuwait's short history, to upgrade and relocate several oil facilities and piping stations over a period of about two years.[77]

Meanwhile, a growing demand for LNG became another major factor in South Korea's energy imports from the Persian Gulf region. The ROK started importing LNG in 1986, following its importation of LPG from Saudi Arabia in 1983, over a period of at least 10 years, but its LNG needs considerably increased throughout the 1990s and especially during the 2000s, when the East Asian state's top three suppliers were Qatar, Oman and Malaysia. In 1996, South Korea signed an LNG supply contract with Qatar for 25 years beginning in 1999.[78] Once South Korea's demand for this clean energy increased further, Qatar, the largest gas producer in the world, attempted to more than double its LNG supply, turning Seoul into its largest LNG market as well as the world's single largest consumer of LNG.[79] The growing importance of LNG in South Korea–Qatar relations led Seoul and Doha to proclaim a so-called "omnidirectional partnership," which would aim, for the most part, to secure a stable, long-term supply of Qatari LNG for the ROK.[80]

Export market developments

Apart from regular economic dynamisms, there were a number of other factors which contributed to South Korea's growing volume of exports to the Persian Gulf region throughout the 1990s and thereafter. With the exception of Iraq, free-trade zones were gradually snowballed in almost all countries of the region, though the Iranian trade zones largely punched below their weight and continue their monotonous function until the present day. Obliged by its expanding commercial connections, South Korea further developed its political ties to a greater number of GCC countries, a move which culminated in the establishment of embassies in and the dispatching of ambassadors to Seoul by those Arab states. Qatar and Kuwait, therefore, became the fourth and fifth GCC countries, respectively, to decide to open a resident embassy in the ROK after Saudi Arabia, the UAE and Oman.[81] By this time, the UAE's ambassador had been in Seoul for seven years, the time it has taken the two nations to formalize their diplomatic ties, thus earning him the title of "Dean of the Diplomatic Corps," which was a position traditionally reserved for the most senior current ambassador to Seoul. Its functions were for the most part ceremonial in nature, consisting as they did in organizing unofficial meetings and even parties for newly arriving or outgoing top envoys to the ROK.[82]

Vastly improved political relationships and high-profile diplomatic envoys brought about more lucrative contracts from Persian Gulf countries, which in due course improved trade imbalances between GCC member states and South Korea. Kuwait, after Iran, asked South Korea to build oil tankers, while Qatar ordered LNG carriers and other types of ships, all of which cost billions of dollars and considerably helped Seoul's trade gaps with the GCC countries.[83] Although South Korea's trade with Persian Gulf nations expanded at a staggering rate in the 2000s, its share of the region's overall imports was significant in the 1990s as well. For instance, Seoul accounted for 6 percent of Kuwait's total imports, more than 4 percent of the UAE's total imports, and around 3 percent of Saudi Arabian and Iranian total imports in 1992. In the case of Iran, the figure of 3 percent was particularly startling, as South Korea moved to become Iran's fourth largest export partner in 1996, 1997, 1998 and 1999 before it rose to be the country's second largest export partner right after Japan in 2000. South Korea was also Iran's third largest import partner in 1999 and soon became its second largest import partner after Germany in 2000.[84]

All in all, South Korea's total exports to all eight countries of the Persian Gulf almost doubled from about $2.1 billion in 1990 to about $4.1 billion in 1999. In the same period, the ROK's imports from the region rose from approximately $5.9 billion to more than $13 billion, an increase of more than 200 percent. This indicates that the ROK's overall trade gap shot up in favor of the Persian Gulf region, increasing from less than $2 billion in 1990 to more than $7 billion in 1999. Considering South Korea's two-way trade with all eight countries of the Persian Gulf region, Seoul's trade deficit with Saudi Arabia was conspicuous in its steady increase throughout the 1990s, jumping from around $986 million in 1990 to about $2.3 billion in 1991 and to more than $4.3 billion in 1999. During the 1990s, Iraq tuned out to be South Korea's smallest trading partner in the region simply because Baghdad had been engulfed by international sanctions, which severely hampered its ability to conduct commercial operations with the rest of the world. From 1990 to 1999, the ROK's total exports to Iraq amounted to $109 million compared to around $391 million in total imports from Baghdad, a trade gap of $282 million. In fact, South Korea's total exports to Iraq, rather surprisingly, did not exceed $163,000 from 1991 to 1995, while the registered data for all Iraqi goods imported by the ROK over the six-year period from 1991 to 1997 shows a sum of only $382,000.[85]

Notes

1 By 1984, South Korea's foreign trade had reached $60 billion, which was more than 22 times larger than that of North Korea ($2.7 billion). See Clough, p. 305.
2 Robert Elegant, *Pacific Destiny: Inside Asia Today* (New York: Avon Books, 1990), pp. 55, 70.
3 Robert E. Bedeski, *The Transformation of South Korea: Reform and Reconstitution in the Sixth Republic under Roh Tae Woo, 1987–1992* (London: Routledge, 1994), pp. 99, 101.
4 Clough, p. 139.
5 Elegant, p. 187.
6 The World Bank, *Water Policy and Water Markets: Selected Papers and Proceedings from the World Bank's Ninth Annual Irrigation and Drainage Seminar*, Annapolis, MD, December 8–10, 1992 (Washington, D.C.: The World Bank, 1992), p. 6.
7 "Japan, Korea See a Windfall in Gulf Peace: Asians Have Major Projects on Hold in Iran and Iraq," *Wall Street Journal*, July 25, 1988.
8 "Korea, Iran Agree to Exchange Ambassadors," *Korea Herald*, January 25, 1989, p. 2.

9 "Common Market OKs Return of Envoys to Iran," *Associated Press*, March 21, 1989.
10 "Iran Upholds South–North Equi-Distance Policy: Mansouri," *Korea Herald*, January 26, 1989, p. 2.
11 "Korea, Iran to Establish Joint Body for Economic Cooperation," *Korea Herald*, July 7, 1989, p. 6.
12 "Korea Could Play Bigger Role in Iran's Reconstruction," *Korea Herald*, July 6, 1989, p. 6.
13 "Iran Rejects Japanese Bid to Quit IJPC Project," *Reuters*, August 22, 1989.
14 "Iran Gears for Reconstruction," *Korea Herald*, February 10, 1989, p. 1 (supplement).
15 "Iran to Diversify Exports to China," *Associated Press*, July 18, 1989.
16 "Baghdad, Seoul Develop Diplomatic Relations," *Korea Herald*, July 20, 1989, p. 13 (supplement).
17 "Iraq, Korea to Raise Ties to Ambassadorial Level Next Week," *Korea Herald*, July 5, 1989, p. 1.
18 "Iraq Makes Every Effort to Rebuild War-Torn Economy," *Reuters*, August 24, 1989.
19 See Sheldon W. Simon, "Regional Security Structures in Asia: The Question of Relevance," in Sheldon W. Simon (ed.), *East Asian Security in the Post-Cold War Era* (New York: M.E. Sharpe, Inc., 1993), pp. 11–27.
20 Edward A. Olsen, *Korea: The Divided Nation* (Westport, CT: Praeger, 2005), pp. 75–76.
21 The GCC countries themselves gradually moved to abandon their anti-Israel rhetoric, and some of them even engaged in covert, and occasionally overt, commercial interactions and political contacts with the Jewish state starting around June 1993, when Kuwait vowed to end its involvement in the 42-year boycott of Israel. See "Kuwait Quits 42-Year Arab Boycott of Israel," *Associated Press*, June 6, 1993.
22 As part of the dual containment policy, the United States' "dog in the manger" mentality virtually nipped in the bud various initiatives by the Iranians themselves to develop better economic connections to other nations. For example, a high-level Iranian official once complained that "everywhere we try to go, we see the Americans there first, trying to convince people not to deal with us." See "European Oil Giants Roiled as US Maps Iran Sanctions," *Christian Science Monitor*, March 20, 1996, p. 3.
23 Dani Rodrik, *The Globalization Paradox: Democracy and the Future of the World Economy* (New York: W.W. Norton, 2011), p. 9.
24 The Asahi Shimbun, *wangan sensou to nihon: towareru kiki kanri* [*The Gulf War and Japan: Questioning Crisis Management*] (Tokyo: The Asahi Shimbunsha, 1991), pp. 38–45.
25 Shirzad Azad, "Japan's Gulf Policy and Response to the Iraq War," *Middle East Review of International Affairs*, Vol. 12, No. 2 (2008), pp. 52–64.
26 "Gulf Crisis Looks Much Like Korea," *Calgary Herald*, September 2, 1990, p. C5.
27 John R. Walker, "Korea an Example for Gulf War," *Edmonton Journal*, January 18, 1991, p. A10.
28 "South Korea: Gulf Implications," *Oxford Analytica Daily Brief Service*, August 28, 1990.
29 "Construction Project Bills Unpaid by Kuwait, Iraq Amount to $1 Billion," *Korea Herald*, January 22, 1991, p. 2.
30 Brian Bridges, "South Korea and the Gulf Crisis," *The Pacific Review*, Vol. 5, No. 2 (1992), pp. 141–148.
31 "Korean Workers in M.E. Advised to Leave for Home," *Korea Herald*, January 8, 1991, pp. 1, 4.

32 "Iraqis Still Friendly to Koreans, Amb. Choi Says on Arrival," *Korea Herald,* January 30, 1991, p. 2.
33 Bridges.
34 "KAL to Stop Flights," *Korea Herald,* January 11, 1991, p. 1.
35 The American request for Koreans to financially support their forces in the Persian Gulf region nevertheless predated the Kuwaiti crisis. In fact, the United States had already asked the East Asian country to provide $20 million for American naval operations in the Persian Gulf waterway at the annual ROK–US Security Conference in June 1988. See William J. Taylor, Jr., (ed.), *The Future of South Korean–U.S. Security Relations* (Boulder, CO: Westview Press, 1989), p. 137.
36 "South Korea to Contribute $220 Million to Gulf Effort," *Wall Street Journal,* September 25, 1990, p. A19.
37 "Korea Likely to Bear More Contribution to Gulf Forces," *Korea Herald,* January 20, 1991, p. 2.
38 "Korean Aircraft to Help Transport Allied Troops," *Korea Herald,* January 19, 1991, p. 1.
39 US Department of Defense, *A Strategic Framework for the Asian Pacific Rim: Looking Toward the 21st Century* (Washington, D.C.: Government Printing Office, 1991), p. 6.
40 In October 1991, the commander of South Korea's military medical unit, Colonel Myong-ku Choi, was awarded the King Abdul Aziz Medal by Saudi Arabia.
41 "Seoul, Riyadh to Sign Accord on Korean Medical Team Members," *Korea Herald,* January 9, 1991, p. 1.
42 "Seoul Denies U.S. Asked for Combat Troops: Local Dailies Run Stories on Wash. Request," *Korea Herald,* January 17, 1991, p. 1.
43 Bridges.
44 "Korea: Will Gulf Help End with Dispatch of Medical Unit?" *Los Angeles Times,* September 30, 1990, p. 2.
45 "'Persian Gulf' out, 'Gulf' in," *Korea Herald,* January 22, 1991, p. 2.
46 *Korea Herald,* January 26, 1989, p. 2.
47 John J. Metzler, *Divided Dynamism – The Diplomacy of Separate Nations: Germany, Korea, China* (Lanham, MD: University Press of America, 2001), p. 94.
48 Glyn Ford with S. Kwon, *North Korea on the Brink: Struggle for Survival* (London: Pluto Press, 2008), p. 192.
49 "Israel, N. Korea Meet on Missile Sales to Iran," *Korea Herald,* June 29, 1993, p. 1.
50 "Korea, Iran Ministers Hold Talks on Joint Construction Firms," *Korea Herald,* July 6, 1989, p. 6.
51 Anthony J. Dennis, *The Rise of the Islamic Empire and the Threat to the West,* 2nd edition (Lima, OH: Wyndham Hall Press, 2001), p. 87.
52 David Reese, *The Prospects for North Korea's Survival,* Adelphi Paper 323 (New York: Oxford University Press for the International Institute for Strategic Studies, 1998), pp. 27–28.
53 Reese, p. 9.
54 In 1996, the DPRK's per capita income out of a GDP of roughly $20 billion was less than $1,000 compared to South Korea's more than $11,000 per capita out of a GDP of roughly $490 billion. See Economist Intelligence Unit, *Country Profile: South Korea, North Korea, 1997–98* (London: Economist Intelligence Unit (EIU), 1997), p. 64.
55 Marcus Noland, "Prospects for the North Korean Economy," in D. Suh and C. Lee (eds.), *North Korea after Kim Il Sung* (Boulder, CO: Lynne Rienner Publishers, 1998), pp. 33–58.
56 Many in South Asia, for instance, were once expressing their concerns about the cultural attitudes of South Korean companies, complaining that "businessmen from South Korea carry their habits with them when investing elsewhere in the

region: a delegation visiting Pakistan demanded changes in the labor law as a condition of opening factories." See Field, p. 69.

57 Japan Institute for Overseas Investment, *Foreign Direct Investment in the East Asia Region: Trends and Outlook* (Tokyo: Japan Institute for Overseas Investment, 1993), pp. 54–59.

58 Clough, p. 307.

59 "Getting into Africa: Investment in Resource-Rich Continent is Choice of Future," *Korea Times*, March 7, 2006, p. 8.

60 Robert A. Manning, "The Asian Energy Predicament," *Survival*, Vol. 42, No. 3 (2000), pp. 73–88.

61 "Saudi Investing More in Korea," *New York Times*, March 17, 1998.

62 "South Korea, Kuwait to Sign Mutual Investment Treaty," *Yonhap News Agency*, March 23, 2004.

63 "Kuwait, South Korea to Sign Investment Guarantee Agreement," *Yonhap News Agency*, December 3, 1998.

64 "Oman, South Korea Sign Investment Protection Agreement," *Yonhap News Agency*, October 8, 2003.

65 Robert Corzine, "Korea Groups in Oman Deal," *Financial Times*, February 22, 1997, p. 2.

66 Roberts, pp. 23, 157.

67 "South Korea Exim Loan to Iran Falters," *Project & Trade Finance*, No. 128 (December 1993), p. 21.

68 "Daewoo-Iran's KAIC Auto Deal," *Korea Herald*, May 16, 1993, p. 8.

69 In spite of all economic hardships and financial troubles, a top Hyundai manager described his Iraqi partners as "very honest people (and) unlike the Saudis, they never asked for bribes." See Kirk, p. 92.

70 "Kuwait, Korea Mark 20 Years of Growing Partnership," *Business Korea*, Vol. 16, No. 2 (1999), pp. 68–69.

71 Roberts, p. 149.

72 "South Korea, Iran to Cooperate in Construction," *Yonhap News Agency*, May 23, 2001.

73 "Korea's Daewoo Wins Barbour Construction Project in Oman," *Yonhap News Agency*, June 4, 1999.

74 Øystein Noreng, *Crude Power: Politics and the Oil Market* (New York: I.B. Tauris, 2006), p. 73.

75 "Korea, Saudi Arabia Energy Ministers Discuss Economic Ties," *Korea Herald*, April 28, 1997, p. 2.

76 "Korea, Kuwait in Storage Deal," *Oil Daily*, October 31, 2006, p. 1.

77 "Korea's SK Wins Kuwait Deal," *International Petroleum Finance*, June 3, 2005, p. 1.

78 "Korea Seeks Development of Gas Fields in Qatar," *Korea Herald*, February 15, 1996, p. 2.

79 "Qatar in Talks to Sell More LNG to Korea," *International Herald Tribune*, November 24, 2006, p. 15.

80 "South Korea, Qatar Declare 'Omnidirectional Partnership'," *Yonhap News Agency*, March 27, 2007.

81 "Qatar, Kuwait to Open Embassies in Seoul," *Korea Herald*, January 8, 1992, p. 2.

82 "Amb. al-Amri of UAE Named Dean of Diplomatic Corps," *Korea Herald*, February 22, 1994, p. 2.

83 See "Kuwait Receives New Oil Tanker from Korea," *Xinhua News Agency*, May 12, 1998; "Qatar to Buy Liquid Gas Carriers from South Korea – Visiting Minister," *Yonhap News Agency*, October 13, 2003; and "Korea Building Solid Partnership with Qatar," *Korea Herald*, March 28, 2007, p. 8.

84 Markaz amar Iran (Statistical Center of Iran).

85 Korean Statistical Information Service.

5 The pinnacle of success in the midst of new challenges

The Korean economy in transition and the Asian financial crisis

After three-and-a-half decades of remarkable industrial achievements and developmental accomplishments, South Korea abruptly encountered its most traumatic and crippling economic setback: the Asian financial crisis of 1997–1998. The crisis, which started when the Government of Thailand made a decision in early July 1997 to allow its currency, the baht, to float after a decline in exports and in the stock market, soon swept swiftly into many other Asian economies all the way to those of Russia and Brazil, though some countries, such as China, conspicuously survived the chaos unscathed. The hardest hit countries subsequently faced massive outflows of foreign capital, economic defaults, financial failures and thereby widespread reverberations to their economies at both the microeconomic and macroeconomic levels. For its part, the South Korean economy registered a negative growth rate of 6.7 percent in 1998, while its real GDP growth plummeted to -2.5 percent from 5.5 percent a year earlier.[1] The unemployment rate also shot up to 6.8 percent in 1998 from only 2.6 percent in 1997, and the situation for many redundant employees got much worse, as the Korean won lost 48 percent of its 1996 value.[2]

Immediately upon the onset of the Asian financial crisis, ardent discussions about and contentious views on the exact causes of the turmoil began to spring up around the world. Many in the West were, for the most part, quick to blame the Asians themselves for the "homegrown crisis," which they largely ascribed to an "Asianesque" capitalism that was considerably hampered by cronyism, irrational economic structures, a lack of transparency and genuine competition, rampant corruption, and an unwillingness to take the sort of risks that were necessary for entrepreneurial activities. However, pundits in the effected countries ran the gamut, blaming various external and internal factors as the main culprits behind the financial calamity of 1997–1998. Some argued that the whole situation came about as a sort of capitalist plot or political putsch, one that was designed to first recycle the recently accumulated wealth of the newly economically developed Asian nations and then shackle them with a new Western-style neoliberalism that would be orchestrated by major global financial institutions such as the International Monetary Fund (IMF) and the World Bank.[3] Others, however, argued that the cause of the crisis lay in the changed interests and expectations of foreign investors and/or the uncoordinated nature of both domestic and foreign financial systems. And still others argued that the political systems of the afflicted societies were to blame for prioritizing economic development over democracy, as "the authoritarian style of government permitted corruption and collusive intimacy between business and government to flourish."[4]

Each view had its own proponents in South Korea, and there are surprisingly still many leading pundits around who tend to blame the IMF for some of their society's economic and social ills, which had only gotten worse during the post-crisis years.[5] Seeds of such condemnation, in fact, had been sown right in the very midst of the crisis, when the South Korean economy had no option but to be bailed out through an unprecedented rescue package of $58 billion underwritten by the IMF in December 1997. Under the IMF conditionality, therefore, South Korea needed to implement certain economic and financial reforms with regard to foreign investment, privatization, trade, and capital accounts (among other issues) with unwelcome and occasionally bitter repercussions for many lower and even middle class Korean citizens.[6]

Whether or not and to what extent the foregoing allegations could hold water, the South Korean economy – and South Korean society – nevertheless underwent considerable developments in the aftermath of the Asian financial crisis. Various reform initiatives were started which essentially followed settlements imposed by the IMF and other global institutions like the World Bank and later the World Trade Organization (WTO); they were started in order to buttress the stability of South Korea's unceasing access to external trade and finance in a rapidly changing system of international commerce. A combination of those implemented policies had to eventually come home to roost. At the microeconomic level, employment opportunities dwindled and those positions still available became much more competitive year after year.[7] Even the birth rate did not remain unscathed, and educational fees had to be adjusted accordingly. The wealth gap, therefore, gradually widened, and the welfare benefits of private and public sector workers were affected simultaneously, prompting many vulnerable people to further press subsequent Korean governments to do something serious about the nation's conglomerates and their welfare policies.[8] On a macroeconomic level, the implications of both the financial crisis itself and the ensuing reform measures were to impinge upon South Korea's external trade, both regionally and globally.

Impact on foreign trade

In the immediate aftermath of the Asian financial crisis, petroleum prices plunged, on average, more than 30 percent. In late 1997 and early 1998, oil prices averaged around $12 per barrel, which was one of the lowest recorded prices in recent history. The occurrence, which some people referred to as a kind of "negative oil shock," instantaneously affected many petroleum producers, forcing them to shut down some of their oil wells and downsize national expenditures, including their development budgets. On the contrary, tumbling oil prices were not a disturbance in the least for major energy consumers, such as South Korea, which were already stuck in the midst of a searing economic slowdown. Cheaper oil prices generally spur energy importers to buy more oil, consume more, and adjust their sharp trade imbalances with some of their petroleum suppliers. And in the case of the ROK, this is precisely what happened. South Korea's trade deficit with Kuwait decreased by more than 50 percent in the *annus horribilis* of 1998 compared to the prior year; this decrease mostly stemmed from cheaper petroleum prices and a considerably reduced demand for energy imports. As soon as the economic situation improved and the East Asian nation stepped back from the financial abyss, however, the old pattern swiftly reasserted itself so that South Korea's oil imports had once again increased by more than 11 percent by late 1999 (that is, 11 percent of its energy consumption in 1998).[9]

Meanwhile, the turmoil created by the Asian financial crisis triggered a sense of solidarity among many in East and Southeast Asia, culminating in the formation of the Association of Southeast Asian Nations (ASEAN) Plus Three (APT) framework. South Korea under Kim Dae-jung in particular played a major role in the materialization of the APT forum, which included the ASEAN countries along with Japan, China and South Korea. It was basically the first time that all these countries acknowledged the urgency of such a region-wide mechanism, which was expected by many to lead to more amicable regional cooperation, if not ineluctably to serve as a catalyst for regional integration – even if only among the three Northeast Asian countries. At least until the ascendancy of Junichiro Koizumi to the premiership of Japan, the APT framework was eminently successful in creating an opportunity for annual summit meetings between the Japanese, Chinese and South Korean leaders; it was also able to stimulate multifold bilateral initiatives that would be negotiated at lower levels through economic, political and cultural officials. Although some of the political and cultural expectations of the APT nations later turned out to be only a *fata morgana*, the economic gains from regional cooperation did much to keep those nations involved in the process.[10]

By the year 2000, South Korea enjoyed a $5.7 billion trade surplus with China; standing as one of Beijing's and Tokyo's top trading partners. This situation coincided with a time when the ratio of external trade to GDP in South Korea had shot up from less than 35 percent (in 1970) to more than 70 percent, contributing tremendously to the ROK's share of global commerce: from about 0.3 percent in 1970 to 2.5 percent in the late 1990s. This achievement was clearly exemplified by the South Korean shipbuilding industry, which had just become the largest in the world, capturing approximately 40 percent of the entire market.[11] Not only did Seoul become Australia's second largest trading partner by 2000, it also became a major trading partner with the United States and Europe, registering a more than $14 billion surplus with the United States alone in 2003.[12] The Middle East, and the Persian Gulf in particular, became a region which came to garner a great deal of attention from South Korea once it had started to rekindle its trade relations with regional markets in the period following the Asian financial crisis.

Impact on trade with the Persian Gulf

During the Asian financial crisis, the ROK's financial institutions turned to their counterparts in the GCC countries for loans and capital assistance. In comparison to the first oil shock, when the Korean government asked the Saudis for financial help, the situation this time was very delicate because the financial health of Korean financial institutions was far worse than it had been in the early and mid-1970s. However, in spite of its poor credit rating, South Korea's Cho Hung Bank was offered capital loans in the amount of $50 million by the Commercial Bank of Kuwait.[13] In the aftermath of the turmoil, the Persian Gulf region attracted once again the attention of the ROK, as rising oil prices and increased wealth spurred an increase in imports and a fresh wave of consumerism among the local population. The Persian Gulf region was, moreover, regarded by Korean companies as an alluring alternative to the widely contested markets of China and India. The issue became more pressing to the South Koreans when European, Japanese and Chinese companies were significantly building up their presence in the region. Although South Korea's white-hot interest in Persian Gulf markets predated the period following the first oil shock, this renewed interest in the region along with the new economic conditions in the region required the ROK to look for new strategies in order to reap the benefits of commercial trade. Such strategies included, but were not limited to, developing and introducing new appealing products; improving its competitiveness in retail markets; and upgrading its logistics and communications networks.[14]

South Korea subsequently became a major trading partner to many GCC states, Saudi Arabia and Kuwait in particular, and commercial interactions between them grew in scope and in volume. The Hyundai Corporation even signed an export contract with Iraq in 2000, which was the largest such deal made by a South Korean company with Baghdad since the Gulf War of 1990–1991.[15] Compared to its commercial relations with other countries in the Persian Gulf region, the importance that South Korea attached to its new economic relations with Iran turned out to be far more staggering. Its rather pivotal position in the region and its use as an overland route for South Korean exports to Central Asia and the Caucasus were part of the reason for the ROK's heavy focus on Iran. Some other factors included the relatively large size of the Iranian population in contrast to the populations of other nations in the region; the country's vast quantity of oil and gas resources; and a slew of new economic programs that the government was planning to introduce. From the end of the Asian financial crisis (more or less), the volume of two-way trade between South Korea and Iran exponentially increased from one year to the next.

In the early 2000s, South Korea was Iran's second largest export market after Japan, while its products soon captured 5 percent of the Iranian market within half a decade. A great number of South Korean companies invested in the Persian Gulf nation, making Seoul the second largest foreign investor in Iran after Germany by the mid-2000s. An agreement on double taxation avoidance signed between the two countries in early 2002 played an important role in the growth of South Korea's economic clout in Iran – the East Asian state's largest export market in the entire Middle East – during the years that followed.[16] As part of the agreement, South Korean firms were allowed to do business in Iran without establishing an office, and those firms which only had liaison offices were not obliged to pay taxes. Construction companies which signed on for projects in Iran that were to last less than a year were eligible for tax exemptions. Moreover, South Korean firms which gave loans to their Iranian counterparts were to be subject to a 10 percent tax on the interest income – which was in sharp contrast to the previous progressive rate which ranged from 12 percent to 54 percent. South Korean financial institutions also did not have to pay taxes while collecting interest from loans they had extended to Iranian businesses. Tax exemptions for aviation and shipping firms and tax avoidance on income from the sale of stocks in Iran were other advantages that stemmed from the agreement.[17] Unlike the situation in Iran, however, the situation in Iraq for South Korean firms was completely different, as it took another Middle Eastern crisis to bring a sea change in Seoul's long-strained relationship with Baghdad.

The Persian Gulf in transition: The Iraq War

In March 2003, the Americans declared war on Iraq on the pretext that Saddam Hussein's (alleged) weapons of mass destruction (WMDs) posed an existential threat to the United States and to its allies all around the world, not to mention their economic and political interests. The declaration of war was not a sudden policy shift, but a continuation of the United States' ongoing approach toward Iraq through military means. When Saddam was soundly defeated in the Gulf War of 1991, Iraq lost roughly two thirds of its military equipment, which included its fleet of fighter jets. Overall, its armed forces were severely depleted, with far fewer warships and around 30 percent fewer soldiers.[18] Iraq was, moreover, not allowed to resuscitate its military strength: The West had imposed a "dual containment" deterrence policy, which aimed to keep Saddam in check in an unambiguous manner; Iraq was hit with a regime of severe economic sanctions, which were occasionally backed up by military action. At this time, Baghdad was still determined to regain its considerable pre-war position in the Persian Gulf region and rebuild its infrastructure and military as quickly as possible; this containment policy was therefore able to effectively deny Iraq access to the financing and the technological know-how it would need in order to swiftly fulfill its goal.[19]

In contradistinction to the clear reasoning behind the punitive measures imposed by the West on Iraq in the aftermath of the Gulf War, the reasoning behind the Bush Administration's claims about Iraq's supply of WMDs and the imminent threat these posed to the security of the United States and its allies were murky at best. Only a small minority of people inside and outside the United States believed these claims – and they were the ones who stood to benefit if the Bush Administration were to follow up on its claims. Not only did Saddam's Iraq unequivocally declare, on various occasions, that the country had no weapons, it could not have possibly obtained WMDs: There was a massive surveillance system that was intently monitoring all of the Iraqi regime's internal and external dealings. Meanwhile, other equally bewildering allegations against the regime – that it had ties to Islamic fundamentalists and that it was involved in planning the attacks of September 11, 2001 (9/11) – also lacked supporting evidence. Once again, only a small minority, which excluded most IR experts, actually believed the accusations held any water. Hampered by an insufficient number of stalwart supporters, the Americans launched a colossal public relations campaign both at home and abroad in order to sell their case (as tenuous as it was) to their citizens around the globe, many of whom have remained cynical about Bush's dubious mission in Iraq until the present day.[20]

While it was eventually possible for the American government in Washington, D.C. to gain enough supporters at home, which it had done rather deftly, the international geopolitical context was not at all well-disposed to the idea of waging a new war in the Middle East. Opponents of an American-led invasion of Iraq were in the majority, and many proponents of the war still preferred to be regarded as skeptics or reluctant backers of the Americans' plan. The United States' efforts to cobble together a "coalition of the willing" ultimately turned out to be more arduous and exhausting among some auxiliary allies than many ancillary partners that the Americans had long taken for granted to endorse their foreign policy decisions (no matter how controversial they may be). In sharp contrast to the Gulf War of 1990–1991, therefore, the Iraq War of 2003 did actually cost many among the perennial defenders of the United States dearly, as several governments were toppled from power, officials sacked, reputations wrecked, careers destroyed, and people jailed. For various political and cultural reasons, such incidents for the most part did not take place among the American allies in Asia, including South Korea. However, the Iraq War did manage to challenge these nations to revisit, even if only for a short period of time, their conventional foreign policies toward the Persian Gulf region.

South Korea's response to the Iraq War

The Iraq War of 2003 broke out less than a month after the commencement of Roh Moo-hyun's presidency in South Korea. Unlike the conservative-led government of Roh Tae-woo during the Gulf War of 1990–1991, Roh

Moo-hyun's government belonged to the Uri Party (previously known as the Democratic Party), which espoused a policy of engaging North Korea as did that of his predecessor, Kim Dae-jung. Kim had upped the ante through enacting various political and economic measures that were favorable to Pyongyang, including an unprecedented summit with the DPRK's leader, Kim Jong-il, in June 2000. When the Americans asked South Korea to dispatch 5,000 to 10,000 combat troops to Iraq, Roh's government was reluctant to yield to the request. Once it realized that failing to heed the request was becoming counterproductive, South Korea had to finally agree to send its military forces to Iraq; Roh justified that move as a matter of preserving the ROK's national interests and securing American cooperation in sorting out the North Korean nuclear crisis – however, the deployment of South Korean troops was referred to by the president as merely a "peacekeeping mission" in the Middle East.[21]

South Korea's initial disinclination to dispatch troops, however, did not imply an overt opposition to the United States' overall policy toward Iraq. Like its Japanese counterpart, the South Korean government had long quietly regarded Iraq's regime as a potential threat to its national interests, especially its energy security, in the Persian Gulf region. Such a threat perception stemmed largely from Saddam's firm opposition to the American military presence in the Persian Gulf region; Baghdad's intelligible demand for an uptick in oil prices; and its unremitting claims, legitimate or not, over its neighboring oil-rich territories, particularly Kuwait.[22] In the first year of Kim Dae-jung's presidency, for instance, when American and British forces led an *ad interim* yet ruinous campaign of airstrikes against Saddam's Iraq as part of Operation Desert Fox in December 1998, South Korea immediately and completely approved the move, and its Ministry of Foreign Affairs and Trade declared unequivocally that "[t]he Korean government understands and supports the position of the U.S. government that its military action was unavoidable."[23]

South Korea was simultaneously careful not to arouse anti-Korean sentiments among the Arabs of the Middle East over the fact that it dispatched troops to the region in the wake of the Iraq War in 2003. As part of a soul-searching maneuver, the South Korean government sent five cabinet-level presidential emissaries to 15 Middle Eastern countries to seek their understanding and sympathy for the military forces it had sent to Iraq. Among the envoys were the then foreign minister, Ban Ki-moon, and defense minister, Young-kil Cho, who met, *inter alia*, a number of top officials in the Persian Gulf region, including their counterparts in Saudi Arabia, the UAE, Kuwait and Oman.[24] The South Korean government also pulled out its nationals from Iraq, Kuwait and Israel, and even looked, in consultation with the justice ministry, to "legally ban" South Korean citizens from visiting Iraq, the nation which the foreign ministry had already designated a "special country" that was "too dangerous to visit."[25] In addition, the government ordered 56 South Korean vessels in the region to take extra precautionary measures when temporarily docking in ports in the Persian Gulf, lest their crews' activities in public spaces spark any anti-Korean sentiments among the local population.[26]

Meanwhile, Roh's government had to face a growing anti-war campaign among South Korean citizens at home. About 80 percent of South Koreans were against the Iraq War and the dispatch of their military forces to that conflict area.[27] Many of them were afraid that the war could actually be a prelude to military action directed against their brethren in the North: The DPRK regime had been warning the South not to "play with fire" and to think carefully about the "disastrous consequences" that its unequivocal support for the Americans would have.[28] The anti–Iraq War campaign in South Korea was, in fact, imbued with some sort of anti-Americanism, as the contentious issue of sending troops to the Middle East further stirred up dissatisfaction with various US policies toward the Korean Peninsula. Although anti-American sentiment was not new to many South Koreans and in fact had its origins in the late 1940s, the American discomfort with, and occasional opposition to, some of the pro-Pyongyang policies championed by presidents Kim Dae-jung and Roh Moo-hyun considerably provoked anti-American feelings and behaviors among many South Koreans – feelings and behaviors that were showcased during numerous anti-war rallies in Seoul and other major cities across the country.[29]

All in all, South Korea first dispatched a unit of around 660 military engineers and medics soon after the onset of the Iraq War in March 2003. The Roh government later capped off its support for the Americans with the sending of an additional 3,000 Korean troops in December 2003. Early opposition to this move was quite strong, but after a long debate at the National Assembly, the government ultimately succeeded in gaining the necessary approvals to carry it out. A small contingent of South Korean air force personnel was stationed in Kuwait, while the rest of the ROK's air force personnel was stationed in a relatively safe area in northern Iraq – though it should be noted that their actual involvement in combat during the war and during the ensuing insurgency that erupted across the country is unknown. What is well known is that the South Korean military contingent that was dispatched to Iraq was the third largest fighting force to be sent to the Middle East after those sent by the Americans and the British.[30] But this fact did not gain the ROK much recognition from the United States because some other coalition partners, such as Australia and Poland, received much more publicity and praise than South Korea for their participation in the Iraq War. This ungrateful, if not disgraceful, treatment of the South Koreans was somewhat reminiscent of how the Americans treated their Japanese allies in the aftermath of the Gulf War of 1990–1991.[31]

Postwar relations

As soon as the major war operation was over in Iraq in early May 2003, the South Korean government made sure to pay closer attention to the safety and well-being of its serving contingent, substituting each division on a rotational basis. Meanwhile, debt relief and reconstruction assistance were two postwar issues that the ROK was asked to help resolve. A pact made by members of the Paris Club in November 2004 permitted it to write off up to 80 percent of the debt Iraq had incurred prior to the Gulf War of 1990–1991. The multi-lateral agreement entailed that the Korea Export Insurance Corporation (KEIC) could get back $84 million out of a total of $212 million worth of overdue export payments from Iraq. The money was to be reimbursed in fixed installments for 17 years beginning in 2011.[32] In late 2003, South Korea had offered to give Baghdad around $260 million, 85 percent of which was pro-vided before the international conference on the reconstruction of Iraq that was convened in the Egyptian city of Sharm el-Sheikh in April 2007. At the Sharm el-Sheikh conference, the East Asian country promised, somewhat reluctantly, to give another $200 million to Iraq, with part of this grudging pledge comprising $100 million in soft loans to be provided through its Economic Development Cooperation Fund (EDCF) over a three-year period from 2008 to 2011.[33]

Such steps were undertaken by the South Korean government in part to bolster the ROK's involvement in the reconstruction of Iraq, especially its dilapidated oil industry. The Iraqi government was planning to bump up its oil production from less than 2 million bpd to about 6 million bpd by 2011, and South Korea wanted to participate in joint efforts to develop new oil fields in Iraq. Since its participation in oil field development in other countries in the Persian Gulf had been significantly hampered – either by government monopoly or by the dominant role of multinational oil companies (if not both) – Iraq was an opportunity that the ROK could not pass up. Still, the involvement of South Korean companies in Iraq was not constrained to the energy sector alone. Once the American and British planes dropped their first bunker busters on Iraq, many South Korean contractors crafted, *sotto voce*, their own plans to enter into a potentially lucrative reconstruction market in the postwar years. Even companies such as LG Construction, with no history of working on building projects in Iraq, were carefully putting together their human and technical resources so that they could win Iraqi contracts once the bout of violence and destruction came to an end.[34]

The desire to benefit from reconstruction projects in postwar Iraq was perhaps most strongly felt by Hyundai. This was because the South Korean firm could count, *prima facie*, on its claim that Iraq was in arrears for unpaid bills in the amount of $1.65 billion; these bills had piled up from various construction projects that the South Korean builder had previously under-taken in Saddam's Iraq. Although Baghdad believed that it owed Hyundai $1.53 billion, the South Korean contractor asserted that its claim also covered accrued interest on the unpaid bills. In spite of this difference of opinion, Hyundai managed to become the first South Korean contractor to win a reconstruction order from the coalition government in April 2004 – due to its extensive experience working on construction projects in Iraq.[35] Although

Hyundai had ceased its main construction activities in Iraq for more than a decade starting in 1993, other branches of the company had not pulled out of the Iraqi market *in toto*. In the early 2000s, for instance, when Iraq was subject to international embargoes, Hyundai Motor Corporation shipped a major order of buses to Iraq, a potentially huge market for vehicles, accounting for 28 percent of Baghdad's bus imports and beating out Germany's Mercedes-Benz, which accounted for 17 percent of Iraqi bus imports.[36]

South Korea and the GCC

By the mid-2000s, the Persian Gulf region was for all intents and purposes providing more than half of South Korea's crude imports, half of its natural gas imports, and more than 60 percent of its overseas construction contracts. And while a decade earlier South Koreans were excluded – due to their lack of expertise and experience – from some of the region's highly sophisticated and expensive undertakings, they could now rather easily beat out many of their European and Japanese rivals to win prestigious projects that brought with them vast sums of cash and a tremendous amount of cachet. Since South Korea was courting the Persian Gulf as part of a strategy aimed at diversifying its portfolio of trading partners, the conventional pattern of South Korean exports to the region was undergoing a dramatic change as well. Shipments of vehicles and heavy machinery were soon to replace shipments of rubber and electrical goods, while electronic items accompanied by iron and steel products were to form the majority of South Korean exports to the region. Moreover, the ROK's connections to the GCC soon went beyond being purely commercial in nature and soon became political as well, even extending into the realm of military cooperation. These newly expanded ties were to be solidified over the following years by a number of unexpectedly high-profile visits on the part of South Korean officials to various Arab states in the region.

The timing of this change in trading strategy coincided with the presidency of Roh Moo-hyun, who later became the first South Korean head of state to visit a number of smaller GCC states, such as the UAE and Qatar, and the first South Korean head of state to visit Saudi Arabia since 1980. The ROK remained one of the latter's top ten trading partners, with the bilateral trade between the two countries totalling around $18 billion in 2005.[37] Saudi Arabia also vowed at that time to spend around $3.5 billion to expand a South Korean refinery so that it could process Bunker-C oil into gasoline and diesel fuels.[38] Soon after this commitment, South Korean companies (including such giants as Hyundai, Daelim and Samsung) would win the greatest number of Saudi construction contracts, obtaining projects valued at $3.6 billion in 2006 and $3 billion in 2007.[39] In order to better adapt to South Korean technology, the Saudi government decided in early 2007 to send a group of 84 engineering and computer-science students to receive training at six South Korean universities, providing each of them with a scholarship of $40,000 per year, which was more than what most entry-level South Korean professors made – though it should be noted that Saudi professors were also paid quite well at this time, out-earning their counterparts around the world.[40]

South Korea's two-way trade with the UAE climbed to around $12.7 billion in 2005, providing various business opportunities to South Korean companies, especially those in the IT, manufacturing, and construction sectors. A large number of South Korean companies set up offices in Dubai and Abu Dhabi, while their counterparts from the UAE invested no less than $8 billion in the ROK during the four-year period from 2002 to 2006. The UAE convened its largest business exhibition ever held at the Convention and Exhibition Center (COEX), located in the East Asian country's capital, in June 2007, a year after the two countries talked about some sort of "hub-to-hub" relationship between Dubai and Seoul: They were anxious to profit from the potential financial and logistical benefits that the two metropolises could bring to their respective regions.[41] South Korea and the UAE additionally entered into discussions in earnest about military and defense cooperation in 2006, a year after the Arab country selected the East Asian state as one of three candidates bidding to work on its next-generation jet trainer project estimated to be worth around $2 billion.[42] The ROK later lost the bid to sell, for the first time, its T-50 trainer jets to the UAE. Although fresh talks on the issue continued for several years, the two nations were to mainly cooperate on other military projects over the course of the following years.

Relations with other members of the GCC developed in a similar fashion, as South Korea's two-way trading relationships with Qatar and Kuwait both amounted to $8.8 billion in 2006, a rather significant increase over the course of just a few years.[43] In 2007, Qatar decided to invest $4 billion in South Korea by 2009, paving the way for an agreement that would allow both countries to avoid double taxation and that would have their companies enjoy truncated tax rates (to be reduced from 25 percent to 10 percent).[44] The ROK's partnership with Qatar gradually became increasingly important, as Doha was supplying 30 percent of Seoul's LNG imports. South Korea was simultaneously the second largest consumer of Omani gas after Japan, the former supplying approximately 22 percent of the ROK's gas imports.[45] Unlike South Korea's relationship with Qatar and Oman, which was predominantly concerned with the energy and construction sectors, the ROK's relationship with Kuwait also involved the defense sector and included the sale and shipment of arms. This military connection between Kuwait and the ROK had been forged in the late 1990s and was subsequently strengthened in the aftermath of the Iraq War in 2003.[46]

Courting the GCC for an FTA

One of South Korea's strategies to deepen its ever-increasing relationship with the GCC was to pursue the conclusion of a free-trade agreement (FTA). The idea was raised, for the first time, during President Roh's official visit to the

UAE, Qatar and Saudi Arabia in May 2006, during which he aimed to further increase the ROK's economic connections to the GCC countries.[47] South Korea had previously signed its first FTA with the Latin American country of Chile, the basic principles of which had been established during the Asia-Pacific Economic Cooperation (APEC) summit meeting in Kuala Lumpur in November 1998. The South Korean government was simultaneously in negotiations with European countries (among others) over the establishment of FTAs. Besides various technical and financial issues, fierce opposition from the agricultural sector and local farmers had long hindered the ROK's government from seeking to establish FTAs with its economic partners in different parts of the world. There were, however, certain advantages inherent in its relations with members of the GCC that encouraged South Korea to seek such agreements with them during the bilateral talks that were scheduled to begin in April 2008 (and continue on into the future).[48]

In the Persian Gulf region, Iraq and particularly Iran have sizable, albeit not quite productive, agricultural and farming sectors, while the GCC countries need to import the bulk of their annual agricultural and dairy requirements. The GCC, therefore, posed no threat at all in agricultural terms to South Korean farmers, and yet the ROK was still reluctant to export agricultural and/or farming products to the GCC in the aftermath of signing an FTA agreement with it. In spite of this impasse in the farming sector, South Korea nevertheless believed that the basic structures of the GCC and ROK economies were mutually complementary in other areas. As a virtual treasure trove of fossil fuels, the GCC states could adequately buttress South Korea's insatiable thirst for energy resources, while an FTA could better facilitate the penetration of more South Korean products into GCC markets – which would partially bring down Seoul's long-term trade deficits with GCC nations. In addition to removing, or at least easing, various bureaucratic and legal impediments that were standing in the way of mutual investment and joint venture opportunities, South Korea also benefited from the fact that many in the GCC nations were looking to place their excess financial resources into special commercial bonds sanctioned by Islamic law – bonds that the South Korean government was all too eager to issue.[49]

Even though the GCC countries were at the same time negotiating among themselves about the feasibility of creating a common market with a single currency in the Persian Gulf region, they were not keen on establishing an FTA with an East Asian nation after China, which had already started to negotiate its own deal in April 2005. It had taken South Korea 14 years of negotiations, for instance, before it finally reached an agreement with Kuwait about a "mutual investment guarantee treaty" in 2004.[50] In a preliminary talk with the Saudis in November 2007, a South Korean call regarding a "high degree" of liberalization for goods and services as well as investment matters turned out to be a thorny and sensitive issue for most GCC countries.[51] The GCC's first FTA was signed with Singapore in 2008 at a time when the Arab bloc's negotiations with a number of Western and Eastern countries for similar accords had almost completely stalled due (at least in part) to each member state's demand for certain national interests to be upheld in a potential deal. The GCC's counterparts had their own specific prerequisites too, as interlocutors from the European Union (EU), for example, were demanding the arrangement of a GCC-wide customs union prior to the signing of an FTA.[52] Despite such hurdles, there were crucial economic and financial reforms being undertaken not only in the GCC countries, but in Iran as well, which prompted foreign countries such as South Korea to strenuously push for greater economic connections to the Persian Gulf region.

Privatization and economic reform

From the outset, the unsound structure, improper management and lack-adaisical performance of the Persian Gulf's economies had a lot to do with their overdependency on energy exports and the ultimately deleterious effects of sudden inflows of oil revenues from the 1970s onward. One particular characteristic of these economies was the accentuated power of governments in both collecting capital as well as managing the entire domestic and foreign affairs of the state from its economy, to its political structure, to its culture. Not only did the task of capital accumulation inevitably move from private hands into the hands of rulers and public sector bureaucrats, the whole process ultimately saw a reallocation of human capital from productive entre-preneurship to ruinous rent-seeking. This, in turn, led to a vicious circle in which the concentration of wealth and resources in the hands of the state further empowered governments and their subservient bureaucracies to monopolize capital at the expense of a relatively independent and prosperous private sector. Things often went awry when a sharp, and often unexpected, decline in energy incomes saddled these states with significant economic and social challenges, some of which even threatened the survival of the estab-lished political regimes in one way or another and forced them to think, if fleetingly, about implementing some fundamental changes to the whole sociopolitical process.[53]

   With the exception of Iraq, the Persian Gulf states have had rather con-trasting experiences regarding economic reform and the process of privatiza-tion. Far from relinquishing the state's tight control over the economy, the GCC put an excessive amount of emphasis on stability and security, while the structural reforms it introduced were modest and fairly limited in scope. And instead of carrying out a unified and unbiased policy throughout the GCC zone, each state implemented reform at its own discretion and pace. Saudi Arabia talked of privatization as a strategic choice for the state, but it was Dubai that turned out to become "the new Arab dream" for many in the wider Middle East region. As for Kuwait, its cachet was never restored in the wake of the various steps it took toward economic and (to a certain extent) political reform. With the long-cherished goal of creating a region-wide common market functioning under a single currency, the GCC has collectively pursued a series of economic reforms, enacting measures related to financial institutions such as banks and stock markets, trade and customs regulations, industrial operations, and FDI laws.[54]

Unlike the GCC, however, Iran enacted economic reforms, which experienced ups and downs, in the late 1980s, and these reforms gained momentum during the past decade when the government engaged in a large-scale privatization project, vowing to rival even Western European countries in terms of selling off state assets. The political system in Iran reached a consensus about economic reforms, removing various legal and administrative barriers to privatization – though the process was never free of problems and a healthy dose of criticism. In addition to a pressing policy of abolishing almost all state subsidies, the reforms aimed to free the government's control over 80 percent of the public sector through the privatization of such industries as banking, mining and transportation. Moreover, the two giant Iranian auto companies were earmarked for privatization, and the NIOC decided to privatize a significant number of its energy firms, which were worth tens of billions of dollars. In tandem with such reforms, the Iranian government also chipped away at various impediments to and restrictions on foreign investment that were present in Iranian labor law in order to promote the growth of the private sector and the success of foreign companies, such as those from South Korea.[55]

Quandary over Iran: Managing relations with the two Koreas

In contrast to the GCC and Iraq, Iran has had its relations with the Korean Peninsula turn out to be a distinctive feature of its foreign policy toward East Asia. Tehran has managed to maintain multifaceted connections to the Korean Peninsula for many decades (almost) without interruption, making Iran one of the few countries in the world that has established political as well as economic relations concomitantly with both South and North Korea. What made this often complex, but not always symbiotic, relationship more peculiar is that Tehran's partnership with Seoul and Pyongyang was able to overcome conventional assumptions, dissimilar patterns of alliance-making, and almost incompatible political ideologies. This rather anomalous diplomatic triangle was unique to the Korean Peninsula's relationship with Iran: Both Koreas tried at various points in time to establish relations with other Persian Gulf nations, but it never happened that both had done so simultaneously. There was indeed something beyond mere national will that sustained the connections between Iran and the two Koreas over the past decades.[56]

As far as Iran's relationship with the two Koreas is concerned, Tehran's foreign policy toward Seoul and Pyongyang was driven by an external and an internal factor. The external factor had much to do with the structure of the international system and its overall impact on the diverse systemic incentives and pressures that shaped Iran's foreign policy behaviors *vis-à-vis* the regimes of the ROK and the DPRK. The internal factor had much to do with the understanding of Iranian policymakers with regard to their country's position in the international system and the way they crafted and implemented Iran's approach to the Korean Peninsula. At times, the international system played a dominant role in Iranian foreign policy, as its diktats inevitably conditioned Tehran's approach to Seoul and Pyongyang. This was more striking after 1980, when prodigious systemic pressures often coerced Tehran into cautiously pursuing its foreign policy goals in the Korean Peninsula.

The relationship between Iran and South Korea followed a strategy of "the separation of politics from economics,"[57] according to which each country strove to follow its own policy goals in regard to the other party while being attentive to its own alliance commitments and the crucial imperatives of the international system. This policy worked to the benefit of each country, but its glitches eventually turned into serious problems. For example, the issue of sanctions against Iran became a stumbling block for Seoul, which was in the midst of, and wanted to continue, expanding its economic relations with Tehran. In the same way, Iran's very first move to approach Pyongyang for military deals in the early 1980s had come as a result of the structural fetters that had been foisted on Tehran at the time. In addition to maintaining their previous military connections, the two parties subsequently established political and even economic ties – though they did not succeed in concluding as many negotiated deals as they had first hoped. While political matters were not quite absent from the Iranian–South Korean relationship, they were heavily emphasized in the Iranian–North Koran relationship in order to partially turn regional and international attention away from the more sensitive aspects of their rather obscure diplomatic connections.

Unparalleled economic interaction

The first decade of the twenty-first century heralded the tidings of a robust economic relationship between South Korea and Iran in spite of a dearth of political interaction between Seoul and Tehran. South Korean companies were encouraged to invest more in Iran, especially in its oil and gas projects, and the Iranian government was subsequently motivated to give preferential treatment to South Korean firms in many other economic sectors.[58] The LG Construction Company was awarded a $1.6 billion contract to develop phases 9 and 10 of the South Pars gas fields project, while Daewoo Motors was invited to further invest in Iran's Kerman Khodro Corporation. Tehran and Seoul set up a joint investment committee in 2008, concentrating their plans on major development projects to be prioritized in Iran. As part of this joint initiative, Daelim Company was offered a lucrative deal valued at around $2 billion in 2009 to participate in the development of the second part of phase 12 of the South Pars gas fields project.[59] At the same time, Iran remained one of South Korea's top suppliers of petroleum, providing 10 percent of Seoul's total oil imports in 2011.[60]

The total value of two-way trade between South Korea and Iran thereby more than quadrupled over a decade from roughly $3.8 billion in 2000 to roughly $17 billion in 2009; it then quickly rose once more to reach $18.5 billion in 2011.[61] There is, at the same time, a strikingly huge gap between the statistics recorded by South Korean authorities and those found in Persian documents. For instance, various South Korean sources contain the total sum of bilateral trade between the two nations and list it at about $10 billion for 2010,[62] but the same calculation found in Persian sources ranged from $10 billion to $20 billion. This bewildering difference had much to do with the informal trade and the *sub rosa* importation of South Korean products by Iran from its neighboring countries, the UAE in particular. And it is this phenomenon that played a major role in the ubiquitous distribution of South Korean brands throughout Iranian markets. These smuggled items included almost any type of South Korean good from familiar Samsung and LG electronic devices to lesser-known products such as Pine cigarettes. The penetration of South Korean products into the Persian Gulf country can be seen in the following statistics: In mid-2005, 70 percent of Iran's TV market went to LG and Samsung; about 40 percent of the entire mobile market was carved out by Samsung Mobile; and more than 70 percent of all automobiles imported by Iran in the first half of 2011 were made by South Korean companies such as Kia Motors, Hyundai and Ssangyong Corporation.[63]

Meanwhile, both South Korean and Iranian governments were indubitably instrumental in the increase in the volume of trade between the two countries. On the South Korean side, the government recognized the importance of economic diplomacy with Iran, channeling resources and support that was needed to maximize the potential benefits of its foreign policy. As part of this strategy, the government assured the availability of some high-tech materials and technological know-how in exchange for more access to Iranian markets. Such facilitation on the part of the government also included encouraging South Korean firms to increase their investments in Iranian projects if they wished to land a larger number of expensive contracts and secure a larger share of the market for manufactured goods. South Korean products exported to Iran were nevertheless fortunate enough not to be in competition with Japanese and Chinese products, though their price and quality were competitive enough to rival those European goods that found their way into the country.

As for Iran, the government's approach of looking toward the East was a specific attempt at obtaining various required technological instruments and financial services which had largely been restricted by a slew of severe sanctions imposed on it by the West. Coupled with this eastward-looking policy, a sudden surge in oil prices filled Iran's coffers, giving the government the financial wherewithal to purchase the technologies and services that it required from East Asian countries such as the ROK. Moreover, privatization and economic reform helped the private sector and a number of influential interest groups to overcome conventional trade barriers and engage more directly in foreign commercial activities, particularly the importation of highly bankable commodities such as automobiles and electronic devices. And one final factor, which has been widely overlooked by interested observers, was the power of Iran's mass media, especially its national television and radio broadcasters, to promote South Korea's consumer and cultural products and thereby boost their popularity among ordinary Iranians.

Why did the Iranian government then offer a substantial share of the country's lucrative markets to the ROK? South Korean products were, by and large, trailing Japanese products when it came to quality, and they were not as price competitive as Chinese products. Politically, there was little motive for Tehran to be more partial toward Seoul *vis-à-vis* its other East Asian partners in Tokyo and Beijing, simply because the regional weight and international clout of China and Japan far outweighed that of South Korea – though it should be noted that the ROK has been punching above its weight both regionally and globally in recent years largely due to the economic and political support it has received from the United States. In spite of this seemingly apparent *non-sequitur*, Iran did have its reasons for generously importing and promoting South Korea's manufactured commodities and luxury goods; some of these goods dominated the Iranian consumer retail space to such an extent that they turned parts of the Persian Gulf country, at times, into a virtual South Korean shopping center.

One important factor behind Iran's preferential treatment of South Korean products could be the possible involvement of South Korea in the Iranian nuclear program, either directly or indirectly, on a temporary or long-term basis. Such reckoning cannot be so easily dismissed as pure speculation when one takes into account the thought-provoking explanation given by the Russians with regard to a significant delay in setting up Iran's Bushehr Nuclear Power Plant, which was supposed to come on line by the end of 2009. When the Iranian authorities voiced their objections, Russian officials informed the Atomic Energy Organization of Iran (AEOI) that a third party was taking too long to provide a few required instruments and that this was the reason why the Bushehr Nuclear Power Plant could not be activated according to the schedule which Iran and Russia had previously agreed upon. Iranian sources, relying on information provided to them by people with close connections to the Iranian Parliament, later revealed that the third party was the ROK; however, it is not known whether it was Iran or Russia that had contracted South Korea to provide those instruments.[64]

The nuclear controversy and the ensuing sanctions

At a time when commercial connections between Tehran and Seoul were undergoing rapid growth, the Iranian nuclear issue and the ensuing regime of economic sanctions implemented by the West negatively influenced the volume of material exchange between the two countries. They also somewhat dimmed the long-term health of the economic and political relationship between the two nations. Despite the fact that Iran had been subject to sanctions since the early 1980s, these punitive measures were greatly extended in number and in scope in the period following the Iraq War because of the nuclear issue. The outcome required the South Korean government to participate in some of the political and economic actions brought against Iran, bringing the East Asian country's trade ties with Tehran to the precipice. While South Korea was able to come up with an excuse to support the political action, it was very hesitant to endorse the relevant economic measures that were enacted against the Iranian government, and it was even twice as reluctant to implement them. When Seoul ultimately toed the line, as it were, on both the political and economic fronts, it had to find a way to deal with the situation and find ways to both mitigate the sanctions and alleviate the indignation of many Iranian officials who had generously opened their country's huge markets to a myriad of South Korean products.

A couple of years after casting a vote in favor of two International Atomic Energy Agency (IAEA) resolutions about Iran's nuclear program in November 2003 and September 2005, respectively, the South Korean government announced a series of broad economic sanctions against Tehran in September 2010. The measures, which South Korea had to excuse by citing its compliance with UN Security Council Resolution 1929, brought almost all financial transactions between Seoul and Tehran under government scrutiny and severely restricted future investments by South Korean companies in the Persian Gulf nation's oil and gas projects. Over a year later, the East Asian government added 105 Iranian entities and individuals to its financial blacklist in December 2011 and cautioned South Korean companies against purchasing Iranian oil; it did not, however, decide to cut energy imports from Iran. This extended list of sanctions precluded South Korea from completing financial transactions with 225 Iranian individuals and organizations, 120 of which had previously been blackballed by the measure enacted in September 2010.[65] In the following year, a European Union ban on insuring Iranian oil shipments forced the South Korean government to stop its importation of Iranian oil *ad interim* – though Seoul was somewhat inclined to adopt a proposal put forth by Tehran to continue supplying petroleum using Iranian oil tankers.[66]

The commencement of the South Korean sanctions on Iran occurred in 2010, when Seoul was Tehran's fourth largest trading partner in the previous fiscal year, accounting for more than 7 percent of the Persian Gulf country's total imports and exports. To counterbalance various irritating moves on the part of South Korea (which had started in 2003), the Iranian government often preferred to try and manipulate its balance of trade with the ROK, though in some cases it took no retaliatory measures whatsoever. Still, Iranian efforts to increase its balance of trade were not wholly embraced, as the government only managed to ban the importation of South Korean products on a temporary basis and to briefly restrict the promotion of South Korean vehicles and consumer goods inside the country. For instance, the Iranian government put a provisional embargo on South Korean products when Seoul backed the November 2005 IAEA resolution,[67] but it only restricted the marketing of South Korean goods in Tehran in early January 2011 for a short period, when it wanted to react to a move made by the South Korean government a month earlier.[68] There was only one occasion which saw Tehran forewarn, publicly and officially, the ROK that it would "fully stop importing Korean goods" – and that was in response to the possibility that South Korea may decide to completely suspend the importation of Iranian oil because of the European Union's ban on insuring oil shipments (mentioned above).[69]

One quiet and less noticeable counterbalancing act undertaken by the Iranians, however, was to look for new opportunities and find potential partners to replace the South Koreans at a time when the possibility for future developments between Tehran and Seoul looked to be quite low. A number of giant car importers in Iran, for example, made arrangements to import Chinese automobiles because their now limited access to South Korean vehicles (due to the economic sanctions) was detrimental to their long-term grip on the Iranian market. These car dealers included Asan Motors and Atlas Khodro, which were previously among the major representatives of South Korean automakers such as Hyundai and Kia.[70] Since the Chinese government ostensibly opposed the stringent sanctions against Iran and since its bargaining power *vis-à-vis* Western countries could far outrun that of the ROK,[71] the new strategy had the potential to cost South Korean automakers quite dearly, as Iran was one of their largest markets in the entire Middle East region. In the absence of major foreign competitors – such as the South Koreans – the success of Chinese brands was evocative of a past scenario in which Japanese products in Iran had enjoyed an extraordinary amount of success.[72]

The unfading North Korean presence

Another result of the Iranian nuclear controversy was the fact that the relations between Tehran and Pyongyang managed to set the world's media and policy circles abuzz: Every single aspect of their bilateral interactions, even their cultural programs, became subject to unremitting international attention. The crux of the problem rested on the close cooperation that was alleged to have existed between Iran and North Korea on Tehran's nuclear and missile development programs. A deluge of biased news stories and policy reports resulted in making more of the issue than was called for by the available evidence. So many outlets worked so hard to substantiate the plausibility of cordial connections between the Iranian government and the DPRK regime with regard to the Iranian nuclear program. In their view, such cooperation could have huge, worldwide security implications. Among those who advocated such (unwarranted) concerns, there happened to be pundits who claimed that the DPRK regime's shipment of missile parts and other military equipment to Iran netted the regime over $2 billion annually, a dazzling figure which, if true, would have been the equivalent of 10 percent of North Korean GDP.[73] A myriad of similar statistics about the net value of military (and other forms of) cooperation between Pyongyang and Tehran during the past decades need, *a fortiori*, to be approached with a hint of caution.

A major problem with these statistics and with the reports that featured them was that reliable information was not readily available: Statements and accounts were largely based on self-made assumptions, and yellow journalism flourished. The bilateral relationship between Iran and the DPRK was of course improving from one decade to the next, but nothing much came of their behind-the-scenes meetings or the many contracts they signed over the years. Iranian officials at the highest levels often used to repudiate vehemently the plausibility of nuclear cooperation between Tehran and Pyongyang; instead, they used to boast about their homegrown knowledge and self-sufficiency in the fields of nuclear technology and missile production, even though they were, at the same time, publicly acknowledging that their country did have good ties with North Korea.[74] More recent news stories about developments in Tehran–Pyongyang relations commonly point to some sort of energy deal between the two countries, but it is not clear whether the cash-strapped DPRK regime is going to import Iranian oil only for urgent and non-commercial domestic consumption or whether it plans to use it for the purposes of certain clandestine development projects.[75]

Besides the deepening of Tehran–Pyongyang relations in the Persian Gulf region and the tremendous amount of media scrutiny about other hypothetical aspects of these relations, there happens to have been some fresh albeit trivial developments in the DPRK's connections to small members of the GCC over the past decade. These new relationships have mostly come as a result of the DPRK's economic interests in the Persian Gulf region. Meanwhile, its conservative counterparts in the GCC have been extremely cautious about making any public announcements about their furtive cooperation with the communist regime of Pyongyang. Apart from some rudimentary diplomatic exchanges between North Korea and the tiny Arab states of the GCC, a new surge in oil prices and a subsequent boom in construction projects motivated the DPRK regime to dispatch many of its workers to the region, including more than 3,000 to Kuwait, about 1,300 to the UAE, and hundreds more to Oman and Qatar.[76] This led North Korea's Air Koryo to establish, and later scrap, weekly flights between Pyongyang and Kuwait City in 2011, catering mainly to the DPRK's laborers in the region during the peak travel season which lasted from April through to October.[77]

Notes

1 Ross Garnaut, "The East Asian Crisis," in Ross H. McLeod and Ross Garnaut (eds.), *East Asia in Crisis: From Being a Miracle to Needing One?* (London: Routledge, 1998), pp. 3–27.
2 Norman Flynn, *Miracle to Meltdown in Asia: Business, Government, and Society* (New York: Oxford University Press, 1999), p. 6.
3 Douglas J. Sikorski, "Global Capitalism and the Asian Financial Crisis," in John A. Turner and Y. Kim, (eds.), *Globalization and Korean Foreign Investment* (Burlington, VT: Ashgate Publishing Company, 2004), pp. 60–80.

4　This statement was allegedly made during an interview with the then South Korean president, Kim Dae-jung. See George B.N. Ayittey, *Defeating Dictators: Fighting Tyranny in Africa and around the World* (New York: Palgrave Macmillan, 2011), p. 18.

5　One of those aggravated societal problems was, for instance, a boom in the sex industry and the subsequent exodus of a rather large number of South Korean sex workers and entertainers to foreign destinations such as the Persian Gulf metropolis of Dubai, whose recent prosperity is based primarily upon a vast *entrepôt* trade with a bustling sex industry. See, in particular, a highly critical piece of editorial by the *Korea Times* published as "Exporter of Prostitution" (June 18, 2012, p. 6). Some other media coverage germane to the embarrassing phenomenon includes "Korean Sex Trade Abroad Surges under Lax Monitoring," *Korea Times*, October 5, 2010, p. 1; "Korean Prostitution Examined in Australia," *Korea Joongang Daily*, April 24, 2012; "10% of Korean Prostitutes Work Overseas," *Chosun Ilbo*, June 19, 2012; "Campaign Starts to Kick Korean Prostitutes Out of Australia," *Korea Times*, August 31, 2012, p. 1; and "South Korea: A Thriving Sex Industry In a Powerful, Wealthy Super-State," *International Business Times*, April 29, 2013.

6　Dani Rodrik, *One Economics, Many Recipes: Globalization, Institutions and Economic Growth* (Princeton: Princeton University Press, 2007), p. 182.

7　For instance, it was possible for Seoul to reply positively to a Saudi Arabian request in early 2000 to send about 1,000 South Korean nurses to the Arab country – though a small group of such workers had already been recruited one year earlier. See "South Korea Asked to Send 1,000 Nurses to Saudi Arabia," *Yonhap News Agency*, February 11, 2000.

8　See Donald Kirk, *Korean Crisis: Unraveling of the Miracle in the IMF Era* (New York: Palgrave Macmillan, 1999).

9　Manning.

10　Amitav Acharya, *Whose Ideas Matter?: Agency and Power in Asian Regionalism* (Ithaca: Cornell University Press, 2009), pp. 156–157.

11　Korea Economic Institute (U.S.), *The Two Koreas in 2000: Sustaining Recovery and Seeking Reconciliation* (Washington, D.C.: KEIA, 2000), p. 99.

12　Gills, p. 179.

13　"Kuwait, Korea Mark 20 Years of Growing Partnership," *Business Korea,* Vol. 16, No. 2 (February 1999), pp. 68–69.

14　"Korea Should Turn to CIS, Middle East," *Korea Herald*, January 6, 2007, p. 6.

15　"South Korea's Hyundai to Export Energy Cables to Iraq," *Yonhap News Agency*, April 13, 2000.

16　"Iran to Emerge the Biggest Export Market," *Business Korea*, November 8, 2004.

17　"South Korea, Iran Sign Double Taxation Avoidance Agreement," *Yonhap News Agency,* January 29, 2002.

18　Azad.

19　Barry Rubin, "The Persian Gulf amid Global and Regional Crises," in Barry Rubin (ed.), *Crises in the Contemporary Persian Gulf* (New York: Frank Cass Publishers, 2002), pp. 5–20.

20　John J. Mearsheimer, *Why Leaders Lie: The Truth about Lying in International Politics* (New York: Oxford University Press, 2011), pp. 3–5.

21　James Brooke, "South Korea Attempts to Bargain over Iraq: It Wants U.S. Help on North Korea Issue," *International Herald Tribune*, October 8, 2003, p. 3.

22　Azad.

23　"South Korea Supports U.S. Air Strikes against Iraq," *Xinhua News Agency*, December 17, 1998.

24　"South Korea to Send Presidential Envoys to Middle East," *Yonhap News Agency*, February 17, 2004.

25 "S. Korea Seeks to 'Legally Ban' Its Citizens from Travelling to Iraq," *Yonhap News Agency*, July 6, 2004.

26 "South Korea Orders Merchant Ship Crews in Persian Gulf Not to Go Ashore," *Yonhap News Agency*, July 10, 2004.

27 The ostensible public outcry of South Koreans against the Iraq War was nevertheless hardly a *crise de conscience*, as it had a lot to do with their own safety; the security of their brethren across the Korean Peninsula; and a collective gesture of anti-Americanism.

28 "North Korea Warns South on Backing U.S. in Iraq," *International Herald Tribune*, March 22, 2003, p. 6.

29 Ted Galen Carpenter and Doug Bandow, *The Korean Conundrum: America's Troubled Relations with North and South Korea* (New York: Palgrave Macmillan, 2004), pp. 88–90.

30 "South Korea Denies Discord with U.S. over Iraq Troop Reduction," *Yonhap News Agency*, April 8, 2005.

31 In the words of Thomas Hubbard, who served as US ambassador to the ROK from 2001 to 2004, "Roh Moo-hyun's decision to send 3,000 troops to Iraq despite opposition from many of his own supporters was very important even though it has received less public recognition in the United States than it deserves." See Korea Economic Institute (U.S.), *Ambassadors' Memoir: U.S.–Korea Relations through the Eyes of the Ambassadors* (Washington, D.C.: KEIA, 2009), p. 186.

32 "South Korea, Iraq Conclude Export Payments Deal," *Yonhap News Agency*, March 10, 2006.

33 "S. Korea Helps Rebuild Iraq with 100m-Dollar Loan, Pushes Joint Oil Development," *Yonhap News Agency*, May 9, 2007.

34 "Korea Builders Seek Postwar Role in Iraq," *International Herald Tribune*, March 21, 2003, p. 15.

35 "South Korea's Hyundai Owed 1.65bn US Dollars for Iraq Projects," *Yonhap News Agency*, December 12, 2005.

36 "South Korea's Hyundai Group to Ship 400 Buses to Iraq," *Yonhap News Agency*, July 22, 2001.

37 "Opening New Era of Saudi–Korean Economic Ties," *Korea Herald*, September 22, 2006, p. 12.

38 Peter Haldis, "Saudi Arabia May Expand Refinery in South Korea," *Octane Week*, Vol. 20, No. 48 (2005), p. 8.

39 "South Korea's Construction Orders in Saudi Arabia to Top 3bn Dollars," *Yonhap News Agency*, March 25, 2007.

40 "Saudi Arabians to Study in Korean Universities," *Korea Times*, February 23, 2007, p. 3.

41 "South Korea, UAE Seeking 'Hub-to-Hub' Cooperation," *Korea Times*, May 13–14, 2006, p. 4.

42 "Korea, UAE to Sign Military Accord," *Korea Herald*, November 15, 2006, p. 2.

43 "A Glance at Kuwait," *Korea Times*, March 27, 2007, p. 5.

44 "South Korea, Qatar Sign Preliminary Accord to Avoid Double Taxation," *Yonhap News Agency*, January 30, 2007.

45 "South Korea, Oman Form Friendship Alliance over Secure Fuel – Paper," *JoongAng Ilbo*, November 13, 2007, p. 1.

46 "Kuwait, South Korea Sign Military Cooperation Pact," *Kuna News Agency*, November 30, 2004.

47 "S. Korea Considers FTA with Gulf Countries: Roh," *Korea Times*, May 15, 2006, p. 2.

48 "South Korea to Start Free Trade Talks with Gulf Cooperation Council," *Yonhap News Agency*, November 22, 2007.

49 Christopher Michael Davidson, *The Persian Gulf and Pacific Asia: From Indifference to Interdependence* (New York: Columbia University Press, 2010), p. 52.
50 "South Korea, Kuwait to Sign Mutual Investment Treaty," *Yonhap News Agency*, March 23, 2004.
51 "S. Korea, Gulf Nations to Launch FTA Talks in 2008," *Xinhua News Agency*, November 22, 2007.
52 Economic and Social Commission for Western Asia (ESCWA), *Survey of Economic and Social Developments in the ESCWA Region 2000–2001* (New York: United Nations Publication, 2001), p. 80.
53 Shirzad Azad, "The Politics of Privatization in Iran," *Middle East Review of International Affairs*, Vol. 14, No. 4 (2010), pp. 60–71.
54 Adam Hanieh, *Capitalism and Class in the Gulf Arab States* (New York: Palgrave Macmillan, 2011), pp. 172–177.
55 Azad, "The Politics of Privatization in Iran."
56 Shirzad Azad, "Iran and the Two Koreas: A Peculiar Pattern of Foreign Policy," *Journal of East Asian Affairs*, Vol. 26, No. 2 (2012), pp. 163–192.
57 In the East Asian context, the concept of separation of politics and economics is derived from the Chinese characters for *zhèngjīng fēnkāi*, which has also been translated to *seikei bunri* in Japanese and *cheongkyong bunri* in Korean.
58 See "Iran and South Korea Sign $500m LNG Contract," *Mehr News Agency*, February 7, 2007; "S. Korea Daelim Confirms Iran Gas Storage Deal," *Reuters*, February 8, 2007; and "South Korea's LG Electronics Begins Producing Mobile Phones in Iran," *Associated Press*, March 13, 2007.
59 "Italy, S. Korea to Develop South Pars Phase 12," *Press TV*, November 3, 2009.
60 "S. Korea's Imports of Iranian Oil Plunge in Dec.," *Yonhap News Agency*, January 18, 2012.
61 "Iran–S. Korea Trade Hits $10 Billion in H1," *Press TV*, October 13, 2011.
62 "Giro-ae seon chungdong wegyo" ["Middle East Policy at a Crossroads"], *Chosun Ilbo*, August 5, 2010.
63 "Tahrime Iran tavasotte KIA shekast khord" ["Kia's Iran Embargo Failed"], *Iranian Students' News Agency (ISNA)*, September 24, 2011.
64 "Roosha gonahe takhire nirugahe Bushehr ra be gardane koreye jenubi andakhtand" ["Russians Blame South Korea for Delay in Bushehr Power Plant"], *Asr Iran*, November 19, 2009.
65 "Korea Follows U.S. Iran Sanctions," *JoongAng Ilbo*, December 17–18, 2011, pp. 1, 3.
66 "S. Korea Mulls Using Iranian Oil Tankers to Resume Crude Imports," *Yonhap News Agency*, July 2, 2012.
67 The *ad hoc* trade embargo, however, extended to a number of other countries, including Britain, Argentina and the Czech Republic, since all of them had backed the IAEA's decision in September to refer Iran to the UN Security Council unless Tehran suspended its ongoing nuclear activities. See "Iran Places Apparent Ban on S. Korean Imports," *Arirang News*, October 20, 2005; and "Britain Fears Tehran Block on Trade," *Guardian*, October 20, 2005.
68 "Iran Tore Down S. Korean Advertising Billboards in Tehran: Official," *Yonhap News Agency*, January 20, 2012.
69 "Iran hangukchepum kumsu kyonggoe cheongbu 'konyok'" ["Iran's Warning about Banning Korean Goods a 'Trouble' for the Government"], *Yonhap News Agency*, June 27, 2012.
70 "Soltane varedate khodro be Iran kist?" ["Who is the King of Car Importers in Iran?"], *Tabnak*, December 24, 2011.
71 "US Clears China, Singapore from Iran Oil Sanctions," *Associated Press*, June 29, 2012.
72 Meanwhile, a myriad of Iranian media outlets displayed their indignation at and trenchant criticisms of South Korea's political posture regarding the nuclear issue

and the ensuing economic sanctions. They were particularly more vocal when South Korean officials were visiting Iran, urging the government to speak out diplomatically and retaliate accordingly for any political and economic move made by the ROK that went contrary to Iranian interests. See "Chera mavazee manfi koreye jenubi aleihe Iran bipasokh mande ast?" ["Why No Response to S. Korea's Negative Positions toward Iran?"], *Tabnak*, April 29, 2011.

73 "N. Korea 'Earning $2 Billion a Year in Arms Deals with Iran'," *Chosun Ilbo*, July 16, 2009.
74 "Ahmadinejad: No Military Cooperation with DPRK," *Daily Yomiuri*, November 30, 2007.
75 "China Holds Up Iranian Oil Shipment to N. Korea," *Chosun Ilbo*, October 21, 2013.
76 "N. Korean Workers Brave Hard Times in UAE," *Chosun Ilbo*, December 25, 2009.
77 "N. Korea's Flag Carrier Cancels Its Air Route with Kuwait," *Yonhap News Agency*, November 10, 2011.

6 The beachhead: Persian Gulf policy under Lee Myung-bak

From "dark corner" to "spreading road"

Although many major cataclysmic events in the modern Middle East temporarily attracted – and occasionally engaged – South Koreans, the region largely remained a "dark corner" of the ROK's foreign policy with little or no serious impact on its national security priorities.[1] Even when South Korean policymakers and business elites were truly enmeshed in affairs connected to the Middle East, they did not perceive any particular need to encourage the general public to think of the region as having long-term importance. It took a convoluted combination of internal and external developments to alert them to the necessity, even the urgency, of encouraging South Koreans, particularly the ambitious younger generations, to pursue their dreams in the Middle East. These developments had much to do with the financial crisis that led to dwindling economic opportunities at home and in other well-known destinations abroad – and, hence, to a growing number of university graduates in search of employment. Given the rising economic prospects of the resource-rich yet hitherto largely unexplored Middle East, and the Persian Gulf region in particular, which had already tempted other East Asians to flock to the region in large numbers, many Koreans now started to look westward.

Less than three months before the end of Roh Moo-hyun's government, Foreign Minister Min-soon Song said, during a trip to the region in early December 2007, that "our country's next spreading road will be in the Middle East."[2] The task of following through on this concept of a "spreading road" then fell to the subsequent government led by Lee Myung-bak (also widely known as LMB) to frame policies pertinent to South Korea's new intentions in the region. In addition to being able to capitalize on lessons learned from years of practical experience in the Middle East, Lee began his presidency at a time when oil prices began to skyrocket and a time which therefore saw enormous revenues flow into the coffers of the oil-producing countries of the Persian Gulf region. By July 2008, oil had reached as much as $147 per barrel, up from about $30 per barrel in 2003 and $50–$60 per barrel in 2005. For many inside the new government, especially Lee himself, this eventuality prompted nostalgic memories of the early 1970s, when petroleum prices swelled from \$3.80 per barrel in October 1973 to \$14.70 per barrel in January 1974.[3] Although oil prices later plummeted, they never bounced back to their original levels, remaining, on average, at least three times higher than the 2003 benchmark.

In the midst of the global financial crisis, when much of the developed world was stuck in an economic depression, the flow of petrodollars into the Persian Gulf offered attractive business opportunities that were hard to find elsewhere. It is true that the idea of a "spreading road" had been raised before the petroleum price hike and that, more importantly, its intended goals meant something far beyond just the recycling of oil revenues. However, the fortuitous combination of "a second Middle East boom" and a new government in South Korea led by someone with practical knowledge of the region – who had already experienced the first Middle East boom during the 1970s – significantly helped facilitate the formation by the ROK government of a new foreign policy. Lee capitalized on his previous personal experience in the Middle East and helped make this new policy a necessary precursor to deepening the East Asian country's established interests in the region. With respect to the Persian Gulf, Lee's "*déjà vu* diplomacy" manifested itself particularly in a flurry of serious attempts to forge multifarious and perennial connections to members of the GCC; a series of efforts to penetrate Kurdistan's energy and construction industries; and numerous strategies to overcome the obstacles posed by Western sanctions against Iran.

Déjà vu diplomacy

As far as contemporary history is concerned, South Korean leaders prior to Lee Myung-bak were seldom prominent in crafting and implementing the ROK's foreign policy toward the Middle East, instead giving the bureaucracy *carte blanche* to create proper policies to secure their nation's interests in the region. The only exception was Park Chung-hee, who briefly played a crucial role in pushing Korean companies into the region following the oil shock of 1973–1974. Despite his overall impact on South Korea's Mideast policy during the 1970s, however, Park Chung-hee never visited the Middle East and his personal encounters were probably limited to meeting the dignitaries from the region whom he occasionally received at the Blue House in Seoul. Lee Myung-bak, on the other hand, made more visits to the region than all previous leaders combined and had already spent many formative years managing projects in various Middle Eastern countries, a bulk of them in the Persian Gulf, during the 1970s and 1980s.

This period marked the heyday of South Korean construction businesses in the Persian Gulf as a global desire to recycle the region's petrodollars lured construction companies from both the East and the West. Lee's performance at Hyundai Construction in the region earned him, at the age of 35, the title of "the youngest ever CEO in Korean business history." For many people in the Persian Gulf, Hyundai came to represent the quintessential characteristics of Koreans to such an extent that "knowing Hyundai meant knowing Korea." To operate in that highly competitive environment, South Korean firms needed to be able to perform, but they also needed strong connections to the centers of power, so that they could rival their Western and Eastern competitors in the region. While the South Korean government played a crucial role in generating this economic boom, senior company executives such as Lee also had to lobby to secure influence and make personal efforts to promote the interests of their affiliated companies – in Lee's case, Hyundai Construction.

When Lee Myung-bak took over the presidency in February 2008, he capitalized on potential economic opportunities in the Middle East in an attempt to fulfill some of the promises he had made during his election campaign. He was one of the first South Korean leaders to draw an analogy between the "second Middle East boom" of 2008 and the "first Middle East boom" of the 1970s, which he had personally experienced and from which he had benefited. For instance, one of the first projects Lee's Hyundai Construction undertook in Saudi Arabia in the mid-1970s generated close to a quarter of South Korea's annual national budget at that time.[4] Recalling such potent memories led Lee to persuade Koreans to take advantage of the various opportunities that the "excellent market" of the Middle East could provide. Lee's expertise and connections to the region, in addition to his administration's behind-the-scenes diplomacy, helped pave the way for South Korean businesses that sought to follow his advice. His frequent visits to Middle Eastern countries and the ensuing number of business opportunities for Korean companies was proof positive that Lee's ambitions for his countrymen could be realized. More importantly, he had already learned how to approach the high-wire act of foreign policy in the region. He was therefore able to help make South Korea's stilted relations with the Middle Eastern countries – and the GCC states in particular – a lot smoother.

Lee Myung-bak's one-man diplomacy is, nevertheless, in no way sufficient in and of itself to adequately explain South Korea's new foreign policy approach toward the Persian Gulf, and the broader Middle East region, during his presidency. Consideration must also be given to the instrumental role played by the international system, represented here largely by the US–ROK alliance. The main guidelines articulated by this security alliance have long served as a blueprint for South Korean foreign policy toward the Middle East, as well as toward other parts of the world. This alliance has brought a lot of benefits – and only a few minor costs – for South Koreans pursuing their interests in the Middle East. When Lee began his term as president, the dust of the Iraq War had settled and the country's reconstruction projects were being awarded primarily to those American allies and close partners that had played a role in the war. For its part, the South Korean government had strongly supported the United States during the Iraq War, providing material contributions just as it had during the Gulf War of 1991.[5]

The South Korean government was thereby well-positioned to secure dozens of lucrative energy and construction projects, particularly those located in the autonomous region of Kurdistan in northern Iraq. The impact of the systemic factor (i.e. the security alliance) was also instrumental in facilitating Lee Myung-bak's close relationships with the members of the GCC, by means of which he was able to obtain their firm assurance that the ROK would be able to rely on a stable supply of energy – at a time when the East Asian country had to scale back its oil imports from Iran *ad interim*. The very concept of the so-called "strategic partnership" that was discussed between the UAE and South Korea would have been far-fetched without the systemic factor, that is, the alliance with the United States. The same goes for the ROK's success in gaining a place on the list of those countries permitted to continue to do business with Tehran despite the tightening by the government of stringent sanctions imposed on Iran. Even though Lee Myung-bak's state-craft and the ROK's security alliance with the United States were extremely important, the overall contribution of the state bureaucracy, as an ancillary factor, to the success of South Korea in the Middle East during this period should not be underestimated.

The GCC: The center of a new Mideast policy

The Middle East is really a large swath of land that encompasses countries with asymmetrical power relations; with contrasting geographical reach and levels of social development; and with variable statuses within the international pecking order. In terms of foreign policymaking toward such a diverse region, a lack of long-term political stability has always been a major concern for all those countries that have significant interests there. Moreover, the political systems of the region have strict controls over all matters relating to external interactions, from diplomatic affairs and international trade to sports and cultural exchanges. The chimera of adopting a single Middle East foreign policy is exacerbated by the lack of cohesion among major regional players and the occasionally hostile relationships between them, which require foreign nations to be cautious in their approach, especially small states – such as the ROK – with significant economic interests in the region.

While the six member states of the GCC share many of the foregoing characteristics, South Korean foreign policy toward these countries has experienced little, if any, radical change since Seoul established diplomatic relations with the GCC's *primus inter pares*, Saudi Arabia, in 1962. Tightly tied to the apron strings of the West as their *arbiter elegantiarum* in many crucial matters of foreign policy, these Arab countries have been ruled by the same political systems, followed the same line of political alliances in external affairs, and have seen their patterns of foreign trade and economic interactions change very little since the time the ROK forged official diplomatic ties with them. For these reasons, the East Asian state has so far experienced few problems in managing its relationship with the GCC countries, and the main issue has often had to do with its level of engagement rather than with its having to change the nature of its policy. South Korea under Lee Myung-bak, therefore, strove to deepen its relations with GCC member states in various political, economic and cultural areas, making the political capitals of these states the destinations for Lee's frequent tours to the Middle East. In fact, whenever Lee was encouraging his countrymen to capitalize on "the second Middle East boom," he was primarily thinking of the GCC states. More importantly, these Arab countries were supposed to be the cornerstone of the so-called "spreading road" policy so passionately followed by the Lee government.

As a former CEO of Hyundai Construction, Lee Myung-bak had a penchant for construction contracts in the GCC countries, and these have long accounted for the majority of the construction orders won by South Korean companies. His abiding interest culminated in a highly praised nuclear deal that was signed with the UAE in December 2009. Estimated to be worth at least $20 billion, it engaged Korean energy giant KEPCO to build four nuclear reactors for the Arab state by 2020. Similar but less lucrative nuclear deals were later signed with Saudi Arabia and energy projects agreed upon with Qatar. Such contracts formed only a tiny fraction of the $600 billion in national development plans that these three countries drafted following a sudden surge in their energy revenues. Consequently, while the total value of all construction contracts for Korean companies in the entire Middle East region was $2.3 billion in 2003, they were able to sign no less than $160 billion in deals with GCC countries alone between 2007 and 2011, an average of more than $32 billion a year.[6] This was a significant achievement, when one takes into account the fact that between 1975 and 1983, in the heyday of Lee's construction activities in the region, the total value of construction orders signed by South Korean companies throughout the Middle East was less than $62 billion.[7]

Despite the importance of construction contracts, energy imports from the GCC countries remained South Korea's main priority. The East Asian country's top four energy providers were all GCC members, with Saudi Arabia as the largest supplier followed by Kuwait, the UAE and Qatar. Though Seoul occasionally increased oil imports from these countries to make up for the loss of Iranian oil imports, the overall pattern largely remained the same. The GCC states provided 70% of South Korea's oil imports and more than 40% of its natural gas imports. This brought the total value of the ROK's energy trade with these countries to around $55 billion annually, more than double China's $22.7 billion and around half of Japan's $115 billion in hydrocarbon trade with those states.[8] In addition, a series of recent oil and gas development projects signed between the GCC countries and various South Korean companies is a virtual guarantee that the current pattern of the ROK's energy trade will not change significantly in the short term. Such a pattern of energy imports, however, has continued to be a key factor behind the East Asian country's ever-increasing trade deficit with some of the GCC states – especially in comparison to its trade balances with other parts of the Middle East. During the period from 2000 to 2009, for instance, South Korea's total trade deficit with Saudi Arabia shot up to $132.54 billion, while those with Kuwait and the UAE amounted to $51.95 billion and $16.55 billion, respectively.[9]

Under Lee Myung-bak's presidency, South Korean exports to the GCC countries experienced a sudden surge, making the region the fourth largest destination for South Korean products after China, Japan and the United States. At the same time, the South Korean government engaged in several rounds of FTA negotiations with the GCC member states in order to prevent the ROK from falling further behind Japan and China, who had already made significant progress in that area.[10] If successfully negotiated, an FTA with the GCC countries would play a crucial role in helping South Korea reach its Middle East export target of $100 billion by 2020. In tandem with these developments, the state-run KOTRA, the main national agency for locating international markets, also provided assistance, organizing the "Made in Korea 2012" exhibition in Abu Dhabi and rolling out plans to establish a "K-Plaza" in one of the GCC member states. Such initiatives could increase the volume of Korean exports to the GCC in the short term, but without an FTA, the $100 billion target would be difficult to reach in the long term.

The second surge in GCC state revenues was not merely reminiscent of the oil boom in the Persian Gulf region during the 1970s and 1980s, it also had other implications, including the creation of state-investment assets known as sovereign wealth funds (SWFs). Although Kuwait had established its own SWF in 1953, even before achieving independence, other GCC members only turned their attention toward SWFs in the wake of the second regional oil boom. By mid-2009, the Abu Dhabi Investment Authority (ADIA), the largest SWF in the region, had net assets of more than $600 billion, roughly equivalent to the South Korean GDP at the time.[11] Lee Myung-bak advised South Korean financial institutions to secure part of this money through hiring talented experts and increasing their international competitiveness. His government also formed a separate task force to readjust related South Korean laws and regulations in order to accommodate the GCC's SWFs. By July 2009, the Korean Investment Company (KIC) was in a position to sign a memorandum of understanding with the Kuwait Investment Authority (KIA) and another with the ADIA in November, courting the major SWFs of the GCC and inviting them to engage in various kinds of mutual investment opportunities.[12]

The Lee administration also sought to cement the East Asian state's long-term interests and the comparative advantages of South Korean companies in the GCC countries by focusing on new areas of bilateral cooperation. Such measures included a wide range of cultural and scientific activities which included educational programs, technical training, medical tourism, and the marketing of sports and movies. Another important issue was the discussion of some sort of "strategic partnership" with the UAE which began in December 2009. Neither Seoul nor Abu Dhabi provided further details about the urgency and scope of such a partnership, but in 2011 the South Korean government dispatched a contingent of 130 soldiers to the UAE on a two-year mission. In a similar development, South Korea and Saudi Arabia vowed to expand the extent of their defense cooperation, engaging in a series of military meetings. One possible explanation here is that the ROK is seeking to become one of the world's leading military exporters, aiming to sell $4 billion worth of arms by 2020 – as compared to the $250 million it sold in 2008.[13] Strengthening links with the GCC countries, therefore, makes strategic sense, as these countries have long been among the largest arms purchasers in the world, tempting even the Chinese in recent years to escalate their arms exports to the region.

By and large, the GCC countries, primarily the UAE, Saudi Arabia and Qatar, became the main focus of Lee Myung-bak's Middle East visits and fertile ground for implementing South Korea's new policies in the region. Qatar's main attraction, besides its gas exports, was its successful bid in 2010 to host the FIFA World Cup in 2022, as preparations for that event could provide lucrative business opportunities for Koreans in various economic and technological fields. The remaining GCC countries, however, were not ignored. In September 2012, for instance, South Korea reopened its embassy in Bahrain after a 21-year hiatus during which the two nations had maintained their diplomatic relations only at the *chargé d'affaires* level. Although Seoul had closed its embassy in Manama in 1991, ostensibly due to financial constraints, the two parties had never terminated their bilateral relationship – even if the meager value of the total two-way trade between them could somehow justify the cessation of political representation at the highest level.[14]

Kurdistan: An investment for the future

While the GCC was at the core of Lee Myung-bak's Persian Gulf policy, he still did not neglect South Korea's interests in other parts of the region. In particular, Lee approached the autonomous region of Kurdistan in northern Iraq, which had begun to attract significant global attention in the midst of undergoing considerable domestic developments. In essence, the previous South Korean government had invested in Kurdistan by sending military forces to the area, and Lee determined that his government would reap some of the rewards of this decision. In the aftermath of the Iraq War and at the request of the Americans in 2004, the ROK dispatched, albeit grudgingly, a contingent of a few thousand troops to Irbil, the capital of Iraqi Kurdistan, in spite of widespread domestic opposition to such a move. These forces, which included medics and engineers, stayed until December 2008, engaging in medical and reconstruction projects and providing a testing ground for similar activities to be undertaken by their civilian counterparts in the future. Such an unprecedented undertaking also provided South Korean officials with a unique opportunity to travel to the area rather frequently – most notably senior South Korean representatives in Baghdad who would often meet with major Kurdish leaders in Irbil to discuss various political and economic issues that were of mutual interest.

However, South Korea's attention to Kurdistan may not be a matter of complete coincidence. Drawing an analogy between East and West Asia, in fact, China comes close to Iran, Japan somehow resembles Turkey, and the

Koreans have a lot in common with the Kurds. This commonality between the Koreans and the Kurds extends far beyond the initial letter "K" – when both are written in English – and has much more to do with politics, geography and culture. Much like the Kurds of West Asia, the Koreans in East Asia are largely disunited, historically marginalized, and often regarded as "a fish among whales" or "a shrimp among sharks." Geographically, both Korea and Kurdistan are hemmed in by imposing mountains, and these heavenly created colossal ramparts of absolutely no cost and harm have played an indispensable role in guarding the identity and achievements of the two nations throughout their turbulent and often neglected histories. Moreover, the Korean fascination with mountains is somewhat reminiscent of the well-known Kurdish proverb that states that "Kurds have no friends but mountains." Considering some relative cultural commonalities, and despite a widening cultural gap between the southern and northern parts of the Korean Peninsula, Koreans and Kurds are, by and large, the most family-oriented, patriarchal and tradition-bound peoples of their respective regions.

The presidency of Lee Myung-bak ushered in a new chapter in Seoul–Irbil relations, although the Korea International Cooperation Agency (KOICA) had been active in Kurdistan since 2004 and the Kurds had signed postwar Iraq's first ever oil contract with South Korea in late 2007.[15] Proof of this new era is the fact that the visiting Kurdish prime minister, Nechirvan Idris Barzani, was among the first foreign dignitaries whom President-elect Lee Myung-bak received in February 2008. The Lee administration would later secure a significant number of oil contracts and construction projects in Kurdistan, laying the groundwork for dozens of other South Korean businesses in the region; future projects ranged from the establishment of the first Korean restaurant to the technical consultancy for Irbil International Airport, the latter being provided by Incheon International Airport Corporation.[16] These projects all played a crucial role in the presence and popularity of Korean products throughout the Kurdish region, particularly automobiles and electronic devices.

Of course, such contracts with Kurdistan were not totally devoid of controversy either at home or abroad. For instance, the ROK's first energy exploration deal with the Kurds, which had sought to secure 1.9 billion barrels of oil, or twice South Korean annual consumption, turned out to be economically implausible and a serious setback for the Lee administration's perpetual quest for foreign energy resources.[17] More importantly, the deal put Kurdish officials and the central government of Iraq at loggerheads over the legitimacy of the act and the legal basis of the contract, forcing Iraqi officials to take retaliatory measures against the ROK, which included the suspension of oil shipments to South Korea *ad interim* and the blackballing of South Korean companies when it came to Iraqi deals with foreign countries.[18] Unlike the energy deals, however, South Korea's construction projects in Kurdistan were more diverse, relatively less contentious, and rather lucrative. Many such projects, worth billions of dollars, have been collectively implemented by a consortium of major South Korean companies and have consisted in the building of basic infrastructure such as dams, roads and sewers in a rapidly developing and flourishing Kurdistan.

Furthermore, South Korea's political and commercial connections to Kurdistan gained in importance as the area served as a beachhead to the rest of Iraq. Postwar Iraq was a total ruin and needed significant national reconstruction, an area the Koreans could count on as their long-established *forté*. More importantly, the gradual stability of the country and its rising oil revenues offered a myriad of other opportunities from energy contracts to export markets for South Korean goods. A sign of this potential was the conclusion of an unprecedented oil deal, valued at more than $3.5 billion, between Seoul and Baghdad during an official visit to South Korea by Iraqi President Jalal Talabani, the first of its kind, in early 2009.[19] Talabani, himself a Kurd and former leader of the Patriotic Union of Kurdistan, was one of the two pillars of the political establishment controlling the autonomous Kurdish region and would prove to be a valuable ally, dampening down the wrath of the Iraqi central government, led by Prime Minister Nouri Al-Maliki, against the East Asian country over its oil deal with Irbil and introducing South Korean businesses to areas of war-torn Iraq beyond his homeland.

All in all, South Korea under Lee Myung-bak regarded Kurdistan more as a site for long-term investment than as a fertile ground for short-term business gains. The ROK became one of the only countries, alongside Sweden and the Netherlands, to upgrade its political presence in Kurdistan to the extent of having an embassy in Irbil, even if it was only occupied by a senior consul general. The KOICA, for its part, played an ancillary role in mapping out various commercial interests *vis-à-vis* its other Western and Eastern rivals, most notably the Japan International Cooperation Agency (JICA), throughout Kurdistan. South Korean attention to Kurdistan, nonetheless, has never been a one-way street, because the Kurds themselves have shown a burgeoning desire to increase Irbil's developing international relations with as many nations as possible. The fledgling polity of Kurdistan needs more investment and technology in order to prosper; its long-cherished goal of fortifying its own international identity independent of Iraq, with more regional maneuvering and freedom of action, requires Kurdish leaders to garner political sympathy throughout the world; build on their previous achievements; and seek commercial and political allies wherever they can find them.

Iran: Overcoming the challenge of sanctions amid rising stakes

While there was no significant change in the political relationship between South Korea and Iran under Lee Myung-bak's presidency, there were numerous economic, and to some extent cultural, developments. Iran remained South Korea's largest trading partner and export market in the greater Middle East, and the volume of two-way trade between the two countries reached an all-time high of more than $20 billion, a sum which included both formal and *sub rosa* transactions. A large number of South Korean businesses were willing to pour their resources into the Persian Gulf country, contributing to the omnipresence of Korean vehicles and electronic goods throughout Iranian markets, which were once dominated by Japanese brands. Additionally, a sudden hike in oil prices in 2008 that had brought increased revenues into Iran; a more vigorous East-looking foreign policy pursued by the Iranian government; and the promotion of South Korean products through official cultural channels each contributed to the dynamics of Seoul's new relationship with Tehran.[20]

In light of this new robust commercial relationship, the sanctions against Iran became a rather large problem for the Lee administration and perhaps the most pressing issue that the ROK had to face in the Middle East since the Iraq War of 2003. As far as South Korea was concerned, the sanctions regime had at least three inconvenient implications. First, the Western powers that were imposing the sanctions had linked Iran's nuclear program to the North Korean nuclear program, putting Seoul in a rather inconvenient position when seeking exemptions from compliance with various sanction requirements. Second, stringent sanctions targeting Tehran's petroleum exports left the East Asian state with no option but to stop importing Iranian oil for about two months in 2012. As South Korea had been dependent upon Iran for 10 percent of its crude imports, even this temporary suspension had serious consequences for domestic consumption and the general health of the Korean economy. Finally, constraints on banking operations and financial transactions between Seoul and Tehran, or any third party beneficiary, were highly detrimental to the fate of 3,000 small to medium-sized South Korean companies doing business with Iran.[21]

Halfway through the nuclear controversy, the Lee administration tried to strike a cautious balance between the ROK's political alliance with the United States and its ever-increasing interests in Iran. Like previous South Korean governments over the past three decades, the Lee administration was prudent enough not to make an analogy between Iran's and North Korea's nuclear programs with respect to its relations with Tehran. Not only are the nature and *raison d'être* of Iranian and North Korean nuclear programs quite different, but such a move would have only antagonized Iranian officials and consequently harmed Seoul's crucial commercial ties with Tehran. In addition, the majority of South Koreans are yet to be fully convinced that Iran's relationship with North Korea has negatively affected the peace and security of the Korean Peninsula. This can be attributed to two major factors: First, Iran has largely been the recipient of North Korean arms and military technology, and has not exported any significant amount of armaments to Pyongyang. Second, the flow of Iranian petrodollars and energy supplies to North Korea plays an indubitably positive role in preventing the DPRK regime from engaging in brinksmanship and saber-rattling against Seoul as a bargaining chip to obtain some basic requirements, particularly when it is very desperate to do so.[22]

The Lee government first attempted to find alternative sources of petroleum once sanctions restricted imports from Iran. Lee himself, following his prime minister, travelled to three members of the GCC, namely, Saudi Arabia, Qatar and the UAE, and Riyadh's subsequent promise to provide Seoul with as much oil as it requested brought some relief to South Korean officials, who were uneasy about the possible consequences of an oil shortage.[23] Despite the indisputable anxiety in South Korea caused by the sudden cessation of Iranian petroleum exports, the crux of the problem was not the replacement of lost energy supplies. When Tehran threatened, through its embassy in South Korea, to implement a total ban on the import of South Korean goods if Seoul were to go along with the decision to stop buying Iranian crude oil, the Lee administration was ultimately left with no other option but to resort to backdoor channels in order to get the ROK exempted from the list of those nations prohibited from making oil deals with Iran.[24]

The Lee government also took some other measures to tackle the implications of sanctions for banking operations and financial transactions between South Korea and Iran. Because of the restrictions on international financial transactions, the Lee administration first tried to iron out the issue through bilateral banking cooperation, opening a special account with the Korean Woori Bank and permitting the Iranian Bank Mellat to open a branch in Seoul. The government also instituted a form of bartering whereby South Korea shipped manufactured products and luxury goods to Iran in return for energy imports. A third measure, taken by both parties, was a sudden temporary increase in the importation of oil and manufactured products, particularly in the run-up to the implementation of various sanctions. One final measure taken by Seoul was to pour South Korean products into the countries neighboring Iran, especially the UAE, so that the Persian Gulf country's "imports mafia," as it was known in the Iranian media, could have easy access to made-in-Korea goods, even if the country itself was out of reach due to certain types of sanctions. It will therefore come as no surprise that Iran has conducted the lion's share of its informal trade with the UAE in recent years, which accounted at one point for 7 percent of the tiny Arab country's GDP.[25]

The cultural dimension in context

While South Korea's cultural overtures to the Persian Gulf harken back to the signing of a document on cultural exchange with Iran in 1953, and while the East Asian country subsequently launched a number of culture-oriented initiatives toward Tehran and the broader Middle East in the 1960s and especially in the 1970s, the ROK's flurry of diplomatic activities in the region under Lee Myung-bak capitalized on this particular area more vigorously than did the previous Korean governments. The aim was to introduce certain aspects of Korean culture and promote some sort of pro-Korean sentiment in the region, particulalry among young people, through official cultural channels. Despite the partial success of the cultural measures taken by South Korea in the region, it is still difficult to call the whole undertaking "cultural diplomacy" or even a kind of "soft power" promotion. Diplomats and official channels are hardly proper instruments and appropriate methods for gaining cultural sympathy among other nations in the long run, and such moves are usually more effective when they are mutually agreed upon and are undertaken through private and non-governmental means. Soft power also comes normally as an offshoot of political power, and its affinity with economic strength is rather unpredictable, if not ephemeral and disproportionate.

As part of "the Korean wave," widely known as "*Hallyu*," South Korea's cultural endeavor in the Persian Gulf region concentrated considerably on entertainment, though educational programs on language and the culinary arts were supplementary components of the endeavor. In July 2008, Korea Global Media Group launched the satellite broadcast of "Korea TV" to promote South Korean culture, covering vast swathes of the Middle East, including North Africa. This media group had commenced its cultural activity in the region in 2005, and the new campaign was to attract a larger number of viewers to Korean dramas and documentaries with Arabic or English subtitles.[26] Other methods of cultural promotion in the region, which were specifically initiated or significantly assisted by South Korean embassies, included sponsored film festivals, movie distribution, traditional dance or music events, taekwondo demonstrations, culture weeks, book fairs, the translation of books and historical records, food festivals, and language classes.

There are a number of ways to estimate how successful such cultural promotion programs were in the Persian Gulf countries. A favorable impression of South Korea directed many Arab consumers toward Korean products, markedly boosting the sales and validating the marketing strategies of Korean companies and their local representatives in the Persian Gulf region.[27] Gripped by glamorous images of movie characters or mesmerized by the excitement of an apparently different lifestyle, more young girls were registering for language courses, while many of their male counterparts decided, out of the blue, to sign up for taekwondo classes. In addition, these young impressionable men and women were searching for their favorite movie actors on the Internet or looking for their films and records in local shops or at department stores. There were also some among them who were influenced to such an extent that – given the fact that they had the financial wherewithal to do so – they went on a tour of South Korea in order to experience the East Asian country and its culture firsthand.[28]

This last group of eager tourists was further courted by the ROK government's various domestic and international programs that were specifically designed to attract a greater number of Arab tourists, especially those who were well-off and who were not bashful about displaying their wealth ostentatiously: those whose swanky lifestyles included a burgeoning desire to spend cash on luxury items, beauty services, and vacations, among other things.[29] South Korea's bustling business of medical tourism, chiefly consisting of visitors coming for cosmetic surgery, has targeted many potential wealthy Arab customers in the GCC countries by launching a slew of marketing campaigns online and through local promotional agents in the region, especially those located in Dubai.[30] The South Korean government has also been keen on relaxing various visa restrictions and required bureaucratic procedures for this group of rich visitors and their accompanying relatives and friends who may end up paying a rather hefty bill for the expenses they run up from their medical procedures, accommodations, and Korean souvenirs. The growing number of tourists and other types of passengers going back and forth from the GCC states, moreover, led some major airlines to try and benefit from the boom, as South Korea's national carrier, Korean Air, decided to resume its services to Saudi Arabia in November 2012 after a hiatus of about a decade and a half.[31]

While South Korea has striven in recent years to promote its cultural products in the Persian Gulf and other parts of the Middle East region, it has done little, if anything, to simultaneously familiarize its citizens with Iranian culture and Arab culture. For instance, South Korea's ambassador to Iran, Woong-yeob Song, revealed during an interview with a Tehran-based educational institution in October 2013 that he had "never read a book about Iranian dishes in Korea, despite the fact that Iranian foods are superior to French cuisine," or "he could not remember any Korean book which specially focuses on Iranian cuisine."[32] The result of such an unbalanced and often prejudiced approach to cultural interaction (and to the cultural campaigns in particular) has been frequent blunders which have generated misperceptions, lost opportunities, and occasionally ruinous behaviors, all of which have had negative reverberations for the whole cultural promotion project undertaken by the South Koreans.[33] Arab visitors to South Korea have also been more vocal recently, complaining about an unbelievable lack of *halal* restaurants and markets; a lack of proper places for prayer and religious festivals; and a growing number of grievous cultural misunderstandings.[34]

Energy security: A new approach to an old obsession

South Korea has long pursued three compelling interests in the greater Middle East region: a safe supply of fossil fuels; easy access to local markets for its manufactured products; and a less challenging way of channeling the region's oil money (which it sought to achieve through construction contracts, touristic programs and Islamic financial instruments). If Lee Myung-bak's *déjà vu* diplomacy concentrated mainly on the second and third of these crucial interests, the oil factor, and energy security in general, was in no way absent from his agenda in the region. The seriousness of Lee's white-hot focus on energy security was especially tested when his government used political persuasion to conclude a groundbreaking nuclear energy deal with the UAE in late 2009. He personally supervised the project during the negotiation process and travelled to Abu Dhabi to attend the signing ceremony at the conclusion of the deal – a deal that pleased Lee so much that he referred to it as a "heaven-sent national fortune."[35]

While the Lee administration considered the nuclear deal to be a better way to bolster the East Asian country's energy security, the UAE took it a step further, calling the contract a new stage in the emerging strategic partnership between Abu Dhabi and Seoul. This starry-eyed attitude was mostly attributed to the nature of the contract because, unlike previous South Korean projects in the region, the nuclear deal with the UAE was (and still is) a joint cooperative venture to operate and maintain the reactors for at least 60 years, thus cementing relations of a different kind with a major oil producer in the Persian Gulf.[36] The first sign of such a multifaceted approach to the region appeared when the Lee administration decided to dispatch a contingent of 150 combat troops to the UAE for a period of two years, insisting that the mission would promote national interests and expand economic and military ties with the Arab nation. Barely flummoxed, many observers instantly connected the mission to Seoul's nuclear energy deal with Abu Dhabi, a connection that was even made by the main opposition party in the South Korean National Assembly.[37]

In fact, the government's understanding of energy security was based on the assumption that old notions of energy security and the conventional methods to achieve it may no longer be applicable to today's fierce global competition for energy resources. The ROK apparently feels uneasy about some explicit challenges to its prospects for energy security, which are mainly related to the emergence of energy-hungry powers from Asia, particularly China and India. Seoul's major Asian rivals are better positioned and better equipped to obtain their energy requirements from the Persian Gulf, a treasure trove of oil and natural gas. Another equally important issue in South Korea's policy circles in recent years has been the prospect of unification and the subsequent implementation of a serious economic development and industrialization plan in the northern part of the Korean Peninsula which would require considerable financial and technological resources from the South. Any such project, extending to every aspect of the economy from infrastructure to manufacturing, would be severely restricted without the required energy resources, a large portion of which would have to come from the Persian Gulf region.

Although North Korea possesses some natural resources, mines in particular, it has no oil or natural gas, and the country has experienced severe energy shortages since the early 1990s, forcing factories to work well below their average capacities. While a bulk of North Korea's energy imports within the past two decades has been supplied by China, this would no longer be the case under a unified Korea, making the provision of basic energy requirements for the northern part of the Peninsula an additional burden for Seoul. According to some predictions, unification and the ensuing economic reconstruction program in the North would drive up the Korean Peninsula's energy demands to levels similar to those experienced in the South during the 1980s.[38]

Cognizant of the potential repercussions of such clear challenges to South Korea's energy security – those posed by the *bête noire* of all East Asian economies – the Lee government tried to implement a new energy policy toward the Persian Gulf region in order to develop a multifaceted relationship with the countries therein, which are staggeringly rich in energy resources. If carefully articulated and skillfully cultivated, this approach would better support the East Asian nation's growing energy needs in the long run.[39]

Rivalry with fellow East Asian states

From their very early encounter with the Persian Gulf, Koreans were pretty much inquisitive about the presence and activities of their Japanese and Chinese counterparts in the region. South Korea's first goodwill mission in 1957 carefully studied Japan's economic maneuvers as well as China's political moves not only in the Persian Gulf but in the broader Middle East region too. The ROK almost duplicated Japan's diplomatic *beau geste* toward the Arab-Israeli wars of 1967 and 1973, while its construction firms engaged in a fierce game of one-upmanship in order to outdo their Japanese counterparts during the building bonanza that followed the first oil shock. During the 1980s, Seoul strove, though somewhat unsuccessfully, not to lag behind China's arms sales to both Iran and Iraq, while its political and diplomatic disposition toward the two Persian Gulf countries hardly differed from that of Tokyo – though the structure of the international system was not irrelevant at all either to the approach that was pursued or the outcome that ensued.

In the 1990s, when China was to gradually emerge as a new economic player in the Persian Gulf, South Korea's previous economic and technological achievements enabled Korean products to compete rather successfully with those from China, but the ROK still had to grudgingly accept Japan's upper hand in various highly coveted areas of the market. When the global quest for energy resources entered into a new era at the start of the 2000s, economic adeptness or technical expertise alone were no longer enough to secure Seoul's sedimented interests in the Persian Gulf given the now multifaceted interests of its East Asian challengers, let alone its other competitors from both the East and the West. Negotiations underway over the conclusion of an imminent FTA between the GCC and Japan and China soon alarmed South Korea, serving as a warning that it not rest on its laurels and that it immediately seek a similar accord in order to secure its ever-expanding interests in the region.

On the cusp of Lee Myung-bak's presidency, the total number of South Korean diplomats in the Middle East amounted to just one-third of those from Japan and China,[40] while the ambitious country's visible political and cultural presence in the region was even further behind that of its East Asian rivals.[41] Enlightened considerably by his previous experience in the Middle East, Lee made some attempts to publicly address the matter on various occasions, aiming largely to arouse a certain awareness among his fellow Koreans about the region and the diverse economic opportunities it had to offer.

The policies which the Lee government followed clearly signified, on various occasions, South Korea's desire to address the many serious challenges posed by its East Asian counterparts in the Persian Gulf and beyond. However, in spite of such necessary and crucial steps, the ROK's various structural weaknesses with regard to the broader Middle East region remain in place. The tip of the iceberg is the fact that South Korea's flagship institute of higher education, SNU, does not have a single Mideast scholar on its faculty, and it does not offer a single course on any aspect of Middle Eastern politics, economics or culture.[42] By comparison, Japan's Tokyo University and China's Peking University can most definitely be considered more resourceful than SNU both in terms of relevant specialists and educational courses they offer to a rather growing number of their interested domestic and foreign students.

Lurking turmoil and transition: What's next for the Koreans?

The ongoing political turmoil in the greater Middle East region, which started with the overthrow of the Tunisian government in January 2011, was another crucial occurrence which the Lee government had to monitor intently. The genesis of the crisis and the unpredictable confluence of events initially prompted perplexing and often contradictory interpretations of its possible implications for the ROK, particularly with regard to foreign and economic policy. For instance, the Korean Ministry of Knowledge Economy was among the first political institutions in the East Asian country to be naïvely optimistic and beguiled by the siren song of the "Arab Spring," predicting that a brighter economic outlook in the Middle East would be an immediate consequence of the turbulence in the region.[43] Despite such a sanguine view, however, the unfolding events soon led South Korean officials to adopt a much more cautious attitude – the crisis proved to be both complex and unpredictable, and they realized that prudence was to be the order of the day. As far as South Korea's Middle East policy was concerned, the Lee government needed to distinguish between the possible ramifications of events unfolding in three particular areas: Libya, Egypt and Syria (taken together), and the GCC.

Libya's former leader, Colonel Muammar Gaddafi, was definitely not a close friend of South Korea, as he had long forged significant political and military ties with his allies in North Korea. Despite Gaddafi's political affiliation and his regime's relations with the DPRK, which dated back to the early 1970s, Tripoli and Seoul managed to establish a diplomatic relationship in December 1980. Later, the South Korean construction industry was allowed to set up significant businesses in Libya, a process which culminated in the groundbreaking contract offered to the ROK by Tripoli to participate in the construction of the Great Man-Made River (GMR) project from 1984 onward. The substantial construction revenues from Libya were only surpassed by those revenues South Koreans generated in the Saudi Arabian market during the 1980s. Until the demise of the Gaddafi regime, there were some other business opportunities for Korean contractors in Libya – though the number of offers depended mainly on Tripoli's oil income and national development plans. Once Gaddafi fell, therefore, the Lee administration was quick to recognize the National Transitional Council of Libya, even providing the council with aid worth $1 million through the World Food Program.[44] In spite of such developments, however, it remains to be seen whether post-Gaddafi Libya will be as stable and lucrative as it was and whether KOTRA's estimates of a $120 billion reconstruction market will actually materialize under the new regime in Tripoli.

Unlike the situation in Libya, the situation in Egypt and especially Syria was, and is, of a different stripe. Egypt under Hosni Mubarak finally agreed to establish diplomatic relations with South Korea only in April 1995, and his regime's praise and public embrace of North Korea was stronger than Gaddafi's. Despite half-hearted diplomatic relations between the two countries from the mid-1990s onward, Cairo always gave lip service to its political ties with Seoul, preferring instead to align itself with Pyongyang.[45] This lack of political will was effectively a stumbling block for the ROK, which wanted to increase its investment and its market penetration in Egypt – which it hoped to do under a post-Mubarak political system. Things were no better in Syria – in fact, Syria is the only Middle Eastern country that has never wished to establish diplomatic relations with South Korea, citing Seoul's political ties with Israel as the main reason for its refusal. Whether or not the current developments will finally lead to the emergence of a new political regime in Damascus, South Korea will continue to seek a way to establish ties with Syria.

In contrast to the foregoing cases, the Lee government's cautious reactions to various internal developments within the GCC countries demonstrated that any seismic change in the political equilibrium of these countries would be an unwelcome change for South Korea, at least for the time being. Although Bahrain has been the only GCC nation to have witnessed serious political unrest thus far, news of political plots, instability and demonstrations in other GCC member states has occasionally made international headlines in recent years. Since the beginning of South Korea's political interactions with GCC nations, these Gulf monarchies have remained under the same political system with similar patterns of government expenditures. While some political pundits and economic experts may argue that the GCC countries will be obliged to continue selling oil to their conventional customers, including South Korea, regardless of who may come into power, two issues need to be noted. First, any new political regime in a GCC country may no longer be willing to spend its oil revenues in the same way as these Arab states have done during the first and second oil booms. Second, an abrupt change in the GCC members' political and economic systems could seriously imperil South Korea's growing connections to the region, if not its current economic investments *in toto*.

Notes

1 This chapter is a revised version of a paper originally published as "*Déjà vu* Diplomacy: South Korea's Middle East Policy under Lee Myung-bak" (*Contemporary*

Arab Affairs, Vol. 6, No. 4 (2013), pp. 552–566). I would like to thank *Contemporary Arab Affairs* for giving me permission to incorporate a bulk of the paper into this book.

2 "Song wegyo 'chungdonge hangukui mire idda'" ["'The Middle East is Korea's Future,' Foreign Minister Song Says"], *Chosun*, December 4, 2007.

3 Ian Skeet, *OPEC: Twenty-Five Years of Prices and Politics* (London: Cambridge University Press, 1988), pp. 99–123.

4 Richard M. Steers, *Made in South Korea: Chung Ju Young and the Rise of Hyundai* (London: Routledge, 1999), pp. 109–110.

5 Spencer Tucker (ed.), *The Persian Gulf, Afghanistan, and Iraq Conflicts*, Vol. 1 (Santa Barbara: ABC-CLIO, 2010), p. 695.

6 "South Korean Contractors Remain Bullish on Middle East," *MEED*, Iss. 18, May 6–12, 2011.

7 "Lee Calls on S. Koreans to Seize Job, Business Opportunities in Middle East," *Yonhap News Agency*, February 20, 2012.

8 Christopher Michael Davidson, "The Gulf Arab States and Asia Pacific: Geo-Economics and Interdependency," in Matteo Legrenzi and Bessma Momani (eds.), *Shifting Geo-Economic Power of the Gulf: Oil, Finance and Institutions* (London: Ashgate, 2011), pp. 183–198.

9 "S. Korea's Trade Deficit with Middle East Widens on Crude Imports: Customs Data," *Asia News Monitor*, May 4, 2010.

10 Fred H. Lawson, "Geo-Political Complications of U.S. Free Trade Agreements with Gulf Arab Countries," In Matteo Legrenzi and Bessma Momani (eds.), *Shifting Geo-Economic Power of the Gulf: Oil, Finance and Institutions* (London: Ashgate, 2011), pp. 190–210.

11 John R. Boatright, *Finance Ethics: Critical Issues in Theory and Practice* (Hoboken, NJ: Wiley, 2010), p. 258.

12 "A New Path for Korea and the Middle East," *Business Korea*, December 15, 2009.

13 "Korea Seeks to Become Major Arms Exporter," *Korea Times*, October 19, 2010.

14 "South Korea Reopens Embassy in Manama," *Gulf News*, September 4, 2012.

15 "S. Korea Secures 1st Oilfield in Iraq," *Korea Times*, November 11, 2007.

16 "Incheon to Support Iraq's Erbil Airport," *Korea Herald*, February 25, 2009.

17 "Korea's Costly Blunder in Iraq," *Chosun Ilbo*, September 19, 2011.

18 "Iraq Warns S Korea against Kurdish Region Oil Exploration," *Xinhua News Agency*, December 24, 2007.

19 "Seoul, Baghdad Agree on $3.55 Billion Deal to Rebuild Iraq," *Yonhap News Agency*, February 25, 2009.

20 Azad, "Iran and the Two Koreas: A Peculiar Pattern of Foreign Policy."

21 "Iran cheje pulddong twilkka: kiobdel noshimchosa" ["Iran Sanctions Make Companies Anxious"], *Yonhap News Agency*, January 18, 2012.

22 Azad.

23 "Iran Sanctions to Affect South Korea Economy, Minister Says," *Bloomberg*, January 13, 2012.

24 "U.S. Extends Waivers on Iran Oil Sanctions for Big Asian Economies, South Africa," *Washington Post*, December 8, 2012.

25 "Dubai Traders Call for Relief on Iran Exports," *The National*, January 3, 2012.

26 "Local Dramas to Air in Middle East," *Korea Times*, May 18, 2008.

27 "Korean Furniture Popular in Mideast," *Korea Times*, October 25, 2013.

28 See, for instance, "Taekwondo Popularity Growing in Kingdom," *Arab News*, October 24, 2009; "Emiratis 'Captivated' by Korean Culture," *The National*, June 5, 2011; and "Youth Forum Promotes Growing Saudi–Korean Ties," *Arab News*, June 21, 2012.

29 "Luxury in the Arab World: Would Sir Like His Goat Wrapped?" *Economist*, June 8, 2013.

30 See "South Korea's Bid to Boost Mideast Tourists by 30%," *Emirates 24/7*, April 14, 2010; "Korea Eyes Saudi Tourists," *Arab News*, October 3, 2011; "Medical Tourism for Arabs," *JoongAng Ilbo*, January 9, 2013; and "S. Korea Promotes Medical Tourism in Middle East Events," *Yonhap News Agency*, April 1, 2013.
31 "Korean Air Flies again in Kingdom Skies after 15 Years," *Arab News*, November 12, 2012.
32 "Korean Ambassador: 'Iranian Cooking Excels French'," *Iran Book News Agency (IBNA)*, October 2, 2013.
33 A very deleterious development took place in June 2013, when hundreds of South Korean fans hurled bottles and debris on members of the Iranian national soccer team, who were running around the Ulsan Stadium celebrating their victory which had allowed them to qualify for the 2014 FIFA World Cup. The occurrence angered many Iranians, who swiftly showed their utter displeasure by disseminating clips, photos and comments related to the incident through various social media outlets. The incident also influenced a decision by the Iranian government to later call off a friendly match between Iran and South Korea. More importantly, it was rather hard then to ignore the fact that the unfortunate development could very well serve to somewhat tarnish South Korea's favorable reputation among many ordinary Iranians. See "S. Korea Media Blame Iran for Angry World Cup Scenes," *AFP*, June 19, 2013.
34 "Arab Students in South Korea Lament Lack of Mosques and Halal Food," *The National*, October 23, 2013.
35 "Seoul's UAE Deal Caps Big Sales Push," *Wall Street Journal*, December 29, 2009.
36 Davidson, *The Persian Gulf and Pacific Asia*, p. 104.
37 "Cabinet Approves UAE Troop Dispatch," *Korea Herald*, November 9, 2010.
38 Robert A. Manning, *The Asian Energy Factor: Myths and Dilemmas of Energy, Security and the Pacific Future* (New York: Palgrave Macmillan, 2000), p. 167.
39 Lack of attention to energy saving issues and wasting away part of the expensive fossil fuels that South Korea imports has also been another serious problem facing the East Asian country for quite some time, harkening back to the very outset of its industrialization and economic development. A few years ago, for instance, a rather scathing editorial by the *Korea Times* summed up this national malaise, warning that "when it comes to saving energy, we Koreans have said one thing and done another ... the current energy turmoil is not political and temporary but structural and lasting. Even more serious than the crisis itself is the lack of a sense of crisis among the nation's major economic players, namely, government, businesses and people generally. The government has only said the strong won would offset the impact. Businesses spend twice as much on energy as their counterparts in advanced countries to produce the same output. The general public is using oil like water. The government dusts off its comprehensive energy program whenever a crisis looms and shelves it as soon as it is over." See "Addicted to Oil: Energy Crisis is still Someone Else's Problem Here," *Korea Times*, June 17–18, 2006, p. 6.
40 "Roh Starts Energy Diplomacy in Middle East," *Korea Times*, March 24–25, 2007, p. 7.
41 It has been reported, for instance, that China spent more than $8 billion to develop the Arabic version of CCTV (China Central Television), which broadcasts a variety of programs in four major categories: news, features, entertainment and education. See "The 'Asian Wave' hits Saudi Arabia," *Saudi Gazette*, July 25, 2010.
42 After advertising internationally for several semesters, SNU's Department of Political Science and International Relations offered in 2010 a faculty position to an Italian scholar who was then teaching at a Canadian university, but the offer

was later declined due to a supposed disagreement over the proposed salary of roughly $50,000 per year. To take over such an academic position, the department would essentially prefer, among foreign candidates, a male PhD educated in the United States who will by and large present a typical American view of the Middle East and who will respect and practice the neo-Confucian values of his conventionally unwelcoming environment – and who, at the end of the day, will get paid $50,000 per year.

43 "Korea Eyeing Middle East Market," *Korea Times*, May 23, 2012.
44 "Korea Stakes Claim in Post-Ghadafi Libya," *CNN*, August 24, 2011.
45 Mohammad El-Sayed Selim, "Korean Investment in Egypt: Status, Problems and Prospects," in J. Rew (ed.), *Korea and Egypt: The Change and Continuity in their Policy and Cooperation* (Seoul: Korean Institute of the Middle East & Africa, 1995), pp. 47–64.

Conclusion

Putting it all together: Koreans and the Persian Gulf region

While a number of Persian Gulf nations had already paid some attention to major developments taking place in the Korean Peninsula, both during and after the Korean War, a corresponding consideration toward the Middle East region did not really exist among Koreans, as they were still utterly obsessed with a myriad of problems, both national and local, that had been plaguing them for more than half a century. By the end of the 1950s, when the dust of immediate national tragedies gradually began to settle and a dire economic situation at home forced Korean leaders to look for a reliable and enduring cure for the nation's ills, the very idea of extending Korea's international relations beyond the frontiers of East Asia slowly started to appeal to policy-makers. The Persian Gulf, the Middle East region's jewel in the crown, was one of the areas which the Koreans subsequently chose to approach for a number of interesting reasons, which included an awareness of the ancient historical connections between the two regions, their relative geographical proximity, numerous economic expectations, and the political need (on the part of both Seoul and Pyongyang) for international recognition and legitimacy.

South Korea's initial steps toward the Persian Gulf region coupled pretty soon with seismic political developments in Seoul in the early 1960s, when the emergence of a new political regime, which had seized power through a bloodless military coup, took the entire nation in another direction, one that was diametrically opposed to the direction in which the country had traditionally gone. One immediate implication of this crucial reordering was that national priorities were redefined markedly and policymaking in almost all areas, from economics to diplomacy, became a serious priority for the new leadership. The bottom line was, in fact, an accentuated appeal for industrialization and economic development of the Korean state. However, the very basic requirements for the ambitious programs crafted by the new political leadership were simply not available. The process of industrialization and economic development was most definitely not an easy one: The entire nation had to put up with the arbitrary imposition of a draconian division of labor and a systematic allocation of resources.

Despite the importance of domestic elements, the new national agenda in South Korea required various external elements in order to succeed – elements that involved changes in its foreign policy and international relations. Among these crucial elements were the contribution of foreign finance, technology, markets, and raw materials to the South Korean economy, without which the project of industrialization and economic growth could not be implemented successfully. Korean policymakers, therefore, rekindled attempts to expand and improve their foreign relations and approached different regions of the world so that they could assure as much access as possible to those resources which their development and industrialization programs required. With regard to the Persian Gulf, some previous experiences in the region meant that South Korean leaders were *au courant* with the labyrinthine complexities of the region as well as the potential contribution it could make to the new agenda developed in Seoul. Still, any approach to the Persian Gulf region needed to get along with the general pattern of foreign policy that the South Korean government was committed to following in one way or another.

In the post–World War II period, the general direction of foreign policy-making and international interactions of the ROK has been largely articulated by the so-called US–Korean alliance. In a nutshell, the major guidelines of this security alliance have long served as the general framework for South Korea's foreign policy approach toward the world at large and the Persian Gulf region in particular. This diplomatic orientation has brought to the Korean state relative benefits from its vested interests in other parts of the globe as well as occasional minor costs that the East Asian country has been willing to shoulder accordingly. Throughout the past few decades, in fact, a delicate, balanced approach to its foreign relations has been of paramount importance to the ROK in trying to achieve its national goals and in trying to counterbalance the paucity of domestic resources as well as its considerably vulnerable position *vis-à-vis* its competitors in the international arena. As a result of this approach to foreign policy (one that was *de rigueur* for a small and susceptible nation), South Korea has been in a very good position to enjoy almost unfettered access to the Persian Gulf in order to achieve part of its long-term national objectives in the region.

Enlightened to a large extent by this convenient approach, the specificity and details of Korean foreign policymaking toward the Persian Gulf were to be fashioned in lockstep with domestic requirements and the opportunities that the region could offer. With the exception of a very few people, such as Park Chung-hee and Lee Myung-bak, South Korea's top leaders have hardly ever played a determining role in crafting and implementing the ROK's Persian Gulf policies over the past decades. The bureaucracy was instead given a principal role in the design of relevant policies and in their implementation. Assigning the task of Persian Gulf policies to the bureaucracy and relevant domestic institutions was more about the required expertise that was needed in order to optimize decision-making processes and minimize the costs of policy failures. The National Assembly was either irrelevant or left to play second fiddle, taking care of the overall policies recommended by the government once they had trickled down through the pertinent bureaucratic channels. Interests groups, and most of the private sector, also needed to rely heavily on the government for varied forms of regular support as well as unconventional assistance when occasional setbacks in the Persian Gulf forced them to be dependent on the state and on state intervention in order to get things done.

An amalgam of the foregoing exogenous and endogenous elements has worked as the key driving force behind South Korea's achievements in the Persian Gulf region which the present research has studied under six distinctive periods. The first period, which lasted for about a decade and a half from the late 1950s to the early 1970s, turned out to be the most passive chapter in the history of South Korea's connections to the Persian Gulf. The East Asian country was then pretty much obsessed with chaotic domestic affairs that had partly stemmed from the new regime's struggle to fortify its power base and later from its attempt to push through a national program of industrialization and economic development which was to further compel Koreans to pay more attention to the Persian Gulf. Diplomatic relationships between the ROK and Persian Gulf nations were, moreover, either non-existent or, those that had commenced, functioning at a snail's pace mostly because South Korea still had little to offer aside from a rather limited share of oil imports from a small number of countries in the region. On top of that, Koreans were really newcomers to the Persian Gulf, and the average knowledge and experience they possessed about the region could hardly rival that of the Taiwanese, let alone their Japanese and Chinese counterparts.

The second period began with the Arab-Israeli war of 1973 and the follow-up oil shock which was soon to give Koreans an indication of the wealth that their firms could amass in the construction industry, and in many other industries, in the region for decades to come. For over half a decade, before the tectonic political shift that was to occur in Iran in early 1979, South Korea experienced unprecedented success in the Persian Gulf on the political, economic, and even the cultural front. South Koreans were able to determine how to deal with the Israeli factor as a stumbling block in their relationship with Arab countries while being able to capitalize at the same time on robust political interactions with Iran and Saudi Arabia to further secure their increasing economic links to the region. The revenues and business generated by the construction bonanza, whose aftertaste still lingers, together with the numerous benefits gained from its exports of manufactured goods persuaded South Korea to work concomitantly on some cultural initiatives to better consolidate its standing among Persian Gulf countries at a time when all the DPRK regime could accomplish in the region were political discussions with the socialist Ba'ath Party of Baghdad.

But, as the saying goes, "every dog has its day." The political turmoil in Tehran in 1979 and the ensuing Iran–Iraq War offered North Korea, on a silver platter, a highly lucrative market for military exports, mesmerizing Kim

Il-sung who was elated by the new situation he was fortunate enough to find himself in. This time, however, was also the harbinger of a third period in South Korea's encounter with the Persian Gulf, a period which extended almost until the end of the conflict between Tehran and Baghdad in 1988. The abrupt political transition in Iran put the country on a different political path, one which would see Iran adopt a unique set of foreign policies and international partnerships; the ROK was therefore left with little choice but to adopt a new path of its own with regard to its foreign policy toward Tehran. The relations between the two nations, moreover, was henceforth to look nothing like the previous bilateral relationship that the two countries enjoyed prior to the demise of the Pahlavi dynasty in 1979. In spite of a downgrade in their political ties with Iran, Seoul still managed to have a commercial relationship with Tehran through increasing its oil imports and winning a number of rudimentary construction projects in areas less affected by the ongoing war with Iraq.

Meanwhile, South Korea tried its best to benefit from the global arms trade to the Persian Gulf that began after the outset of the Iran–Iraq War in spite of its ostensibly neutral position toward the warring parties. Seoul could sell weapons, either from its own stocks or those belonging to a third party, to both Tehran and Baghdad, but it was not allowed, in the end, to cross a certain red line with regard to military shipments to the region during the course of the war. Still, this loss in arms sales for the ROK was more than balanced by the enormous revenues that it received from the thriving construction market of Saudi Arabia in the first half of the 1980s. That period also marked the arrival of the highest number of Korean workers in the region – even though a majority of them were gradually leaving the region in the mid-1980s and shortly thereafter once oil prices had sharply plummeted and the employment situation in South Korea had vastly improved. Besides Saudi Arabia, the ROK either established or upgraded its relations with smaller members of the newly formed GCC in order to achieve energy security through diversification and long-term investment in these source countries. The second oil shock had recently justified such a strategy, underlining the importance of obtaining energy security.

In the fourth period, the conclusion of the brutal conflict between Iran and Iraq provided South Korea with an opportunity to rekindle its past policies and try to mend fences with both Tehran and Baghdad. But the East Asian state was not able to renew friendly political ties with Iran, being convinced instead to follow a policy of separating its economic and political connections to the Persian Gulf state. By doing so, it would be able to meet its alliance requirements (that is, with the United States) while enjoying uninterrupted economic interactions with Tehran. Owing to a variety of regional and international circumstances, South Korea was obliged at times to stay within tighter alliance constraints far beyond the leeway it wished to be granted for its special relationship with Iran. One can contrast this special relationship with the ties between Iran and the DPRK, which were completely unimpeded by any third party requirements or constraints. In addition, Seoul's dalliance with Baghdad was soon over when Saddam's combatants crossed the Kuwaiti border in 1990, triggering yet another sore spot in South Korea's Persian Gulf policy. Of course, part of the problem can be attributed to the fact that it was an era of transition and uncertainty for almost everyone: for South Korea, for the Persian Gulf states, and generally for the countries that lay beyond the last vestiges of communist rule.

The fifth period roughly coincided with the ROK's preparations to expand its trade horizons with Persian Gulf states in the wake of the Asian financial crisis of 1997. In the decade that followed the financial turmoil, South Korea reached the pinnacle of its commercial relations with many Persian Gulf countries, most notably with Iran. As the ROK's stakes in the region were rising, South Korean companies were encouraged to invest more than ever in the region in order to put their country in a better position to vie with new ravenous competitors from other Asian countries, particularly those from China and India. Apart from the GCC zone, however, the political environment in the region morphed from bad to worse when the Americans invaded and occupied Iraq in 2003 based on the pretext that the latter possessed WMDs. The United States was intent on replacing the Iraqi regime with a democracy and believed that this would help the country prosper. South Korea could not escape the calamitous outcome of this war, as Seoul was eventually pressured into providing military and financial support to the American-led coalition. It also had to deal with the subsequent rise of anti-Americanism among its citizens, which led to occasional protests in the streets.

The Iraq War had barely vanished from sight when the issue of Iran's nuclear program started to plague Seoul's ever-expanding trade relationship with Tehran. What added insult to injury was the fact that North Korea had been implicated in the whole affair, forcing the South Korean government to seek backdoor channels to keep its ties with Tehran on track. The crux of the crisis was palpably obvious to many, but what had made things somewhat convoluted was Iran's unusual connections to both Koreas: The nature of these connections was rivaled by only a few contrasting cases in the world, and it had absolutely no parallel among other countries in the Persian Gulf region. Following a pragmatist approach toward the Korean Peninsula, Tehran has largely ignored the ideology factor in its relationship with Seoul as well as Pyongyang, aiming to get all the goods and services the Koreans on both sides of the DMZ have been able to offer it. On the Korean side, Seoul has not bothered much with Iran's continuous relations with the DPRK regime, taking care instead of its vastly increasing commercial interactions with Tehran and seeking to keep a low profile with respect to its political ties with Iran. Pyongyang's policy toward Iran does not seem to be very dissimilar to that of the ROK's interest-oriented approach, as the communist state has benefited prodigiously from its uninhibited relationship with Tehran since the early 1980s, gaining access to a great sum of invaluable hard currency, technical exchanges, and energy supplies (among other things).

Finally, the presidency of Lee Myung-bak presaged a distinctive, sixth period when South Korea refocused its policies toward the Persian Gulf, which it saw as a crucial gateway to the greater Middle East and which one Korean official had just dubbed a "spreading road of the future." Under Lee, the ROK made numerous attempts to forge multifarious and long-lasting connections to members of the GCC; penetrate Kurdistan's energy and construction industries; and work on various strategies to overcome the quandary posed by the Western sanctions levelled against Iran. Embodied in the concept of "*déjà vu* diplomacy," Lee drew heavily on his previous experience in the region in a nostalgic sense of thrill and action, striving to foster South Korea's policy goals and to extend the East Asian country's vested interests in the Persian Gulf. Regional and international circumstances also remained relatively favorable for the ROK's Persian Gulf policy during Lee's presidency, although the emergence of new Asian rivals made the working environment in the region much more competitive than it used to be and the achievement of long-term objectives and aspirations by non-regional contenders less assured.

Lee, the former CEO of Hyundai Construction, concentrated both on short-term gains, to be obtained from the region's second oil boom, and long-term goals through establishing a myriad of political and economic connections – particularly to member countries of the GCC. Exemplified by his frequent visits to the Persian Gulf – where he travelled more often than all previous South Korean leaders combined – Lee's *déjà vu* diplomacy met some notable successes, ranging from new achievements in the GCC countries and Kurdistan to solutions to the problems posed by the sanctions against Iran and plans to move his country forward in the post-oil-boom era. Lee Myung-bak's policy in the Persian Gulf was not, evidently, devoid of blunders, as some of his actions or rather his inaction turned out to lead to what one may call a "demure diplomacy." He overplayed South Korea's abundant fortune in the nuclear deal with the UAE and oil contracts in Kurdistan. His government's multifaceted and future-oriented policies toward the region were contradicted by his narrow focus on the smaller states of the GCC, and they shunned long-term investments in larger countries such as Iran and Iraq; they also almost completely ignored some old yet sensitive issues pertinent to high politics in the region. One such case was his government's abstinence from voting on a resolution about the status of Palestine at the UN General Assembly in November 2012. The diplomatic mischief came to light when South Korea's East Asian neighbors and regional rivals, China and (interestingly enough) Japan, both voted in favor of the measure, leaving Seoul in a dubious position regarding its long-term policy concerning the issue.

When his term in office was over, Lee Myung-bak was replaced by Park Geun-hye, who had no background in, and few, if any, connections to the wider Middle East region. Only time will tell whether she will need to follow the Lee style of face-to-face diplomacy with leaders of the male-dominated countries of the region or whether she can once again put the relevant state bureaucracy at the helm of the ROK's diplomatic affairs. Caught between two divergent worlds of *paterfamilia*s politics, intrinsic to South Korean and Middle Eastern societies, Park is further handicapped by the lack of her predecessor's assertiveness toward and knowledge of the region. Consequently, Park's maneuvers toward the Persian Gulf may increasingly be subservient to the diktats of ambitious bureaucrats in Seoul and, from time to time, to today's huge corporations, both once absolutely obedient to, and ready to serve, future-oriented policies and state-initiated strategies, particularly during the reign of her father, Park Chung-hee, in the 1960s and 1970s. While attempting to avoid any unnecessary risks, as befits a small and susceptible player with considerable stakes in the region, the Park government is still widely expected to fall in line with the "spreading road" policy, even if direct responsibility for such a policy falls to the bureaucrats, and stay focused on South Korea's ever-expanding interests throughout the greater Middle East and the Persian Gulf region in particular.

Bibliography

Acharya, Amitav. 2009. *Whose Ideas Matter?: Agency and Power in Asian Regionalism.* Ithaca: Cornell University Press.

Al-Farsy, Fouad Abdul Salam. 1980. "King Faisal and the First Five-Year Plan," in Willard Beling (ed.), *King Faisal and the Modernization of Saudi Arabia.* London: Croom Helm Ltd.

Al-Mashat, Abdul-Monem. 1995. "The Egyptian Perception of Korean Issues," in J. Rew (ed.), *Korea and Egypt: The Change and Continuity in their Policy and Cooperation.* Seoul: Korean Institute of the Middle East & Africa.

Al-Sayyid, Mustapha. 2001. "International and Regional Environments and State Transformation in Some Arab Countries," in Hassan Hakimian and Ziba Moshaver (eds.), *The State and Global Change: The Political Economy of Transition in the Middle East and North Africa.* Richmond, UK: Curzon Press.

Alnasrawi, Abbas. 1984. "Middle East Oil and Economic Development: Regional and Global Implications." *Journal of Asian and African Studies*, Vol. 19, No. 3–4.

Anvari Tehrani, Ibrahim. 1993. "Iraqi Attitudes and Interpretation of the 1975 Agreement," in Farhang Rajaee (ed.), *The Iran–Iraq War: The Politics of Aggression.* Gainesville, FL: The University Press of Florida.

Ayittey, George B.N. 2011. *Defeating Dictators: Fighting Tyranny in Africa and around the World.* New York: Palgrave Macmillan.

Azad, Shirzad. 2008. "Japan's Gulf Policy and Response to the Iraq War." *Middle East Review of International Affairs*, Vol. 12, No. 2.

——. 2010. "The Politics of Privatization in Iran." *Middle East Review of International Affairs*, Vol. 14, No. 4.

——. 2012. "Iran and the Two Koreas: A Peculiar Pattern of Foreign Policy." *Journal of East Asian Affairs*, Vol. 26, No. 2.

——. 2013. "*Déjà vu* Diplomacy: South Korea's Middle East Policy under Lee Myung-bak." *Contemporary Arab Affairs*, Vol. 6, No. 4.

Bedeski, Robert E. 1994. *The Transformation of South Korea: Reform and Reconstitution in the Sixth Republic under Roh Tae Woo, 1987–1992.* London: Routledge.

Bello, Walden. 1989. "Asia's Miracle Economies: The First and Last of a Dying Breed." *Dollars & Sense,* Vol. 143.

Boatright, John R. 2010. *Finance Ethics: Critical Issues in Theory and Practice.* Hoboken, NJ: Wiley.

Bozdaglioglu, Yucel. 2003. *Turkish Foreign Policy and Turkish Identity: A Constructivist Approach.* London: Routledge.

Bridges, Brian. 1992. "South Korea and the Gulf Crisis." *The Pacific Review*, Vol. 5, No. 2.

——. 2001. *Korea after the Crash: The Politics of Economic Recovery.* London and New York: Routledge.

Brown, Gilbert T. 1973. *Korean Pricing Policies and Economic Development in the 1960s.* Baltimore: Johns Hopkins University Press.

Brzoska, Michael. 1987. "Profiteering on the Iran–Iraq War." *Bulletin of the Atomic Scientists*, Vol. 43, No. 5.

Burchett, Wilfred G. 1968. *Again Korea.* New York: International Publishers.

Burke III, Edmund. 1988. *Global Crises and Social Movements: Artisans, Peasants, Populists and the World Economy.* Boulder, CO: Westview Press.

Buss, Claude A. 1982. *The United States and the Republic of Korea: Background for Policy.* Stanford: Hoover Institution Press.

Carpenter, Ted Galen and Doug Bandow. 2004. *The Korean Conundrum: America's Troubled Relations with North and South Korea.* New York: Palgrave Macmillan.

Chaudhry, Kiren A. 1997. *The Price of Wealth: Economies and Institutions in the Middle East.* Ithaca: Cornell University Press.

Choe, S. 1971. *Relations between Korea and Arabia.* Seoul: Omungak.

Clifford, Mark L. 1994. *Troubled Tiger: Businessmen, Bureaucrats, and Generals in South Korea.* Armonk, NY: M.E. Sharpe.

Clough, Ralph N. 1987. *Embattled Korea: The Rivalry for International Support.* Boulder, CO: Westview Press.

Cumings, Bruce. 1987. "The Origins and Development of the Northeast Asian Political Economy: Industrial Sectors, Product Cycles, and Political Consequences," in Frederic C. Deyo (ed.), *The Political Economy of the New Asian Industrialism.* Ithaca: Cornell University Press.

Davidson, Christopher Michael. 2010. *The Persian Gulf and Pacific Asia: From Indifference to Interdependence.* New York: Columbia University Press.

——. 2011. "The Gulf Arab States and Asia Pacific: Geo-Economics and Interdependency," in Matteo Legrenzi and Bessma Momani (eds.), *Shifting Geo-Economic Power of the Gulf: Oil, Finance and Institutions.* London: Ashgate.

Dennis, Anthony J. 2001. *The Rise of the Islamic Empire and the Threat to the West*, 2nd edition. Lima, OH: Wyndham Hall Press.

Dent, Christopher M. 2002. *The Foreign Economic Policies of Singapore, South Korea and Taiwan.* Cheltenham, UK: Edward Elgar.

Disney, Nigel. 1977. "South Korean Workers in the Middle East." *MERIP Reports*, No. 61.

Economic and Social Commission for Western Asia (ESCWA). 2001. *Survey of Economic and Social Developments in the ESCWA Region 2000–2001.* New York: United Nations Publication.

Economist Intelligence Unit. 1997. *Country Profile: South Korea, North Korea, 1997–98.* London: Economist Intelligence Unit (EIU).

El-Sayed Selim, Mohammad. 1995. "Korean Investment in Egypt: Status, Problems and Prospects," in J. Rew (ed.), *Korea and Egypt: The Change and Continuity in their Policy and Cooperation.* Seoul: Korean Institute of the Middle East & Africa.

Elegant, Robert. 1990. *Pacific Destiny: Inside Asia Today.* New York: Avon Books.

Feld, Lowell S. 1995. "Oil Markets in Crisis: Major Oil Supply Disruption since 1973," in Siamack Shojai (ed.), *The New Global Oil Market: Understanding Energy Issues in the World Economy.* Westport, CT: Praeger.

Field, Graham. 1995. *Economic Growth and Political Change in Asia.* London: Macmillan Press.

Flynn, Norman. 1999. *Miracle to Meltdown in Asia: Business, Government, and Society.* New York: Oxford University Press.

Ford, Glyn and S. Kwon. 2008. *North Korea on the Brink: Struggle for Survival.* London: Pluto Press.

Frank, Charles R., K. Kim and Larry E. Westphal. 1975. *Foreign Trade Regimes and Economic Development: South Korea*, vol. 7, National Bureau of Economic Research. New York: Columbia University Press.

Garnaut, Ross. 1998. "The East Asian Crisis," in Ross H. McLeod and Ross Garnaut (eds.), *East Asia in Crisis: From Being a Miracle to Needing One?* London: Routledge.

Garver, John W. 2006. *China and Iran: Ancient Partners in a Post-Imperial World.* Seattle: University of Washington Press.

Geldenhuys, Deon. 1990. *Isolated States: A Comparative Analysis.* Cambridge: Cambridge University Press.

Gills, Barry. 1996. *Korea versus Korea: A Case of Contested Legitimacy.* New York: Routledge.

——. 1997. "The Political Economy of Diplomacy: North and South Korea and Competition for International Support," in D. Kim and T. Kong (eds.), *The Korean Peninsula in Transition.* London: Macmillan Press.

Gosfield, Frank and Bernhardt J. Hurwood. 1969. *Korea: Land of the 38th Parallel.* New York: Parents' Magazine Press.

Grayson, James H. 2002. *Korea: A Religious History.* New York: RoutledgeCurzon.

Haggard, Stephen and C. Moon. 1993. "The State, Politics, and Economic Development in Postwar South Korea," in H. Koo (ed.), *State and Society in Contemporary Korea.* Ithaca: Cornell University Press.

Haldis, Peter. 2005. "Saudi Arabia May Expand Refinery in South Korea." *Octane Week*, Vol. 20, No. 48.

Hanieh, Adam. 2011. *Capitalism and Class in the Gulf Arab States.* New York: Palgrave Macmillan.

Hapdong News Agency. 1987. *Korea Annual 1987.* Seoul: Hapdong News Agency.

Hartung, William D. 1990. "U.S.–Korea Jet Deal Boosts Arms Trade." *Bulletin of the Atomic Scientists*, Vol. 46, No. 9.

Hedberg, Hakan. 1978. "International Government Financing Survey: Special Report on South Korea." *The Institutional Investor*, Vol. 12, No. 4.

IBP USA. 2011. *North Korea: Energy Policy, Laws and Regulations Handbook, Volume 1: Strategic Information and Development.* Washington, D.C.: International Business Publications.

Japan Institute for Overseas Investment. 1993. *Foreign Direct Investment in the East Asia Region: Trends and Outlook.* Tokyo: Japan Institute for Overseas Investment.

Khan, Haider A. 1997. *Technology, Energy and Development: The South Korean Transition.* Cheltenham, UK: Edward Elgar.

Kirk, Donald. 1994. *Korean Dynasty: Hyundai and Chung Ju Yung.* Hong Kong: Asia 2000 Ltd.

——. 1999. *Korean Crisis: Unraveling of the Miracle in the IMF Era.* New York: Palgrave Macmillan.

Korea Economic Institute (U.S.). 2000. *The Two Koreas in 2000: Sustaining Recovery and Seeking Reconciliation.* Washington, D.C.: KEIA.

——. 2009. *Ambassadors' Memoir: U.S.–Korea Relations through the Eyes of the Ambassadors.* Washington, D.C.: KEIA.

Lall, Sanjaya. 1997. "Industrial Development and Technology," in D. Kim and T. Kong (eds.), *The Korean Peninsula in Transition*. London: Macmillan Press.

Lawson, Fred H. 2011. "Geo-Political Complications of U.S. Free Trade Agreements with Gulf Arab Countries," in Matteo Legrenzi and Bessma Momani (eds.), *Shifting Geo-Economic Power of the Gulf: Oil, Finance and Institutions*. London: Ashgate.

Lie, John. 1998. *Han Unbound: The Political Economy of South Korea*. Stanford: Stanford University Press.

Looney, Robert E. 1994. *Manpower Policies and Development in the Persian Gulf Region*. Westport, CT: Praeger.

Malkasian, Carter. 2001. *The Korean War*. Oxford: Osprey Publishing.

Mangum, Garth L., S. Kim and Stephen B. Tallman. 1996. *Transnational Marriages in the Steel Industry: Experience and Lessons for Global Business*. Westport, CT: Quorum Books.

Manning, Robert A. 2000. "The Asian Energy Predicament." *Survival*, Vol. 42, No. 3.

——. 2000. *The Asian Energy Factor: Myths and Dilemmas of Energy, Security and the Pacific Future*. New York: Palgrave Macmillan.

Mardon, Russell. 1990. "The State and the Effective Control of Foreign Capital: The Case of South Korea." *World Politics*, Vol. 43, No. 1.

McCormack, Gavan. 2004. *Target North Korea: Pushing North Korea to the Brink of Nuclear Catastrophe*. New York: Nation Books.

McLachlan, Keith. 1979. "Iran," in *Middle East Annual Review 1978*. Essex, UK: Middle East Review Co.

Mearsheimer, John J. 2011. *Why Leaders Lie: The Truth about Lying in International Politics*. New York: Oxford University Press.

Metraux, Daniel. 1992. "The Economy," in Andrea Matles Savada and William Shaw (eds.), *South Korea: A Country Study*, 4th edition. Washington, D.C.: Library of Congress, Federal Research Division.

Metzler, John J. 2001. *Divided Dynamism – The Diplomacy of Separate Nations: Germany, Korea, China*. Lanham, MD: University Press of America.

MobileReference. 2010. *Travel Seoul, South Korea: Illustrated Guide, Korean Phrasebook and Maps (Mobi Travel)*. E-book. Boston: MobileReference.

Moon, C. 1980. "Korean Contractors in Saudi Arabia: Their Rise and Fall." *Middle East Journal*, Vol. 40, No. 4.

Navias, Martin S. and E.R. Hooton. 1996. *Tanker Wars: The Assault on Merchant Shipping during the Iran–Iraq Conflict, 1980–1988*. New York: I.B. Tauris & Co. Ltd.

Noland, Marcus. 1998. "Prospects for the North Korean Economy," in D. Suh and C. Lee (eds.), *North Korea after Kim Il Sung*. Boulder, CO: Lynne Rienner Publishers.

Noreng, Øystein. 2006. *Crude Power: Politics and the Oil Market*. New York: I.B. Tauris.

Oliver, Robert T. 1954. *Syngman Rhee: The Man behind the Myth*. New York: Dodd, Mead and Company.

Olsen, Edward A. 2005. *Korea: The Divided Nation*. Westport, CT: Praeger.

Park, Chung-hee. 1963. *Kunggawa hydngmydngiwa na [The Country, the Revolution, and I]*. Seoul: Hyangmunsa.

——. 1979. *Korea Reborn: A Model for Development*. Englewood Cliffs, NJ: Prentice-Hall Inc.

——. n.d. *Major Speeches by President Park Chung Hee, Republic of Korea*. Seoul: The Samhwa Publishing Co.

Porter, Michael E. 1990. *The Competitive Advantage of Nations*. New York: Free Press.

Reese, David. 1998. *The Prospects for North Korea's Survival*, Adelphi Paper 323. New York: Oxford University Press for the International Institute for Strategic Studies.

Reeve, W.D. 1963. *The Republic of Korea: A Political and Economic Study*. London: Oxford University Press.

Reich, Bernard. 1987. *The Powers in the Middle East: The Ultimate Strategic Arena*. New York: Praeger.

Reischauer, Edwin O. 1967. *Beyond Vietnam: The United States and Asia*. New York: Vintage Books.

Republic of Korea, Ministry of Foreign Affairs. 1970. *Daehan minguk wegyo yeonpyo* [*Annual Report on Foreign Policy*]. Seoul: Ministry of Foreign Affairs.

——. 1994, 1996, 2001, 2003, 2004, 2005, 2006, 2007, 2009. *Wegyo Munseo* [Diplomatic Archives]. Seoul: Republic of Korea, Ministry of Foreign Affairs.

Roberts, John. 1995. *Visions & Mirages: Middle East in a New Era*. Edinburgh and London: Mainstream Publishing.

Rodrik, Dani. 2007. *One Economics, Many Recipes: Globalization, Institutions and Economic Growth*. Princeton: Princeton University Press.

——. 2011. *The Globalization Paradox: Democracy and the Future of the World Economy*. New York: W.W. Norton.

Rubin, Barry. 2002. "The Persian Gulf amid Global and Regional Crises," in Barry Rubin (ed.), *Crises in the Contemporary Persian Gulf*. New York: Frank Cass Publishers.

Sampson, Anthony. 1975. *The Seven Sisters: The Great Oil Companies and the World They Made*. London: Hodder & Stoughton.

Scalapino, Robert A. and H. Yi. 1986. *North Korea in a Regional and Global Context*. Berkeley: University of California, Berkeley, Center for Korean Studies.

Shim, U. 1983. "Korea's Economic Progress Owes Much to Saudi Arabia." *Diplomacy*, Vol. 9, No. 11.

Sikorski, Douglas J. 2004. "Global Capitalism and the Asian Financial Crisis," in John A. Turner and Y. Kim (eds.), *Globalization and Korean Foreign Investment*. Burlington, VT: Ashgate Publishing Company.

Simon, Sheldon W. 1993. "Regional Security Structures in Asia: The Question of Relevance," in Sheldon W. Simon (ed.), *East Asian Security in the Post-Cold War Era*. New York: M.E. Sharpe.

Skeet, Ian. 1988. *OPEC: Twenty-Five Years of Prices and Politics*. London: Cambridge University Press.

Soysal, Ismail. 1997. *Soguk Savas Donemi ve Turkiye: Olaylar Kronolojisi (1945–1975)*. [*The Cold War Period and Turkey: Chronology of Events (1945–1975)*]. Istanbul: ISIS Yayincilik.

Steers, Richard M. 1999. *Made in South Korea: Chung Ju Young and the Rise of Hyundai*. London: Routledge.

Stern, Thomas. 1986. "Korean Economic and Political Priorities in the Management of Energy Liabilities," in Ronald C. Keith (ed.), *Energy, Security and Economic Development in East Asia*. New York: St. Martin's Press.

Suzuki, Hideo and Yoshii Satoshi. 1999. *Rekishi ni miru nihon to kankoku & kitachousen* [*Japan's Relations with South and North Korea from a Historical Perspective*]. Tokyo: Akashi Shoten.

Taylor, Jr., William J. (ed.). 1989. *The Future of South Korean–U.S. Security Relations*. Boulder, CO: Westview Press.

The Asahi Shimbun. 1991. *Wangan sensou to nihon: towareru kiki kanri* [*The Gulf War and Japan: Questioning Crisis Management*]. Tokyo: The Asahi Shimbunsha.

The Financial Times. 1983. *Financial Times Oil and Gas International Year Book.* London: Longman.

The World Bank. 1992. *Export Processing Zones.* Washington, D.C.: The World Bank, Industry and Energy Department & Country Economics Department.

——. 1992. *Water Policy and Water Markets: Selected Papers and Proceedings from the World Bank's Ninth Annual Irrigation and Drainage Seminar,* Annapolis, MD, December 8–10, 1992. Washington, D.C.: The World Bank.

——. 1993. *The East Asian Miracle: Economic Growth and Public Policy – A World Bank Policy Research Report.* New York: Oxford University Press.

Tucker, Spencer. (ed.). 2010. *The Persian Gulf, Afghanistan, and Iraq Conflicts,* Vol. 1. Santa Barbara: ABC-CLIO.

US Department of Defense. 1991. *A Strategic Framework for the Asian Pacific Rim: Looking Toward the 21st Century.* Washington, D.C.: Government Printing Office.

Varhola, Michael J. 2000. *Fire and Ice: The Korean War, 1950–1953.* El Dorado Hills, CA: Savas Publishing Company.

Wade, Robert. 1990. *Governing the Market: Economic Theory and the Role of Government in East Asian Industrialization.* Princeton: Princeton University Press.

Waltz, Kenneth N. 1979. *Theory of International Politics.* New York: Random House.

Westphal, Larry E. 1990. "Industrial Policy in an Export-Propelled Economy: Lessons from South Korea's Experience." *Journal of Economic Perspectives,* Vol. 4, No. 3.

Whitehill, Arthur M. 1987. *Doing Business in Korea.* Beckenham, UK: Croom Helm Ltd.

Wilber, Donald N. 1976. *Iran: Past and Present,* 8th edition. Princeton: Princeton University Press.

Willetts, Peter. 1978. *The Non-Aligned Movement: The Origins of a Third World Alliance.* London: Frances Pinter.

Wilson, Rodney J.A. 1984. "Japan's Exports to the Middle East: Directional and Commodity Trends and Price Behavior." *Middle East Journal,* Vol. 38, No. 3.

Yager, Joseph A. 1984. *The Energy Balance in Northeast Asia.* Washington, D.C.: Brookings Institution.

Yusuf, Shahid and Kaoru Nabeshima. 2006. *Postindustrial East Asian Cities: Innovation for Growth.* Palo Alto, CA: Stanford University Press.

Index

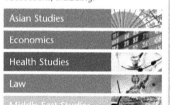

www.ingramcontent.com/pod-product-compliance
Ingram Content Group UK Ltd.
Pitfield, Milton Keynes, MK11 3LW, UK
UKHW020351010325
455677UK00021B/395